'Rory Spowers is a real environmentalist, genuinely engaged with the problems we must all face as we heat up the earth and trash its resources. But he also writes with candour and wit about the agony and ecstasy of trying to build and live the green dream with his young family on an abandoned Sri Lankan tea plantation. It's inspiring stuff, and left me more convinced than ever that all this really matters – and that to ignore it is as much a threat to our present sanity as our future security.'

Hugh Fearnley-Whittingstall

'This is a book of great charm and warmth. It is about huge events and tiny moments, and captures perfectly the restless spirit of all of us who have pursued a life yet, like a distant rumour of war, suspect something more important was happening elsewhere. It is most of all a book about waking up, recognizing that connection to the world isn't about romance and whimsy, but straining to hear the voice inside you when the background noise is deafening. I heartily recommend this lovely book.'

Tim Smit, co-founder of the Eden Project

A Year in Green Tea and Tuk-Tuks

My unlikely adventure creating
an organic farm in Sri Lanka

by Rory Spowers

HarperElement
An Imprint of HarperCollins*Publishers*
77-85 Fulham Palace Road,
Hammersmith, London W6 8JB

The website address is:
www.thorsonselement.com

and *HarperElement* are trademarks
of HarperCollins*Publishers* Ltd

First published by HarperElement 2007

1

Map illustration by Nicolette Caven

A catalogue record of this book is
available from the British Library

ISBN-13 978-0-00-723309-0
ISBN-10 0-00-723309-4

Printed and bound in Great Britain by
Clays Ltd, St Ives plc

Contents

Notes from a Forest Garden

for 'Doc Man'

What the caterpillar calls the end of the world,
the master calls a butterfly.
Buddhist saying

Acknowledgements

I would like to thank my father, my mother and my two brothers, Hugo and Adam, for their support for the Web of Hope and Samakanda; my wife Yvette and our two sons, Sholto and Xan, for their patience and inspiration as the book came to fruition; my agent Robert Kirby for persevering and making it possible; Belinda Budge, Katy Carrington and all at HarperElement for their enthusiasm and Gavin Lewis for his skills at transforming an unwieldy manuscript into what you are now holding. In Sri Lanka, a big hug to Viren, Giles, and Pat for being so instrumental in our making the move. Full respect to all our other friends in and around Galle for being so solid after the tsunami - you know who you are. Most of all, I would to thank Mr Pitchamurtu and the whole team at Samakanda for bringing this dream closer to reality. None of this would have been possible without your hard work.

Prologue

Full Moon at Sunset

25 December 2004. Wijaya Beach, Talpe, Sri Lanka.

A full moon rises at sunset as waters from three oceans mingle at our feet. The Arabian Sea, Indian Ocean and Bay of Bengal swirl together in one foaming jade curtain that crashes over the rocks and reef.

It has been one of those magical days; the air clean and crisp after months of monsoon rain, light sparking on the water, glinting off the sand, a million dancing crystals swirling around us. Our two sons are splashing around in shallow pools as local boys play cricket on the beach. All our friends are gathered together – some full-time residents in the area, others here for a few months of the year, some out on holiday.

As the light fades, we gravitate to the bar, soaking up the last of the sunset with cold beers and cocktails. All seems so right with the world. It's Christmas Day, the start of another season, the mood is buoyant all along the south coast, bookings higher than they had ever been during 20 years of civil war. Everyone is looking forward to a few months of fine weather, weekends at the beach and nights dancing under the stars.

I look at Yvette and know, really truly know, that moving to Sri Lanka has been the best decision we have ever made.

A few hours later, a vast wall of water advances from the southeast of the Indian Ocean and completely obliterates this tropical idyll we now call home.

In the space of five minutes, some 217,000 people are killed and five million made homeless within the tsunami's sphere of destruction. In Sri Lanka, 32,000 die, 70,000 homes are destroyed, leaving 500,000 homeless, and 1,100 children lose both parents. For several days, the world watches in horror as the full impact of the tragedy is beamed into their living rooms.

For those of us left amid the debris, life at the beach will never be quite the same.

26 December 2004. Galle.

At first, we have no idea that anything has happened. Yvette and I had moved into our house days before, with our two sons, Sholto and Xan, aged three and one. After six months in rented houses within the ramparts of Galle Fort, a sleepy walled town on the south-western tip of the island, the renovations of a house we have rented for 10 years are nearly complete. Our house in Karapitiya, a suburb of Galle, is perched on a small hill, four kilometres inland. For the first time in years, we have all our belongings in one place. A container has just arrived from England and the hallway is stacked with cardboard boxes, ready to be unpacked as we finally install ourselves into this 'dream home'.

Our first inkling of the disaster comes soon after nine in the morning, in a text message from our friend Henri. I read it out to Yvette, bemused by the contents: 'Are you OK? We're safe and high at Wijaya.'

'What does that mean?' Yvette asks. 'Is last night's party still going?'

'Maybe. Bit odd, though, isn't it?'

Virtually everyone we know in the area had been celebrating Christmas at the beach only hours before.

Yvette calls Suneth, who is restoring some furniture for us in Bentota, which is about halfway between Galle and Colombo, the capital city some three hours' drive along the west coast.

'Hi Suneth,' she starts. 'Just wondering how you are getting on with those cabinets . . .'

'Sorry, I can't talk right now.' She hears panic in his voice. 'Water's coming into the shop, and sand. We have a disaster happening . . . the tide is rising . . .'

'That was strange,' she says, putting down the phone. 'He sounds totally freaked out.'

The reality starts to strike home. First the power goes down. This is not unusual; power cuts happen on an almost daily basis. But then the sirens start, followed by the helicopters, which will turn into a steady stream of traffic over the next few days, since our house is just 200 metres from the main hospital for the south of the island. The landlines and mobile phone network are down for hours and will be intermittent for days.

With no TV or Internet access in the house, we turn to the car radio. Builders gather round and translate as news comes in of rising sea levels around the island, from Trincomalee in the northeast to Batticaloa, Pottuvil and Arugam Bay on the east coast, then Hambantota, Tangalle and Galle in the south, followed by Hikkaduwa, Bentota and Kalutara on the west coast. Remembering that we have almost no petrol in the car, I set out with Sholto to fill up at the nearest pump, half a kilometre away.

By the time we hit the junction by the hospital, it becomes clear that something momentous has occurred. The road is chaos. It seems that the whole island is on the move. Entire families on motorbikes, mopeds, even bicycles. Trucks filled with shouting men pick their way through the traffic. An impenetrable queue has developed around the petrol station.

'What's happening, Daddy?' Sholto asks from the back seat.

'I'm not sure, Sholt. Something very weird.'

I turn round and head back to the house, the sound of helicopters above the palm trees already creating the air of a war zone, like the opening scenes of *Apocalypse Now.*

Our friend Eduard appears at our house, on the back of his neighbour's motorbike. 'Have you heard what's happened?' he asks. I detect a trace of panic disrupting his usual calm.

'Not really,' I reply. 'Only what we've heard on the car radio. Is it some sort of tidal wave?'

'Something like that. The water almost came up to our house.' This is hard to believe. Eduard lives nearly 3 kilometres from the coast.

'Are you all OK?' I ask.

'Everyone's fine. Not so sure about people in the Fort, or on the coast, though.'

'Are you getting any signal on your phones?'

'Not any more.' We both light cigarettes. I have to sit down, suddenly overwhelmed.

'What we have to watch out for now is disease,' Eduard says. 'Epidemics, typhoid, stuff like that. How's your water here?'

'Our well should be fine. We must be far enough inland.'

'I'd better get back to the house. Just wanted to check on you guys.'

'Thanks, mate. And look, if it gets too hairy where you are, head up here.'

'Thanks. I'm wary about leaving the house though. They've started looting.'

For the following three days, the chaos that has struck the coast is enveloped in an eerie stillness. A hot humid blanket stifles the stagnant air, as if the atmosphere itself is pregnant with shock, grief and despair.

There are moments when it really does feel like the end of the world. Sholto watches one scene from Walt Disney's *Fantasia* over and over, Mussorgsky's 'Night on Bald Mountain', an operatic, apocalyptic nightmare, in which a Satanic beast is awoken from his slumbers and descends on the unsuspecting inhabitants of his world.

'Why do you keep watching that, Sholto?' I keep asking. 'Don't you find it scary?' He looks at me blankly.

27 December 2004. Galle.

The weather is intense – so static, so sultry, so humid. It feels not only oppressive, but somehow portentous.

Feeling helpless without transport, I continue trying to get petrol. I manage to get a call through to Rob, a friend in the Fort. His car had been carried down the street and deposited on top of another one. It does, however, have petrol, so I set off with a length of hosepipe to try to siphon some out.

The roads between our house and the coast are jammed with trucks, mopeds, 'tuk-tuk' three-wheelers. At every junction, wild-eyed men wielding wooden sticks are trying to direct the chaos. I am sent down narrow lanes, into oncoming traffic. It takes 45 minutes to cover what should be a 10-minute journey. The thought of running out of petrol in this mayhem and being forced to abandon our car makes me turn for home.

Of course it's a huge relief to hear that Rob is safe, as are all our other friends in the ex-pat community – miraculously. Rob had been staying with his step-brother Jack and his wife Jo in the Fort. He said goodbye shortly after 9 am and opened the front door to be greeted by 2 metres of water rushing towards the house.

Henri had been 'safe and high at Wijaya Beach', but only just. The water destroyed the restaurant below her and rose to within a foot of her bedroom door. Her boss, hotelier Geoffrey Dobbs, had been swimming in Weligama Bay, about 40 minutes' drive down the coast. To begin with, the vast approaching swell had virtually emptied the bay, before sweeping Geoffrey inland and depositing him in the crown of a palm tree. We discover that others we know have been swept from their beachfront cabanas, many naked after a night's sleep, and left clinging to concrete columns.

But we also learn how many have not been so lucky. The death toll continues to rise every time we hear the news, climbing by tens of thousands each time. Many local people we know have lost relatives – brothers, sisters, mothers, fathers, children, even whole families. Everybody has been exposed to scenes of absolute horror. Dead babies in pools of mud, bodies piled high in trucks on the way to the hospital, where they are stacked up in the suffocating humidity. I feel permanently nauseous and smoke incessantly.

News filters in about others we know but have been unable to contact. Olivia, manageress of Amangalla, the recently opened luxury hotel in Galle Fort and an old friend, watched from the hotel balcony as water shot through the Old Gate like a massive high-pressure fire hose, carrying boats, palm trees and bodies. Knowing that her two children were still asleep in her house, she raced back home, relieved to find the water had only just seeped under the garden gate.

Fritz Zwahlen, the chef at Amangalla, had only just arrived with his family from the Philippines. Fritz was at a little seafront super-market about 400 metres from the ramparts of the Fort. 'The tide's high today,' he remarked casually as he stood at the checkout and watched the waves spill over the road outside.

Seconds later, this 'high tide' had turned into an enormous swell, a vast wall of water advancing across Galle harbour. Before Fritz had a moment to register what was happening, the owners of the shop had ducked outside and rolled down metal security shutters, leaving him on his own inside. Soon he was floating through the supermarket, surrounded by packets of Corn Flakes, cartons of cigarettes and tubes of Pringles. The water rose. And rose.

'I thought that was it,' Fritz tells me later. 'As I moved up to the ceiling, I realized that if I didn't drown, I would soon be electrocuted by the lighting or the fridges. I thought, OK, I've had a nice life. That's it. Then I saw light coming from the floor above through a gap in the metal shutters. By this time, there was only a few inches of air left between me and the ceiling. I took a deep breath, swam down and came out through this small gap onto the first floor balcony.'

Minutes later, the water subsided. In his soaking chef's clothes, Fritz started the short walk back to the Fort. Then the second wave struck, picking him up and carrying him the length of Main Street, along with cars, palm trees and other screaming people, depositing him near the Buddhist temple. Once again, Fritz brushed himself down and started back to the hotel, soaking wet and covered in mud. He had a quick shower, then set about cooking lunch for 400 people as the lux-ury hotel became a five-star refugee camp for the next few days.

Meanwhile in Bentota on the west coast, our friend Viren and his girlfriend Pat were celebrating Christmas at Viren's sister's new villa, with a party of about 20 friends and relations. The villa had been completed only days before.

'We were all having breakfast and watching some fishermen try to haul their boat further up the beach.' Viren tells me later. 'Some of us went down to help. We could see the tide was behaving strangely. A fisherman pointed to a rock about a hundred metres out to sea, which I'd swum to the day before. The water had receded, so far back, the whole rock was revealed. The fisherman said he had never seen that before. Only then did we register that something was seriously wrong and rushed back to the villa. We all ran upstairs as my niece tried to close the glass doors on the ground floor. She only just escaped as the water ripped through.'

'One of the weirdest things was just how different the impact was over short distances,' Pat recalls. 'We were relatively unaffected, but the railway line just a hundred yards away was ripped apart and deposited on the other side of the road.'

Over on the east coast, in a small village north of Komari, the inhabitants knew something was on the way. For several weeks, a village elder had been having recurring dreams about a wave that would devastate the coast. His visions so impressed the villagers that they had conducted rituals for the days leading up to the event. The whole village survived.

Across the entire region, wild animals and indigenous peoples had responded to their own early warning signals. In Thailand, elephants cried and moved inland. In Sri Lanka, not a single dead wild animal was found in Yala National Park. As others ran onto beaches to pick up stranded fish and were swept away by the incoming waves, indigenous people in Banda Aceh moved to higher ground.

28 December 2004. Galle.

Most of the coast road to Colombo is impassable, but convoys are making it through on inland roads, extending a three-hour journey to at least eight. There are rumours of hijackings of aid trucks, as well as widespread looting. The tension feels like it could snap into unrest on a huge scale, which along with epidemics, now becomes everyone's greatest fear.

As ever, a tragedy on this scale seems to bring out the best and worst of human nature. Stories of selfless heroism clash with tales of absolute depravity. Like the three men who rescued a young girl from the waves, only to gang rape her later.

29 December 2004. Galle.

We arrive safely in Colombo during the middle of the night and spend the day trying to decide what to do. My mother had been due to arrive the day before from Australia, where she was visiting my brother Adam. Should she still come here, or should we go there? Finally we decide that she should come and we will spend a few days upcountry in Dambulla. She is now booked to arrive on the 2nd.

By this time, the British High Commission has established an office in the Fort and I speak with volunteer Eric Coleman, who had been on holiday at the nearby beach of Unawatuna and would now play a key role in the immediate aid effort. I offer the use of our house. Resourceful people, from ex-pats and Colombo socialites to local grassroots organizations like Sarvodaya and SEWA Lanka, are orchestrating a lot of the primary humanitarian aid, sending trucks to disaster zones around the country, from Galle in the south to Batticaloa in the east. Giles and Viren, our friends who run the Ulpotha yoga retreat, have started Lanka Real Aid and launched an online appeal for emergency aid in badly hit Arugam Bay. Rob, Jack and Olivia are all directors of Friends of the South, a charity started some months before to improve livelihoods in the southern province. They too have managed to mobilize very quickly, funds are coming from abroad and supplies being dispatched to critical areas.

30 December 2004.

I drive back to Galle with a car packed full of rice, lentils, bottled water, milk powder, petrol and medical supplies. Fires smoulder beside the road, the smell of melting plastic mingling with burning flesh from bodies being cremated. We arrive to find our house occupied with teams from the UN, International Labour Organization and Christian Children's Fund.

31 December 2004. Galle.

Eric calls a meeting at Amangalla, attended by local officials, expats and some tourists with aid experience. Everyone looks shellshocked. I see many familiar faces. Most look like they have not slept in days. There's Piero, the Italian artist who has lived here for 30 years; Anthony, the eccentric author and publisher and another long-term resident; Angela, aka 'Woody', who will soon swing into action cooking meals for volunteers. Olivia introduces the meeting and Eric outlines the immediate needs. Eduard offers his house in the Fort as an office. Robin, who had been living in Galle for 18 months with his wife and children and had been one of the founders of the Eden Project in Cornwall, offers computers. Everyone lists their skills and anything they can offer. Within hours, an office is up and running in Pedlar Street and Project Galle 2005 has been born.

Part One

'Always Travelling, Never Arriving'

Chapter One

An Indian Walk

You can only be lost if you are trying to get somewhere.

Ram Tzu

Easter 1974. Surrey, England.

I am seven years old. I wake to the sound of Canada geese flying overhead, their guttural shriek increasing in pitch as they swoop in to land on the lake beside the house. Nobody else is up. I put on my clothes, creep downstairs and out through the kitchen, taking the tool shed key. I find a small wheelbarrow and a pair of clippers, then head down the top and bottom lawns towards the stream, into the area we had been clearing the day before.

A huge bonfire has burnt to the ground, leaving a ring of green leaves and charred sticks around a core of smouldering cinders, like a giant crown of thorns. I start to throw these into the middle, rekindling the heat. Within seconds, little flames appear, which I feed with half-burnt branches.

Then I take the clippers from the barrow and start lopping small branches off an alder, felled by one of my brothers the day before. A misty silver light hangs over the lake, slowly dispersing to reveal the full bloom of spring: the budding leaves on old oaks; pink-white blossoms on weeping cherries; daffodils rearing their orange-yellow heads.

July 1976. Surrey, England.

I am cutting grass in the late afternoon, driving a white Bolens mini-tractor. There's been drought all summer and my father is pumping water from the lakes to revive trees planted in the spring, using a huge bowser mounted on a trailer.

I'm James Hunt at Brands Hatch. The challenge: to cut the grass, as well as possible, as fast as possible. I swing through chicanes, between apple trees and garden furniture at full throttle, in top gear, making sure that I clip the last tuft of grass at the border, allowing the cutting edge of the rotating blades below me to sweep over the turf boundary with the flower bed. My father will be pleased.

Later, after tea, I race around the garden on my bicycle, surveying the day's work. The manicured grass highlights the furrowed trunks of old oak trees, the massive splaying branches of Amazonian *gunaras* drooping to the ground, the trailing tentacles of weeping willows forming tunnels on the banks of the lake.

Now I'm Barry Sheene, shifting weight through corners and out-braking Kenny Roberts to clinch the world title. The light is soft, golden, velvet. The smell of freshly mown grass fills the air. Two white swans drift across the water as the sound of the M3 motorway seeps into Eden.

October 1977. Surrey, England.

Sunday lunch. My father is holding court. Sir James, the headmaster of his old school in Australia, is seated at the other end of the table. In a few days, Sir James will make a speech to those assembled for the opening of my father's magnum opus, an extension to the house, filled with books, pictures and eccentric objects collected from his travels. A shrunken human head from Papua New Guinea, with flowing black silk hair, the lips and eyelids sewn up with thread to prevent them from cracking; a haunted sedan chair containing a Prussian officer's hat decorated with deep-blue feathers; a sketch of temple murals in Ceylon by Australian artist Donald Friend; a Roman bath, carved from a single block of marble, retrieved from the rose garden when my parents first bought the house.

My father is telling the story of how he ran away from school in 1940, lied about his age, joined the army and set off to rescue my grandfather from a PoW camp at the age of 15. I am enthralled.

'I went to Sir James and told him what I wanted to do. And do you know what he said? He said if that was what I really wanted to do, he knew he couldn't stop me.' Sir James smiles as my father recalls his reaction.

'And what about your mother?' another guest asks.

'Oh, I told her I was joining a scout group, called Force X. It was only after talking to someone at a drinks party in Melbourne that she discovered what that was. By then, I was on my way to Ceylon.'

'Ceylon?'

'Ceylon was the first place I saw outside Australia. I remember standing on deck as we approached Colombo. All I could see was palm trees and sandy beaches. Surely this must be paradise, I said to myself.'

My fascination for the East stemmed from these stories. Ceylon, Calcutta, Cooch Behar, all sounded so exotic, fertile with mystery, heavy with intrigue. After the war, my father lived and worked in Calcutta for the two years leading up to Indian independence in 1947, working as ADC to the last Governor-General of Bengal, his godfather. My brothers and I had grown up with near-mythic tales about my father's catalogue of accidents on a Harley-Davidson, which he had been required to ride at more than 30 miles an hour at the front of the Governor-General's motorcade, to reduce the risk of assassination. An ambulance followed, ready to scoop my father up after collisions with cows and bullock carts, or wayside drains.

I loved tales of his bearer, Rai Bahadar Bibhuti Baba Mookerjee, who walked the streets of Calcutta barefooted, before toasting bread between his toes for the Governor-General's breakfast. The romance and horror of these stories made a deep impression on me, and I knew from an early age that I would head for India at the earliest opportunity.

Although my brothers and I would groan and lift our eyes to the ceiling as my father launched into yet another rendition of 'the Harley story', or one of his many war adventures, I was always secretly glad to hear them again. They filled my mind with fantastic images of Kipling's *Jungle Book,* fused with my father's colourful exploits.

At the same time, I felt a resonance with the more mystical attraction of the East. I was drawn to films about Buddhist monks, intrigued by words like 'zen' and 'yoga'. I liked the idea of walking through burnt, dusty landscapes in bare feet, of living very simply. The concept of enlightenment fascinated me.

My childhood vision of God was of an imposing bearded man with flowing white hair, seated on a throne in the clouds, controlling life on earth with some sort of giant computer. When I was five, I was stunned to hear one of my two brothers reveal that the air we breathe encompasses the entire globe. The concept of air being everywhere, that the breath I took into my lungs could be shared by people on the other side of the world, completely entranced me. God was everywhere. In everything and nothing.

Later, my image of a great man in the sky came into conflict with a belief in some kind of universal energy. I found it difficult to equate the Christian vision of God with the feeling of oneness sparked by the summer sun falling on yellow roses. Nature, rather than the Bible, became synonymous with God.

By the time I was a teenager, I had come to believe that the only way to find 'happiness' was through pursuing the techniques offered by the Eastern mystics. Those guys had been at it for thousands of years. They must have discovered the secret, the key to 'being happy, all of the time'.

I borrowed a book from my mother about basic meditation and started staring at a candle in my bedroom, waiting to be transported to a transcendental paradise. Nothing happened.

Despite my disappointment, I persisted. I read and re-read Herman Hesse's *Siddhartha*, developing a naive fascination with the life of wandering ascetics. I continued to meditate and dabbled in a form of yoga brought to the West by an Indian saint called Paramahansa Yogananda at the beginning of the last century.

When I left school and finally travelled to India, the experience proved more powerful than I had ever imagined. It was freedom, vitality and life as I had never known. The air was heavy with possibilities. I was intoxicated by India, not just by the smells, colours and sounds, but by the energy of ordered chaos that permeated everything I saw. I felt like I had come home.

One day in February 1990, I was sitting on a sand dune in northern Sudan, staring at a rising full moon in a star showered sky. For nine months I had been cycling through Africa with three friends, riding through vast expanses of wild untarnished bush on a mountain bike and the three-seater 'trandem' originally used by *The Goodies*, a zany BBC series from the 1970s.

The deserts of Sudan had presented new challenges, forcing us to walk long distances on narrow donkey tracks connecting settlements beside the Nile. Although I was converted to the benefits of bicycle travel, the physical process of walking began to attract me even more. I found that the direct contact with the earth created a primal connection with the landscape, linking the sense of self with all that lay around, like a glimpse of something eternal, infinite and universal. Sitting on that sand dune, I suddenly knew that, one day, I would undertake a long walk. I did not know when, or exactly where it would take me. But I knew that I would travel alone on the dusty paths of rural India, the country that I had been obsessed with for years.

I returned from Africa in April 1990, disenchanted with the Western world. After a year of living like a nomad in the bush, life in London seemed totally divorced from what I now perceived as reality. I found it hard to see how I could fit into a massive economic machine that was systematically destroying the planet. The compromises appeared too great.

This period coincided with huge media interest in environmental problems, from rainforest destruction to global warming and holes in the ozone layer. I could not help feeling that we were heading for a planetary emergency, and that most people were living in a state of denial about the implications. It was hard to see what kind of career I could pursue without being a part of the problem. So I resolved to do whatever I could to raise awareness, through research, writing and, if possible, making films. To try to make ends meet during this period, I used my increasing passion for cooking to secure a series of jobs in London pubs and restaurants, most notably a six month stint at the renowned River Café in Hammersmith.

After making a film in India about pollution in the Ganges, which re-united Bill Oddie, one of the original Goodies, with the trandem, I started working with Herbie Girardet, an environmental writer and film-maker based between London and Wales. As the media interest waned during the 90s, and corporate 'greenwash' tactics were used to discredit the science behind climate change, my understanding and passion for the issues increased.

At the same time, I found myself on a spiritual quest. I began to believe that the world was engaged in a transition, shifting our values from competition and greed to cooperation and synthesis, giving birth to a new vision, the 'divine marriage' of inner and outer, male and female, reason and intuition, Matter and Spirit. My determination to embark on a long walk in India seemed to form an integral part of the quest. It was now or never.

I walked out of the town of Kanyakumari, the southern tip of India, on 30 September 1996, carrying a small pack on my back and a black umbrella. Six months later, I walked into Calcutta, having walked more than 2,000 miles and experienced the heaven and hell of India on a daily basis. I had been surrounded and attacked in a remote fishing village on the coast of Orissa; spent a night lost in a forest known for leopards, tigers and elephants; witnessed ancient festivals and rituals in the temples of Tamil Nadu. My guts were populated with battalions of alien bacteria and my feet felt like hardened leather soles.

A few days later, I was back in Bombay, ready for my return flight to England.

However, I delayed my departure to see Ramesh Balsekar, a spiritual teacher I wanted to meet. Before becoming a 'guru', Ramesh had studied at the London School of Economics, then he rose to the highest echelons in one of India's largest banks, living his life very much in the material, modern world. Rather than prescribing rituals, meditation techniques or magical formulas, he showed his students how to undermine the conditioned processes of the mind.

Every morning in his living room, Ramesh held *satsang*, a spontaneous discourse with anybody who turned up. Although he fulfilled the traditional role in the guru–disciple relationship, there was none of the razzmatazz that surrounded the personality cults of most modern teachers.

For the next week, I spent every morning listening to Ramesh expound his radical teaching, which supported a concept I had nurtured since childhood and was increasingly verified by modern science – that our sense of freewill is ultimately an illusion. One afternoon, lying under the fan in my hotel room and flicking through one of Ramesh's books, my attention was caught by one sentence: 'What you are trying to find is what you already are.' I had heard, or read, similar words on countless occasions. Usually I found them rather annoying: if it's so simple, why can't I grasp it? Why am I so miserable, searching for something which is staring me in the face?

This time however, something happened.

I had a sudden intuitive flash that lasted a split second but lit up the room. My spine jolted. I burst into laughter. It was tragic, but funny at the same time. After years of seeking something, I suddenly realized that 'it' has been too close to see. I walked over to the mirror. I was in my reflection and my reflection was in me.

Ironically, the confusion in my life was being dissolved by the words of a retired bank manager, rather than some wizened ascetic sage in a Himalayan cave. There was, however, one conundrum that I found hard to resolve. My passion for environmental problems seemed to be at odds with the core precepts of the teaching. If everything was as it should be, why would I bother concerning myself with such things?

Some years later, I saw that this was misconceived. Given my 'programming', that combination of genes and continually evolving social and environmental conditioning that creates our individual personality, I have no alternative but to do what I do. I began to see that, right now, in this moment, everything is perfect. It could not be any other way. However, that acceptance need not imply agreement. For example, although I *accept* that the current form of free market capitalism is a reality, it does not necessarily imply that I *agree* with it. If I feel driven to work towards environmental awareness and an ecological lifestyle, then that is the part that I am destined to play. Ultimately, I have no option.

Chapter Two

Lanka or La-La-Land?

Don't be afraid to go out on a limb.
That's where the fruit is.

Anon

31 May 1997. London.

I'm in the upstairs bar of a Notting Hill pub with my old friend Toby, where a friend of mine is running a club on Sunday afternoons. The members are mostly fashionistas and media types, pop promo directors and a few grungy models, eating lunch, drinking, playing backgammon, powdering their noses in the loos. It's the usual London scene. I've been back from India for three weeks. Nothing has changed. We order a bottle of red wine and start setting up a backgammon board.

'Who did you say was coming?' Toby asks.

'A girl called Rosie. I met her at that yoga retreat in Scotland before going to India. She's bringing a friend.'

'All right!'

'Don't get too excited, mate. No idea who she is.'

An hour later, Rosie appears. I walk over, give her a hug, introduce Toby. 'And this is Yvette,' Rosie says. A dark-skinned girl with long curly hair appears from the top of the stairs, wearing a dog-tooth jacket and black pants. In profile, she looks almost Ethiopian, her slender neck and fine features balanced with a pronounced fore-head. She is stunningly exotic.

'Hi,' she says, holding out her hand. Is that accent Irish, American?

'Hi, Yvette,' I reply. 'So, where are you from? I can't place your accent.'

'Barbados, originally. I live in LA now.'

I'm entranced. We sit down, order more wine, continue with our game, Rosie and Toby playing against Yvette and me.

'So, Rosie tells me you've been walking through India.' Yvette throws the dice and turns towards me. 'Why on earth did you do that?' I hate this question, since I have no adequate reply.

'You know what? I really don't know.' I had to be honest. 'It was just one of those things that evolved, took on a life of its own ...'

'What did you get out of it?' She's direct, penetrating. I like it.

'I met a teacher, a guru. An old man in Bombay. Kind of made sense of my life for the first time.'

We talk for hours. She wants to know about India. I want to know about California. When I wake the next day, I am enraptured.

In July, I flew west for the first time in my life, to see Yvette. She had moved to Venice Beach three years before, where she had started her journey as a ceramic artist. She met me at LAX, wearing a short black dress and driving a red pick-up. The city baked under a sun-drained sky, full of space, hazy white light and adrenalin dreams. The white noise of 'the grid' burnt the ends off my nerves, like flaring match heads. California was a buzz, but so alien to the world in which I had recently been immersed.

13

'Come travelling with me in India,' I kept saying to Yvette. 'This all seems so unreal by comparison.'

'OK,' she said one day. 'Let's do it. I've always wanted to go there.'

A month later, Yvette had left her life in LA and we were heading to India, where we planned to travel together while I was to write a book about my walk. At the time, I really believed that I wanted to live there and was intent on convincing Yvette that Tamil Nadu was far more attractive than Venice Beach.

After a few weeks, I had been completely cured of that aspiration. The frustrations of India got the better of me. Rather than revelling in the sensory stimulation, I could see only escalating pollution and desperate poverty.

The same week that Yvette and I had met, Rosie also introduced us to Giles. South African by birth, Giles had been a property developer in London before moving to Sri Lanka in the mid-90s. With his old friend and now business partner, Viren, a Sri Lankan by birth but educated in Canada, Giles was developing the Ulpotha Sanctuary, an eco-tourism venture in the heart of the island, which was preparing to receive its first group of budding yogis for two-week retreats. 'You have to come over,' Giles was adamant. 'You'll love it.'

Giles's advice came back to us and we sought refuge for a while in Sri Lanka. We arrived in the capital Colombo in November, shortly after a Tamil Tiger bombing in the city centre had destroyed parts of the Hilton, the World Trade Centre and surrounding office blocks. Luckily, the attack happened outside office hours. Viren described how shards of broken glass had flown across his office and been embedded like daggers in the opposite wall. One sliver had pierced the back of his chair.

Within hours of our arrival, Yvette was comparing the country to the island of her youth. 'It reminds me of Barbados when I was growing up,' she kept saying.

With a British mother and Bajan father, Yvette had been born and raised on the quintessential tropical island with swaying palms and white sand beaches, surrounded by a clear turquoise sea. Moving to London when she was 21, she endured the British climate for seven years before returning to Barbados, vowing never to subject herself to such miserable weather again. The Barbados Yvette knew as a child had largely disappeared. Recently rated as the fastest developing nation on earth, the island was enjoying a level of affluence and prosperity hitherto unknown in the Caribbean. The simplicity and charm that she now observed in Sri Lanka had given way to vulgar faux-Palladian villas, gated communities, traffic jams and crack-related crime. Although we were to spend many months there, and often weighed it up as a place to live, it was simply unaffordable. In those terms Sri Lanka was very different. We could live well, and relatively cheaply. Giles and Viren provided the perfect introduction and we spent memorable weeks taking trips to Ulpotha, down south to Galle and hanging with their friends in Colombo.

We stayed in Colombo with Giles and Pat, a Canadian recently divorced from her Sri Lankan husband but so smitten with the country that she had stayed. Her stunning spacious apartment overlooked the sea and railway just off Galle Road and formed the nexus for a floating population of intriguing people. There was Lalith, aka Leftie, who shared my interest in ecology; Amrik, a member of one of the country's political families, who shared Giles's passion for paragliding; Rukman, whose Galapita eco-lodge in the southeast of the island had a similar vision to Ulpotha. When we left Sri Lanka, after six weeks, for California, it was with considerable regret. Our overwhelming impressions were of smiling, friendly people and a stunningly beautiful island, perversely protected from the rapid changes seen in other parts of Asia by nearly 20 years of civil war.

Almost from the moment we met, Yvette and I started a seven-year conversation about where in the world to live. The decision centred on a few key places, focusing mainly on Barbados, California and Byron Bay in Australia. We made occasional forays into other ideas, from the Pyrenees and Morocco to South Africa and southern Italy, but these never lasted too long. Our reservations varied from the economic to the climatic, from the prevailing culture to the fact that, in the case of Australia, 'it's so bloody far away'.

As this seemingly endless discussion continued, Yvette found herself doing precisely what she had vowed never to do again – living in London. This was partly down to her wanting to sell the flat she owned, partly down to my inertia about leaving friends and family. London in the late 90s was a fun city to live in and, although we could not really afford it, we took full advantage of all that was on offer. Then, when it all got too much, something radical happened. I fell in love with a small cottage in Wales.

One bright Spring day in late March 1999, I was taking the train up to London from my father's house in Surrey, my eyes glued to the estate agent's details for Lower House, near the tiny village of Llanbadarn-y-Garreg. The train pulled into Staines and I watched as a man with a bicycle and trailer manoeuvred into the guard's van in the next carriage. He then wandered through and sat down opposite me.

'You thinking of moving to Wales?' he asked later, having seen the document I was studying so intently.

'Oh, dreaming of it really,' I replied, looking up. 'Why, is that where you live?'

'No, but I have lots of friends down there. It's a beautiful place.'

Minutes later, I discovered that Andy Langford knew my old boss from the film world, Herbie Girardet. But more importantly, he taught permaculture, a system and design philosophy for sustainable lifestyles.

'Permaculture isn't just about growing some of your own food,' Andy explained. 'It's a complete philosophy, covering every aspect of sustainable living. I'm teaching a course up at the Findhorn community in Scotland later this year. If you do buy the property, maybe you should come and join us?'

It sounded like a good idea. In a sense, this serendipitous meeting on the train changed my life. It was there and then that I resolved to move to Wales and start practising permaculture.

We spent the next four years living at Lower House, two winters of which we escaped to Barbados. Despite some reluctance, Yvette enjoyed the life we had there, especially during those rare moments when the sun shone. The location was stunning, the house perched on a south-facing hillside on the edge of the Edw Valley, about 12 miles west of Hay-on-Wye. Perfect rainbows would span the valley, dropping into green pastures like divine reflections. In the late summer of 2000, we were married in the small parish church, becoming the second couple in a hundred years to do so. For the next three years, we grew vegetables, walked the hills, foraged for wild mushrooms, planted fruit trees and Yvette kept bees.

Our time in Wales was productive for both of us. I was able to explore my interest in ecological building, constructing a straw-bale house rendered with lime mortar, which served as a studio for Yvette and an office for me. Yvette started a collection of work, developing her own distinctive style, while I researched and wrote *Rising Tides*, a history of ecological thought.

Then, on Boxing Day 2000, Yvette announced that she was pregnant. Sholto was born on 5 September, three weeks late and after 42 hours of labour. Like every couple with their first baby, our lives changed from that moment. Six days later, 10 fanatics flew two commercial airliners into the World Trade Center in New York, and the whole world changed forever. The global events that followed only fuelled the desire for a new life overseas, somewhere a bit out on a limb.

Living on a Welsh hillside, with a small baby, 20 minutes' drive from the nearest pint of milk, with torrential rain and gale force winds pounding the doors and windows, proved quite a challenge, especially for my Caribbean wife. We rented our house to Zoe, an ex-groupie to a Swedish punk band and custodian to a menagerie of gerbils, then flew to Barbados and rented a flat for four months.

Chapter Three

'Doc Man'

Only when the last river has been poisoned,
the last tree cut down, the last fish has been caught;
only then will you realize that money cannot be eaten.

Cree Indian saying

Within days of our arrival in Barbados in late 2001, I was introduced to Dr Colin Hudson by a friend of Yvette's, who saw that my increasing fanaticism for all things ecological might resonate well with the man who had become the island's most prominent environmental campaigner. Although some people dismissed him as an eccentric alarmist, few could fault the integrity of his beliefs. I was intrigued to meet him but, at the time, had no idea just how much he would influence the direction my life has taken since, providing the key inspiration for the major decisions we would soon be making.

Stepping from the dust and din of Barbados roads, into the lush green abundance of Little Edgehill, we found ourselves in Colin and his partner Mo's garden. It created a palpable shift in perception, like an oasis in the desert. Wearing a wide-brimmed straw hat, Mo waved from a corner of the garden, where she sieved compost through what looked like a giant hamster's treadmill, made from rolled up wire fencing. Her movements were slow and methodical, seemingly effortless, despite the midday heat.

'Hey, Doc Man,' she called to Colin. 'Rory and Yvette are here.'

Dressed in tatty shorts and a T-shirt, his arms and legs covered in scratches, Colin, 'Doc Man' to his friends, emerged from behind a stack of cleared branches, piled into a long row below a towering *ficus*. After a brisk introduction, I explained the core ideas behind my recent book *Rising Tides*. Then Colin wiped the sweat from his brow and shot off on a whirlwind tour of the plot, while I struggled to keep up, both with the pace of his step and the torrent of information that poured out of him.

'This half-acre represents, almost exactly, the Ecological Footprint for a couple on this island,' he said.

Although familiar with the Ecological Footprint analysis, an ecological accounting tool which reflects the real impact to the biosphere from human activities, I still found Colin's explanation tremendously illuminating.

'Imagine a vertical cylinder, around you, or your house, your car, your holiday, whatever it may be. You have to work out how big that cylinder must be to maintain whatever it is indefinitely. The energy embodied in the components of your car, for example, includes not just the resources used to make it, but also the petroleum products used in its manufacture and transport. Then add that to the amount of atmosphere required to absorb the carbon monoxide, nitrous oxides and other pollution generated by the manufacturing, maintenance and the driving of the car, and you arrive at a figure that tells you how much of the planet's bio-productive capacity is needed to absorb the full life-cycle impact of your car, from design to disposal.

'This can be applied to anything, from cars and houses through to what we eat, like having a farmed trout on your plate once a week for example. The Footprint will not only reflect the area of land required to grow what the fish is fed, but the impact of transporting it to the fish farm, as well as the processing, packaging and transport which brings the fish to your supermarket shelf.'

'It's a very clever tool,' I said, already feeling the contagious quality of Colin's enthusiasm. 'At last we can reduce these intangible issues to concrete terms, and make informed decisions about what is truly sustainable.'

'Exactly!' beamed Colin. 'And it produces some surprising results. For instance, a car is made of some 15,000 components. The energy used in their manufacture and assembly is more than 10 years' driving in terms of fossil fuel use.'

Colin's message was also aimed at those who assumed that their Footprint was light. 'Ironically, long distance cyclists, who need to replace the thousands of calories they burn through, can be very high Footprint users if they eat energy bars produced from lots of different ingredients, flown in from around the world. Of course, if they eat locally grown organic produce, their Footprint is very low.'

And contrary to what many believe, our modern industrial agriculture is hugely inefficient, yielding only six units of energy for every 15 used in its production. 'Compare that with some forest gardens, or permaculture systems, which produce 15 times more energy than they use in their production,' Colin said. 'Now *that's* efficient!'

Our conversation came full circle as Colin looked around his garden.

'With the current population of Barbados, this garden represents the per capita fair share of Footprint available for a couple,' continued Colin, as he sped off through terraces made of old stacked tyres, brimming with rocket, exotic lettuces and medicinal herbs.

'When Mo and I moved here, about two years ago, we set out to see what we could do with it. We are now living within our Footprint, growing more than enough calories to feed ourselves. We've found that more than 70 per cent of our waste was compostable, so we've cut our landfill waste by over 90 per cent. We recycle our "grey-water" from sinks and the washing machine, using it for our watercress.'

As he spoke he turned and headed over to an elevated trough, made from recycled plastic containers, brimming with a thick blanket of watercress. 'The pump is driven by that solar panel,' he said, pointing to the corner of the garden. He then hurdled a terrace of tyres, sped over to the panel and turned it a few degrees. 'Solar panels are up to 200 per cent more efficient if they track the movement of the sun,' he said, wandering back to where I stood.

I wondered how the changes in their lifestyle had affected Colin and Mo's basic living costs. 'Inevitably, we are still locked into the system to some degree. We have insurance payments, pensions, a few utility bills, but our overall spending is about a quarter of what it was.'

'Do you ever feel that you are depriving yourselves of anything?' I asked rhetorically, sensing what the answer would be. 'Absolutely not!' he said. 'Quite the reverse. This has been the most fun thing I have ever done in my life. We have learned so much, just by trying to live "intelligently". This is what indigenous people had to do, on a daily basis: devise intelligent ways to use the resources available to them.' Colin believed it was crucial to distinguish 'intelligent' human activities from technologies which are merely 'clever'. As examples he cited biomimicry as an approach to design, permaculture systems and photo-voltaic solar cells. 'While I agree that genetic modification is very clever, I'm not sure whether it's really intelligent,' he said. 'Intelligent living is fun. In fact, we have started a consultancy here, called Treading Lightly, trying to help people with sustainability issues, trying to show them what's possible. Our motto is "Using Less, Living More". Living this way may seem like a challenge, but it should be fun to do it, not a drag.'

As I followed Colin past a line of passion fruit vines, I reflected on how rarely people 'walk the talk' to such a degree. Although I had spent many years involved with 'the movement', I was often struck by how seldom people had been able to integrate these principles into their own lives.

We stopped for tea under a long, low shelter made from recycled aluminium sheets, curved over a frame of wooden poles. Running the length of the structure, hanging from pieces of cord with clothes pegs, were laminated sheets of printed A4 paper. My eyes skimmed over a few pages. One held a cartoon showing the planet under maximum stress from pollution and diminishing resources, with a huge tap attached to it and one dismal drop of water hanging off the end. Below it stood two besuited figures. 'There's only one solution,' says one. 'A much bigger tap.'

Next to this hung concise descriptions of the Footprint analysis, accessible to both adults and young children. Tips on how to make your own domestic cleaning products from non-toxic materials hung next to ways of keeping your house cool without using electricity; a successful car-pool scheme in Berlin next to windmill water-pumps in the Colombian community of Gaviotas.

Another cartoon struck me deeply, summing up three responses to the issues we face at the start of the 21st century. The drawing was of a yacht, struggling against strong winds in high seas. The caption read: 'The optimist waits for the wind to change. The pessimist says it won't. Meanwhile, the realist sets the sails.' It seems that most of us fall into one of these categories. The optimists, or technologists amongst us, insist that human ingenuity will prevail, enabling us always to stay one step ahead of nature. The pessimists don't care and think we're heading for extinction, whatever happens. Then there are the realists, those rare men and women, like Colin and Mo, who actually seem to be doing something.

'This is designed like a funnel,' Colin said, pointing to the roof above us. 'One end is wider than the other, so that the air passes through and keeps it cool.'

The room was indeed noticeably fresh after the midday heat, and we sat on low sofas made from strips of foam spread across old plastic milk crates.

'What brought you to Barbados?' I asked Colin.

'Well, it was the product of those strange synchronicities which seem to happen only two or three times in one's life. While I was studying at agricultural college, I became fascinated with the prospect of population increase and how the world would keep feeding itself. This became the subject of an essay I wrote for a competition and, while doing the research, I came across a report by the FAO – the UN's Food and Agriculture Organization – which listed Barbados as one of the role models for sustainable agriculture in the tropics.

'This was partly the result of naval blockades during the Second World War, when the island was forced to feed itself, creating an incredibly sophisticated system, from planting firewood to cooking the local sweet potatoes – rather than relying on imported rice – through to distilling their own vinegar. Anyway, after leaving college

I saw a job advertised for a soil physicist here, applied for the position and got it. Not long after, I found myself working for Sir John Saint, the visionary who has been responsible for much of the island's success.'

'So when you arrived here, 40 years ago, the island was pretty much self-sufficient?'

'Absolutely.' Colin's sparkling eyes reminded me of a wise owl. 'It was almost like a picture book it was so perfect. I was completely awe-struck by the productivity, which was more horticulture than agriculture, revolving around some 26,000 allotments, or small-holdings of about quarter to half an acre, integrated with modest-sized farms of about 200 to 300 acres. It was certainly labour intensive, but so ingeniously devised and so competently managed.

'Someone with quarter of an acre had access to the same genetic base as the biggest farmer, the same seed store, the same animal stock. At the time, this was the most densely populated agricultural nation on earth, with an holistic subsistence economy. Barbados was like a crucible, a tropical laboratory for self-reliance.'

'And what remains of those 26,000 allotments?' I asked.

'Oh, a thousand, if that,' said Colin, visibly pained at the thought.

'So what made you stay?'

'Towards the end of his life, Sir John saw that the whole thing would fall apart, as development and tourism took hold. At the time, I could not believe that it would, but he just looked at me and said: "Young man, it will." And he was right. Anyway, I stayed out of curiosity I suppose, to see what would happen and whether there was any chance of preserving what was here.'

'Do you see evidence of the island's ecology being under strain?'

'All the time. And it's not just old nutcases like me,' he said. 'It's in the newspapers every day – people wondering what to do about the traffic, the pollution, the reefs, the beaches disappearing, the water ...'

'So when the island was self-reliant, was it living within its Footprint?' I wondered.

'It was. It had to. Nothing was imported. Today we need five times more than the area of the whole island to sustain ourselves. Most of our food comes from Canada, America and Europe. Should any of these supply lines be disrupted, we would find ourselves in a lot of trouble.'

I looked around. 'Places like this would become much sought after.'

'I know,' said Colin. 'That's what I keep telling Mo. We'd have to barricade ourselves in here with a shotgun!'

Among Colin's portfolio of activities was his role as leader of the National Trust hikes, taking residents and visitors alike on long rambling walks through the nooks and crannies of the island.

I was to accompany him on several hikes, and was increasingly amazed by his energy and enthusiasm for everything about Barbados. One day I asked him where the inspiration had come from.

'A man called Richard Goddard,' he said, striding out through an avenue of sugarcane with his rolled up brolly. 'He was Bajan but went to live in Canada. When he came back, after many years, he was terribly saddened to see that his friends and family were losing touch with their country – the culture, the history, the flora and fauna.'

'It often seems to take someone coming from the outside to notice these things. Like yourself,' I said.

'Well I don't know about that,' he replied modestly. 'But the idea for the hikes has spread. Some visiting Indians came on a few and, from what I hear, they are now running hikes in New Delhi!'

'It seems to be another strange irony of the Information Age. Despite being saturated with information, we're losing all contact with our roots and immediate environment.'

'Indeed,' said Colin, turning down a footpath towards one of the island's gullies. 'That's what bio-regionalism is all about, learning to understand how things work around you, the trees, the hydrology, the flora and fauna.'

'Apparently children in the developed world can recognize up to one thousand brand logos but fewer than 10 local plants,' I said as we zig-zagged down a steep bank.

'It's funny you should say that.' Colin was now beating a path through thick undergrowth with his umbrella. 'When I take school-children round our garden, I often tell them how Amerindian children, by the time they are 10 or 11, can recognize over a thousand indigenous plants. They may not be able to read and write, but they can identify the medicinal properties of herbs, which plants are poisonous, which can be eaten and so on. Then I ask the children which do they think are the better educated. And do you know what? To my absolute amazement, the vast majority of them say the Amerindian children are. I find that fascinating.'

Colin had started out life as an engineer, but ended up an environmental campaigner. When Barbados played host to Rio+2 in 1994, he hatched a plan to raise the spirit of the event. It was the first international UN conference after the Earth Summit two years earlier and a focus for the Small Island Developing States most at risk from rising sea levels.

His Village of Hope fired the imagination of over 3,000 people on the island, working together to build a temporary exhibit to showcase examples of sustainability, or 'Initiatives of Hope', from around the world. Traditional water purification techniques from the area stood next to the latest solar technology from California, hydroponic farming initiatives from the slums of South America next to permaculture systems from Australia, local recycling and composting initiatives next to appropriate and intermediate technologies in use throughout rural Africa.

'We wanted to recognize the horrors but provide solutions at the same time,' Colin said. 'Rather than telling people that things should be like this, we wanted to say, "Look, these people are already doing this in Gaviotas, in Curitiba, in small villages in south India." Rather than wagging the finger, we wanted to show what was already possible, what was already happening. This simple four-letter word – hope – incites such resonance within people; more and more so as the world reels from one crisis to the next, and the media bombards us with doom and gloom.'

I nodded. 'The debate seems to start from the position that there are no solutions, that sustainability is nothing more than a pipe-dream, or a buzz-word.'

'Precisely,' said Colin. 'But the fact is that thousands of people around the world *are* living sustainably. We just don't hear about what they're doing, because it's not news, there's no drama involved!'

The time I spent with Colin over the next two years was inspiring and intensely rewarding. Not only was he a man with a vision, but a man with the energy and dynamism to live it. Looking at the scale and speed of the development on the island – the brash, almost vulgar opulence of the new hotels, the huge scars on the landscape where natural habitats had been cleared for yet another golf course, coral limestone excavated to build yet another sumptuous villa (only to be occupied by the owner once a year) – I began to reflect on the nature of wealth itself. Despite the material trappings, I wondered just how much better off Barbados was now than 40 years ago.

Sure, most people were no longer toiling in the fields, or living in cramped wooden chattel houses. They were sitting in air-conditioned cars and concrete office cubicles, breathing recycled polluted air, developing RSI at their computers, incubating road rage, suffering from soaring rates of cancer and adult onset diabetes from nitrate and pesticide run-off in the water and learning how to cope with stress, that peculiar modern phenomenon which technology and progress seem to have accentuated rather than diminished.

As Colin liked to point out, 'Eco-nomics' and 'Eco-logy' share the same Greek root, *oikos*, meaning house. Both words refer to the management of the household to the mutual benefit of all who live there. Unfortunately, the two words followed divergent paths. Our economic system is concentrating money and power into a smaller and smaller elite, the gap between rich and poor is widening, the biosphere is riddled with toxic pollutants, global warming threatens to extinguish life as we know it, basic resources like water and topsoil are disappearing and evidence from all around the world has exposed the fallacy of the 'trickle-down' benefits of capitalism.

Colin and I agreed that the only way to reverse this situation was to bring economics and ecology back into synergy, to apply ecological truths to our corrupted economic thought and make it beneficial, not only to all human beings, but to all forms of life. As Colin liked to point out: 'Many economies have been built on ecologies, but not one ecology has ever been built on an economy.' For sustainability to become a reality, we had to learn to live off 'nature's interest', rather than our 'natural capital'. As eco-economists like Paul Hawken point out, we are currently burning through our collective inheritance of natural capital, using as much oil in one year as nature took a million years to create.

From our many discussions, I began to realize that real wealth is what surrounds us – the topsoil, trees, plants, water and planetary life-support systems that constitute our natural capital. Unfortunately, these 'ecosystem services' are ignored by conventional economics. Hence the pickle we find ourselves in. Are wealthy people really rich, I began to wonder? Are they happy? Is a successful person a 'rich' person, or a 'happy' person? I have repeatedly been struck by the fact that some of the poorest people I met in Africa or Asia, appear to be some of the happiest. I thought about the charm of villages I had walked through in Tamil Nadu and Andhra Pradesh, the selfless hospitality we had been shown while cycling in northern Sudan, or the simplicity of traditional life in a refuge like Ulpotha. These places seemed to exist outside time, like T. S. Eliot's 'still point of the turning world', divorced from amplified modern pressures by the lack of television, cars and telephones. I began to yearn for more of that in our own lives.

Chapter Four

The Web of Hope

You never change things by fighting the existing reality.
To change something, build a new model that
makes the existing model obsolete.

Buckminster Fuller

At the time that we met, Colin was working with others from around the globe to develop a Village of Hope, similar to the one he had created in Barbados, for the World Summit on Sustainable Development in Johannesburg later that year. He suggested that I start compiling a 'Book of Hope' to coincide with this, a compil-ation of 'best practice' role models for sustainability drawn from around the globe. Soon I was ploughing through Colin's dusty files and 30 years of *Ecologist* back issues, depressing myself about the state of the planet. But, once in a while, I would find little seeds of hope that would provide the basis for the book: the forest gardens of Kerala; the hydrogen fuel-cell; micro-credit schemes like the Grameen Bank in Bangladesh. As the weeks and months passed, the concept evolved from the original booklet into an ever-expanding online database, which it seemed natural to call the Web of Hope, an educational resource that would highlight ecological solutions and make them accessible to a more mainstream audience.

Back in Wales, the project gathered steam. Colin and Mo made a visit and, following an introduction from my graphic designer friend Paddy, a virtual neighbour in the Golden Valley, we all trooped off to a meeting in Stroud with a small IT outfit working from some converted farm buildings. Sitting in on the meeting was Tim Willmott, who had been working with them for some months. He looked uncomfortable in a navy blue suit, and I had the sense that the corporate world was no longer his bag. Our embryonic idea clearly resonated with Tim, and it became apparent that we had a core team ready and willing to move this forward. Paddy designed a logo and I started preparing copy for the first *Little Book of Hope*, which we aimed to launch and distribute for free at the World Summit in Johannesburg. Tim used his long career in IT and experience in the corporate world to start preparing funding proposals and, bit by bit, the pieces came together. We found a few core supporters prepared to offer seed money, others willing to be trustees.

In August 2002, I joined Colin in Johannesburg for the lamentable Summit, at which governments from around the world abdicated responsibility for looking after the planet, preferring instead to promote public-private partnerships with the very corporations responsible for most of the world's ecological problems.

However, on another level, the air was buzzing, as activists and NGOs from around the world fused their networks, shared resources and expanded their global reach. I could almost hear the nodes of this expanding global network fizzing as new connections were made. Although funding for Colin's Village of Hope was withdrawn at the last minute, the Web of Hope was now making itself visible.

During 2003, the Web of Hope (WoH) became a registered UK charity and we started our educational roadshow, which has since been performed for children around the south of the country.

Life in Wales was becoming increasingly difficult. I was travelling a lot for WoH meetings and Yvette felt marooned up a valley with Sholto demanding all her attention. We were also broke, since Tim and I were rarely paid, and what little money we did raise was earmarked for the WoH.

It was at about the time that we found Yvette was pregnant again, in February, that the seven year conversation finally came to an end. I was cooking dinner in Wales, ruminating on the globe and the myriad possibilities it offered. As we had found for seven years, when confronted with the whole world, it was hard to pin down a place that appealed to both of us. This time however, it happened.

'How about Sri Lanka?' I said suddenly.

'What? To live?' Yvette looked startled.

'Yup. To live.'

'OK,' she replied. 'Let's check it out. Sounds like things have moved on over there with the peace process.'

I was also feeling the urge to move on. Aspects of life in Britain were starting to wear me down: the omnipresent speed cameras and CCTV, the Americanization of British politics upheld by New Labour, the 'nanny state' syndrome, the hypocrisy of the state clamping down on basic freedoms, the blatant lies of politicians and their pathetic attempts to deal with the most urgent problems facing humanity, all combined with the sheer expense of living there.

This was also a period in which my eco-fundamentalism reached a peak. Almost every action we took was considered in relation to the planet: from which saucepan to use and how much water to put in the kettle, through to Ecological Footprint studies on the impact of disposable nappies compared with the cotton ones we washed at home. At times this bordered on the insane, but my anger at those I saw responsible for the state of the planet was real enough. What right did these people have to inflict poisons on us, 'medicating' society with enforced vaccinations, chemical additives in food, fluoride in the water supply? Following 9/11, I had begun to see a rotten core at the heart of the Western world and the American Empire, now ruled by a group of people I found positively spooky. My research into the US 'neo-con' cabal and their vision for the 21st century did not comfort me. It seemed these guys would stop at nothing, openly referring to recent advances in genetics that could transform biological warfare into 'a politically useful tool – by targeting specific genotypes'. The invasion of Iraq was the final straw.

Part of the attraction of Sri Lanka was the escape from the endless bombardment of propaganda from the Western media; the spice of a life less controlled, and the possibilities that this afforded; the option of being able to build an ecological house without having to conform to absurd building regulations, or the possibility of realizing dreams that were simply untenable in the UK, like leading a lifestyle that was largely self-sufficient and within ecologically sound parameters. The fact that the kids would grow up close to a tropical beach was an added bonus, and my beloved India would be on our doorstep.

In March 2003, we were back in Sri Lanka for the first time in seven years, making a three-week 'recce' to see if this was really the place where we wanted to put down roots. The civil war in the north had reached a ceasefire, the peace process was holding and foreign investors were knocking at the door. Giles, whose enthusiasm had prompted our first visit, was currently in the property business to cater for those who were now looking at the country as a stable and viable place to live.

Within hours, the trials and tribulations of the tropics started to strike home. We had rented a beachfront cabana on Wijaya Beach near Talpe – a truly stunning location for much of the year. However, the season was ending, the sea starting to change and horizontal rain lashing into our hut. Inevitably, we had all come down with colds and a hacking cough on the plane. Yvette, already nauseously pregnant, was really suffering. In addition, the salty humid air made the mattress, sheets, pillows and mosquito nets damp. This was far from comfortable and less than ideal conditions for recovery.

Fortunately, a good spell of weather followed, the hut dried out, we dried out and vitality was restored. The pendulum swings of Sri Lanka had already started. We spent a few days making forays with Giles to look at property, then adjourned for a few days at Ulpotha, soaking up the secluded tranquillity for which this traditional mud village has become so renowned. We swam in the freshwater tank, feasted on sumptuous local curries and indulged in ayurvedic pamperings.

One piece of land down south had intrigued me, on a hilltop outside Galle, with fabulous panoramic views. At the time, the fact that the previous owners had been the Aum Shinkyo cult from Japan, and the only building on the land was a large concrete bunker that looked suspiciously like a sarin gas factory, was not enough to put me off. So started some ambitious plans.

A combination of Colin's influence, my work with the Web of Hope and the inspiration provided by places like Ulpotha, all now converged into one dream: to develop a place in Sri Lanka that was both an ecological learning centre as well as a living example of some of the ideas that had found their way onto the WoH database, from permaculture and forest gardening to rainwater harvesting, mud-building and photo-voltaic solar panels – like Colin's Village of Hope, but more permanent. Ultimately, I envisaged this becoming another 'node' within a global network of such initiatives, a place where teachers could share their knowledge with those who passed through. Over three days at Ulpotha, this idea was nurtured through the presence of one wise old man.

When he was first interviewed for *The Ecologist* by Teddy Goldsmith in 1984, the late Mudiyanse Tennekoon was described as 'a prophet of traditional rural life in Sri Lanka'. Descended from a long lineage of traditional farmers, Tennekoon was a living encyclopaedia of indigenous wisdom and knowledge. Much of this was evident in the interview, where he listed many traditional methods for controlling pests, from pouring cactus milk into paddy field inlets to spreading crushed coconut refuse at the corner of fields to attract the *Demalichch* bird, which feasted on the paddy bugs and *Godewella* worms.

Tennekoon was dismissive of the Green Revolution hybrids and chemical applications so applauded in the 1950s, noting that 'the traditional varieties of paddy had long stems so they blew in the wind, which made it very difficult for the insects to land on them', and their 'big droopy leaves which shaded the soil underneath and prevented weeds from growing through'. By planting a diverse crop from the 280 or so varieties of rice cultivated in the country, traditional farmers were also less prone to poor harvests through drought and climatic variations. He pointed out that certain rice varieties were grown for a particular purpose, some being good for lactating mothers, others for those working in the fields. Of these 280 varieties, only 15 or so are now left.

Over the previous 10 years, Tennekoon had become the mentor at Ulpotha, now a thriving traditional community in a previously deserted village near Kurunegela, in the middle of the island. In 1833, the British had abolished Sri Lanka's traditional system of *rajakariya*, a form of community service responsible for maintaining the sophisticated upland irrigation system, which they regarded as feudal and abusive. Ulpotha, which translates as 'water source', was one of many important watersheds abandoned as a result of this process.

Tennekoon oversaw the rehabilitation of the system of reservoirs, known as 'tanks' (from the Portuguese *tanque*) at Ulpotha, thus restoring the watershed and providing an irrigation system for communities throughout the area. (Viren and Giles have since enabled the community to become self-sustaining by opening the village up for small groups of ecotourists and yoga students, with a limit of 16 weeks in the year to minimize the impact.) Spartan but comfortable mud huts provide accommodation for guests, who gather in the central *ambalama* (pavilion) for meals, or just to sit and absorb the serenity that seems so intrinsic to the place. In addition, various reforestation projects were implemented, along with traditional paddy field and agro-forestry systems. The village is now almost entirely self-reliant.

The indigenous wisdom that informed Tennekoon's perspective was only half the story. He was also a man of great wit, writing incisive but humorous letters to both George W. Bush and Saddam Hussein in the run-up to the war in Iraq. His humour could also convey those direct and simple truths that modern man so easily overlooks. When asked by Goldsmith if he had ever used a tractor, Tennekoon pointed out that it not only disturbs the soil structure but 'neither defecates nor urinates, hence makes no contribution to soil fertility ...

nor does it reproduce itself – when it dies one simply has to buy another tractor.' As he wryly concluded, 'What is the point of saving labour in a country which has such high unemployment?'

Tennekoon also possessed an extra-sensory level of communication with the biological world. In the same way that some indigenous people, elephants and other wild animals were able to sense the tsunami on its way, he could sense imbalance or unease within the natural world around him. Giles recalls one day at Ulpotha, when he went to bathe at the tank with Tennekoon. As they came back to the steps, Giles saw Tennekoon break down in sobs and start wailing.

'I asked him what was wrong,' Giles remembers. 'He pointed towards the bank at the end of the tank, saying that something terrible had happened. Later that day, some villagers came rushing to tell me that two cows had fallen in and been trapped between rocks, at the precise point where Tennekoon was pointing. When I mentioned this to him later, he just remarked, "Oh, that must have been it", and carried on with his business.'

In terms of 'walking the talk', Tennekoon could hardly be faulted.

'He was a one-off who actually lived in the world he talked so much about,' Viren said. 'He believed that spirits were all around us and needed to be respected and revered, that nature was a powerful force to be treated at least as well as the gods, and that there was much to be learned from the way man traditionally lived in ages past.'

The last time I saw Tennekoon, before he died in February 2005, he gave me a pamphlet entitled *Universal Welfare Organization*, his blueprint for a governance system that would respect the rights of the natural world and the role that humanity could play within it. It was a lucid and far-reaching document, tracing the globalization process from the fall of Constantinople in 1453 through the Industrial and Technological revolutions to the present day. His conclusions serve as a fitting legacy to the vision and ideals of a man whose passing has left the world without much of the wisdom we so urgently need.

'Both nature and the human race face total destruction. It is the urgent duty and common task of all progressive individuals, who seek to safeguard the common future of humanity and the equally vital conservation of nature, to devote themselves to the organization of the global mass-movements directed towards these historical objectives. They will necessarily have to engage in a relentless struggle to abolish the power of big corporations and the bureaucracies, and to establish the supremacy of civil society through democratic revolution.'

As far as Tennekoon was concerned, modern man had been brainwashed by a 'story' – one that needs to be replaced with a 'new story' that integrates indigenous, traditional wisdom with progressive ecological thinking.

By the time we flew back to the UK in late March 2003, Yvette and I were on a mission. We needed to complete work on the house in Wales so that we could offer it for sale. This was not as straightforward as we had initially thought, and it would take some months and several prospective buyers before we secured a deal.

It was a fraught and emotional time. Although I was excited by the move to Sri Lanka, it also seemed a huge step into the abyss. Was this such a good idea? How would we survive there? What would we *do*? Where would the kids go to school? Would it be it safe with a new baby? Most of our friends thought we were insane. 'Sri Lanka? Why do you want to go there? Isn't there a civil war going on?'

Apart from these concerns, I was also gutted to leave a house and a landscape that I had become so attached to. Then there was my commitment to the Web of Hope. Would my geographical separation affect the success or failure of the organization?

Over the next few months, life moved in to a new dimension. When you are having a child, the universe seems to conspire to make life as complicated as possible. Suddenly you are changing jobs, moving house, having the child, all at the same time.

In our case, we were doing all this, as well as planning to move countries. We had decided to move lock, stock and barrel, liberating ourselves once and for all from that lurking sense of responsibility for what lay back home – be it a house, or merely stored possessions rotting in some warehouse. The levels of stress began to ratchet up.

In addition, we had taken on a full summer schedule for the Web of Hope. This kicked off with a one-week conference coordinated by the Gaia Foundation, a global network of prominent activists. It was built around a visit from theologian and writer Father Thomas Berry, author of *The Great Work* who was described by *Newsweek* at the time as 'America's greatest living philosopher'.

One of the many inspiring points raised by Thomas really struck a chord with me, adding further momentum to plans nurtured in Sri Lanka. 'Of the institutions that should be guiding us into a viable future, the university has a special place because it teaches all those professions that control the human endeavour.' His voice was frail with age as he read from his book, but the words were concise and considered. 'Our educational institutions need to see their purpose not as training personnel for exploiting the earth but as guiding students towards an intimate relationship with the earth.' Gaia Foundation's concept of 'ecological learning centres' acting as nodes around the globe, spoke directly to my desire to do something similar, making me wonder if the project in Sri Lanka could add to this in some way.

The question most often raised about our move regarded the children's education. What would we do? Being disillusioned with the British system, and in no way able to afford the education I had been privileged to enjoy, I had long felt that we could hardly do worse than what was on offer in England. I fancied the notion of starting a small school, which would place as much emphasis on ecological education and practical skills as on the conventional curriculum. Maths and history would co-exist with cooking, gardening, growing vegetables, carpentry and basic building skills, similar to a Rudolf Steiner school, but without the restrictions of a single ideological basis. The original Small School started by *Resurgence* editor Satish Kumar in his village of Hartland, Devon, was a role model I had in mind, but I knew it posed a major challenge.

On the last day of the Gaia Conference, Colin Campbell, a shaman, threw the bones for Yvette and me, using ancient divination techniques to see the pattern displayed by the random casting of 54 pieces of crocodile tooth, rhino bone and other relics from the African bush.

Colin's story was fascinating. He had grown up in the bush of south Botswana, bizarrely in the very village where I had spent the first night of my year-long cycle through Africa, and had been adopted by the local medicine men from an early age, learning about the properties of plants from the age of six. He first felt 'the calling' in his late teens. But because he knew that the initiation as a *sangoma* was gruelling, often killing people in the process, he committed to it only many years later. Without doubt, there was a quality and a presence about this man that was different. He had a quiet humility

41

matched with an incisive wisdom that cut through the verbal baggage of some group discussions.

I remember looking at Yvette as Colin removed the pieces from a bag and prepared for the throwing. The atmosphere was charged, almost visibly electric. From the moment that the bones fell, Colin's usually taciturn nature was transformed. A torrent of information then flowed from him: precise, exact and delivered in a way quite distinct from his usually withdrawn demeanour. It was astounding – as though our minds had been x-rayed, revealing all.

Sri Lanka, Colin concluded, should be good for both of us, but California would be even better. Oh dear, I thought at the time. Lanka or La-La-Land? Have we made the right decision?

Somehow, the jigsaw fell together. In July we had an official launch for the Web of Hope at my father's house in Surrey. We then planned another visit to Barbados, where Number Two was due in early October. I could spend more time with 'Doc Man' Colin and we would all avoid another British winter. The house in Wales sold, we stored our belongings at my father's house and flew to Barbados in September. We rented a house from a friend of Yvette's and prepared for the new arrival. Xan was born on 9 October, in a birthing centre in Barbados, with Yvette's mother, Sholto and me all standing by.

Our greatest concern for the future, especially now that we had two children, was how to make our lives economically sustainable. *Rising Tides* was clearly not a 'beach read', nor destined for the bestseller lists. The Web of Hope moved forward in fits and starts but was unlikely to be a reliable source of income during these embryonic stages, if ever.

We had been in Barbados a few weeks, when one day I received an e-mail, followed by a phone call, from Michael Baldwin, who had read about the Web of Hope in an article I had written for *Resurgence* magazine. The founder of the Marion Institute near Boston, Michael had been contemplating starting something similar. Why reinvent the wheel if others were already working on it? Could we not forge some sort of collaboration? Within a few days, Michael had arranged to fly to Barbados for one night so that we could meet.

'How will I recognize you at the airport?' I asked.

'Oh, I'll be wearing a blue blazer and looking like another boring American,' he replied in a throwaway Bostonian drawl.

Michael proved to be the very antithesis of 'another boring American'. After a successful career on Wall Street, his passion for 'the alternative' found expression by laying the foundations for what was to become the Marion Institute. His initial interest in the more extreme edge of unexplained recent phenomena, like crop circles and alien abduction, led him to set up a series of conferences and events that had enlisted a veritable Who's Who of the prime movers from a wide spectrum of disciplines. People like Nobel Peace Prize Winner and founder of Kenya's Green Belt Movement Wangari Maathai; 'new physicist' Peter Russell; global energy guru and pioneer of the hydrogen fuel-cell Hypercar concept, Amory Lovins; visionary eco-economist Paul Hawken.

Michael was so different from what I expected – as clearly I was for him – that we stood staring around each other outside the airport for a full two minutes. Eventually, I zeroed in on the blue blazer.

'Michael?' I asked tentatively.

'Rory!' He shook my hand with gusto and we walked towards the car. As we loaded his bags into the boot, Michael took off his blazer and rolled up his shirtsleeves, revealing large tattoos on one

43

forearm. An unlikely adornment for a Wall Street financier, I thought.

As we drove to his hotel, Michael further shattered any preconceptions I had of an East Coast WASP. His far-reaching intellect, grasp of diverse issues and passion for it all was astounding. Our conversation swung from climate change to *The Da Vinci Code*, from Tibetan Buddhist teachers to new economic theories developed by Paul Hawken, from biodiversity to the connections between ancient mysticism and modern physics made by writers like Fritjof Capra and Peter Russell. The discussion continued over dinner and we made an informal arrangement to see how the Web of Hope might be aligned with Marion Institute. Michael would talk to the board and see how we might progress. It all seemed very positive.

Xan was three months old when we flew back to the UK in the January 2004 and made our final plans for departure. We packed a few tea chests of essentials to be shipped out to Sri Lanka and left the rest of our belongings stacked in a garage at my father's house, planning to be back in six months to send them out in a container.

This felt strange, a final severing of ties, not only with our home in Wales but also the house and country in which I had grown up. Although I had travelled a good deal, spending many months overseas at a time, this felt very different. This was it – a final departure. However things turned out in Sri Lanka, I knew the chances of our returning to the UK were slight.

Just before we had left Barbados in mid January, Colin had returned from a month in Pakistan, where he was advising rural communities on sustainable agricultural techniques. On his last night in

Pakistan, he had been asked to smoke a traditional hookah pipe of perfumed tobacco after a celebratory dinner. With a history of lung infections, Colin was nervous but knew it was rude to decline. He took a tentative puff.

On the flight back to London, he developed a severe cough. While staying with his 90-year-old father near Bristol, his condition deteriorated. Tim went over to see him and reported that 'he looked like death'. He was prescribed heavy antibiotics and told by the local doctor it was OK to fly back to Barbados.

We spent Christmas in a rented house on the wild Atlantic coast of Barbados. Mo called several times from their house, sounding concerned. When we saw Colin in the New Year, he seemed better, joking that he had decided either to be well again by the end of the week, or drop dead. On 15 January, we went to his 65th birthday party in the garden at their Barbados home, Little Edgehill. Mo and friends had cooked up a storm, the garden was lit with flares and the assembled company was appropriately eclectic. We gave Colin a hammock, with strict instructions to take it easy, slow down and actually lie in it, knowing full well that this plea would fall on deaf ears.

On a Sunday in late February, Yvette and I took Sholto and Xan to stay with my mother in Wales for the last time before our departure for Sri Lanka. It was a clear but bitterly cold morning.

I set off on my own to climb Mynedd Troed, the pyramidal peak that dominates the landscape around Talgarth. It had played an important part in my life during the previous years, as the point to which I could retreat for solace and that sense of connection.

I was ill-equipped for the conditions, wearing just a T-shirt and light jersey. By the time I reached the summit, it was too cold to hang around. I jogged down through heather and bracken, thinking about what lay ahead: our huge leap into the unknown.

Back at the house I sank into a hot bath, then sat beside the wood-burner, thawing out my frozen extremities. My mother was making lunch and offered me a glass of wine. The telephone rang.

'Rory, it's Tim.' My mother passed the handset.

'Hi, Tim.'

'Hi, mate. I'm afraid I have some bad news.' He paused. My heart jumped.

'Colin died this morning.'

Few times in my life have I experienced such a profound sense of shock. I put down the phone, walked outside and looked up at Mynedd Troed. Brittle light sparkled in a pristine sky. The world felt quite empty.

The following days were complicated. We were booked to fly to Colombo on 12 March. Prior to that, Tim and I were going to meet Michael and his board at Marion, just outside Boston, flying out on 27 February. Colin's funeral was scheduled for the 28th in Barbados, the same day that I would be presenting my pitch. Much as I wanted to be in both places at the same time, we agreed that Colin would have wanted me to be at Marion, making a bid that would ultimately lead to his Web of Hope becoming more of a reality, the initiative which, towards the end of his life, he described as the most exciting thing he had ever done.

So, as hundreds of fellow environmentalists and hikers followed Colin's coffin on a final tour of Farley Hill in Barbados, forming a long human spiral, I made my presentation to the Marion Institute board. By some bizarre synchronicity, at almost the precise moment Colin was laid to rest, the Web of Hope was born as a sustainable organization, a living testament to a man who upheld all he believed in with such passion and integrity.

Sometimes, it seems, the universe cannot resist such connections.

Chapter Five

The Resplendent Isle

The emerald island encircled by the sapphire wave.
Ramayana

Galle Fort dangles like a teardrop from the southwestern lip of Sri Lanka's coastline, poised over blue sapphire waters stretching south to Antarctica. Monumental stone ramparts encircle a small headland on one side of the harbour, forming bastions of apparent impregnability against the crashing surf and encroaching forces that have occupied it over the centuries.

It is thought that the biblical port of Tarshish referred to Galle, from where spices and precious stones have been traded ever since. During the colonial era, the Portuguese, Dutch and British have all held sway within these walls, along with Phoenician and Moorish traders who passed through before them and occupied the area first fortified by the Portuguese from 1588, then known as the Black Fort, or Santa Cruz. The Dutch took Galle in 1640, after a siege that lasted 18 days and ended with a bloody battle on the beach. They started constructing the ramparts some 20 years later. In contrast, the transition from Dutch to British took place in 1796 without a single shot being fired. Ceylon remained a British colony until independence in 1948, and changed its name to Sri Lanka in 1972.

Across Galle harbour, the Rumassala headland is rooted in legend. In the Hindu epic *Ramayana*, the warrior Lakshman is wounded by the demon king Ravana while trying to rescue his abducted princess Sita. He sends the monkey-god Hanuman to bring medicinal herbs back from the Himalayas which will save his life. Having forgotten which herbs were necessary, Hanuman makes the wise decision to uproot a whole mountain, parts of which fall into the sea, one of them forming Rumassala hill. Similar hills exist in south India that legend also attributes to Hanuman's expedition and which I walked past on the first day of my trek to Calcutta. Like Rumassala, these hills are renowned for rare ayurvedic plants that are found nowhere else in the world outside of the Himalayas.

Just beyond Rumassala lies magical Unawatuna, which translates as 'it fell from the sky'. Sci-fi writer and long-term Sri Lanka resident Arthur C. Clarke is not alone when he attributes rare qualities to this beautiful bay. Clarke believes the area has the most intense gravitational pull of any point on the globe – a feature he attributes to a huge meteorite impact thousands of years ago. This theory is supported by a recent study of gravitational anomalies, pinpointing an area off the south coast of the island as a vortex comparable with the North Pole. Many people who come here seem to feel an intense pull to the environs. Like others, Clarke has postulated that the ruins of an Atlantis-like city lie just off the coast, which may have been Ravana's capital in the *Ramayana*, Sri Lankapura, but was submerged soon after his death around 2387 BC, a date linked with the biblical flood in Genesis.

Like many people, my brief periods spent in Sri Lanka had created an immediate, albeit superficial impression, of a 'mini-India'. This was reaffirmed the moment we landed. Frazzled by a long flight with two small children, stewing in a strange blend of trepidation, exhaustion and excitement, the sheer pandemonium enveloped us as we stepped through the terminal doors to be engulfed by muggy polluted air. This was not like arriving for a holiday. We were here to live. It felt very different indeed and I could not help but wonder if this had been such a good idea after all.

Then you are hit with the insane but somehow functioning anarchy of the roads, filled with roaring Ashok Leyland buses, driven by wide-eyed betel-chewing speed-freaks, slewing round bends into oncoming traffic like Hollywood stunt drivers; the belching Tata trucks, grinding along like giant mechanical crabs, the lopsided chassis sometimes twisting off the cambered roads and leaving the rear axle hanging like some rear appendage in the slow act of detaching itself completely; the little three-wheeled tuk-tuks, buzzing through traffic like angry hornets and prone to trying any manoeuvre at any instant; the bullock carts, the swerving cyclists, the cyclopic tractors with one headlight and pedestrians' apparently genetic inability to stop at a junction, or look at the oncoming traffic when crossing the road.

The comparisons with India continue wherever you go – the profusion of temples and the omnipresence of religious imagery, paraphernalia and worship; the food, the roadside stalls, the markets, the battles with Kafkaesque bureaucracy.

Like all such generalizations, these descriptions soon fall short. A new reality emerges. One begins to notice that the air is not quite so pregnant with a kaleidoscope of smells. That distillation of smouldering *beedi* cigarettes, *dhoop* incense, spiced *chai* tea, diesel fumes, rotting fruit and roadside excrement is somehow less intense. The streets seem cleaner, the overpopulation and poverty less in your face. The food can be very fine, but less varied and less exotic than say, in southern India.

As a predominantly Buddhist land, the heightened pulse that comes with Hindu worship is of a more placid nature. In India, Hindu temples are geared for full-on sensory stimulation, the sights, colours, smells and sounds converging in one overwhelming synaesthesia which can make the pyrotechnics of modern Western dance culture look tame. As the months and the miles clocked up in India, I would never tire of the Hindu temple experience. It was always a buzz.

In contrast, the Buddhist temples in Sri Lanka are sedate and serene. My experience of Hindu temples in Sri Lanka also stands distinct from those of India. In the same way that Pettah, the main market area of Colombo, never quite matches the colour and decay of Old Delhi or Calcutta, so the Hindu culture of Sri Lanka appears more restrained, as though the contrast levels have been turned down. For me, even the ancient pilgrimage centre of Kataragama, the most revered site on the island and held sacred by every religious persuasion, lacks the vitality of a Tiruchendur, Chidambaram, or the other temple towns of Tamil Nadu.

The exception is Esala Perahera, the annual festival of the July-August full moon and noted for its widespread and prolific consumption of marijuana, ingested like the *bhang* paste used in India's Holi festival. This form of psychedelic pain relief is presumably connected with extraordinary levels of self-mortification with which Kataragama is associated, most notably fire-walking, but including every conceivable form of body-piercing, using hooks, spears, spikes and tridents.

To make these distinctions is not to imply that Sri Lanka is any way less complex or less interesting than India. Far from it. The diversity may not be on such a vast scale, but it is there, just more subtle, more buried below the surface. In India, every street scene is like an epic movie, full-on, frenetic, relentless. In Sri Lanka, there is the outward appearance of equilibrium but, as the country's on-going political crisis shows, divisions run deep and dysfunction is never far away.

Our cursory understanding of Sri Lankan politics was soon revealed since, quite unwittingly, we had arrived in the country a month before a general election, the outcome of which would have ramifications for foreigners seeking residency.

We landed on 15 March. The election was scheduled for soon after Sinhalese New Year in mid-April. In a bid to win a majority, President Chandrika Kamaratunga, the matriarch of the ruling Bandaranaike dynasty, which had held the country in its grasp for decades, was forming alliances with fundamentalist minorities, most notably the neo-Marxist JVP and the JHU, a party of Buddhist extremists (a contradiction in terms if ever I heard one).

I have to admit that I had never heard of the JVP. Like the Khmer Rouge of Cambodia, the JVP had evolved from radical left-wing student groups in the south of the country during the mid-1960s, particularly in and around Matara, Tangalle and Hambantota, the main towns on the south coast beyond Galle. Major JVP insurrections in 1971 and 1987 had left thousands dead, as innocent people were killed for little reason beyond their alleged political affiliations. Brutal atrocities took place, such as the use of car tyres to 'necklace' unfortunate victims within a ring of flaming petrol, a practice usually associated with South African townships. By all accounts, these were bleak and fearful times, with curfews, roadblocks, informers, people being followed and bodies hung from trees and telegraph poles. Death squads descended on the south, eliminating entire families in a desperate bid to flush the JVP out. All this had happened just over 15 years before.

It was recent history but, compared with the war with the Tamils in the north, had hardly registered on the international news radar. Now, nobody seemed to know how strong the JVP really were, or how radical their policies. What was evident was that a group of agitators had now been given legitimacy through their association with a major political party, namely Chandrika's SLFP (Sri Lanka Freedom Party). In practical terms, it was hard to pin down exactly what this might mean.

'They have very nationalistic views and dislike foreigners', was the usual refrain. Beyond that, we had little idea about what to expect. Besides, the accepted wisdom was that the opposition would win.

Since emotions are known to run high at election time, many of our friends had chosen to lie low, or even skip the country for a few days. Quite by chance, we were booked to fly to the Maldives for five days, where I was to do some consultancy at a resort with good eco-credentials that was trying to minimize its impact. When we returned, we found that Chandrika's coalition had won and the JVP now held four cabinet posts.

Quite rapidly, the political climate began to change. Rumours abounded, with lawyers predicting a tax on foreign property ownership. We began to sense an element of urgency, feeling some pressure to secure a house, or at least some land, before these measures came into effect. At this stage, we were open to anything, having formulated few clear ideas about where we wanted to live. I still harboured the desire for some land big enough to pursue ecological projects, but this was possible on an acre or even less. Although the Fort had its charm, its cramped conditions were too claustrophobic and urban for my liking. I needed green spaces.

Soon we had fallen into an almost daily pattern of going to look at land and houses, from small plots of beachfront to old *walawwas* (colonial manor houses) tucked away inland, or parcels of land surrounded by paddy fields, like little palm covered islands encircled by an emerald sea. Word spread. Tuk-tuk drivers would appear at the door, offering 'antique houses', 'paddy islands', 'beach land', whisking us off for arduous rides, most of which proved futile but, once in a while, sparked a glimmer of interest.

After buying maps from the Survey Department in Colombo, we were able to hone in on the areas that met our criteria. There was the issue of proximity to Galle, to schools, the beach and friends. Then there was the 'super highway', the country's first dual carriageway, being constructed between Colombo and Matara. Inevitably, this sliced through some of the most exquisite landscape in the south of the island and effectively ruled out a strip about 2 kilometres wide, especially any land with elevation, to which the discordant cacophony of Sri Lankan road noise would inescapably drift.

A bit of land at the beach appealed as a safe investment, but we did not relish being on the coast throughout the year. For a start, the local politics with small fishing settlements was known to be a minefield, and many Sri Lankans regard these coastal communities with trepidation. 'The south has always been associated with murders, thuggery and black magic,' one Sri Lankan friend would tell me later. Not a great recommendation.

Then there was the weather. As we had discovered, the coast is under attack from sea spray and high humidity for much of the year. The spray coats everything from sheets and clothes to computers and books with a corrosive film of salt. And besides, we were not here to speculate on property. We were here to create a home to live in full-time, and the idea of displacing an impoverished fishing family from their ancestral land, then building a villa behind a concrete wall, seemed like a perfect recipe for antagonizing our neighbours. As Yvette had witnessed in Barbados, the coast can rapidly become colonized by foreigners, blocking any access to the sea, then eroding the beachfront with callous development. This was not a route we wanted to follow.

I was also fixated with rising sea levels. In fact, my primary concern at almost every property we looked at – which must have been over 50 – was how it would be affected by a sea-level rise of 2 metres. This was not restricted to the coast. Many of the low-lying areas of paddy field were also at risk if water rose in the estuaries and the surrounding network of inland waterways.

My other concern was with water generally. The groundwater and wells near paddy fields can be contaminated with pesticides, nitrates and, in some cases, heavy metals. Also, how reliable would these wells prove during the dry seasons, especially if climate change started to reverse conventional rainfall patterns, as was now being observed around the globe? For much of the year, when the rain falls in relentless solid sheets, it is hard to imagine that a lack of water could ever pose a problem. However, the speed at which it drains from the landscape is almost equally impressive, leaving parched, dusty conditions for months every year.

What I was looking for was the potential for total self-reliance – the possibility of depending on our own water and our own land, minimizing the number of utility bills in the process and increasing our capacity for riding out future complications, be it escalating oil prices or changing rainfall patterns.

This may sound dramatic, but I was approaching the process with a long-term view, not so much for Yvette and myself, but more for Sholto and Xan. Judging by the speed at which ecological changes are starting to take hold across the globe, it is hard to imagine what conditions will prevail in 30 years' time. However, from my point of view, one thing was certain: when the shit really does hit the fan, which it will, those that have developed self-reliant lifestyles will be those best prepared for the transition and most immune to the challenges they will face. In a sense, I was here in Sri Lanka to prepare my family for the global economic and ecological meltdown that I had begun to see as being inevitable within my children's lifetime. The evidence had started to appear overwhelming, with even conservative commentators speculating about crossing the climate change tipping point within a decade and 'peak oil' before 2010, beyond which we slide down the 'bell curve' of the graph. Since everything from the global food supply to our transport systems and the pharmaceutical industry are so dependent on the black gold, the implications are overwhelming.

In addition to tuk-tuk drivers and shifty types who would spring out of dark doorways offering 'big land with antique house', there were brokers and agents offering their services, scouring the coastal strip for anything that might appeal to this new and burgeoning market. At times, the speculation seemed excessive. There were stories of Hong Kong bankers flying along the coast in helicopters, shooting digital video of attractive plots, then almost instantly securing sales with their friends back home over mobile phones. Inevitably, prices were constantly on the rise, especially in the Fort and along the coast.

The first agent to take us out was Sean, a young Christian from Kandy who spoke fluent English and whose manner was instantly reassuring, lacking the typical hard-sell bravado. He was working with Ibrahim, an old Muslim friend of his from Kandy who we had met the year before on our 'recce'. We had bumped into Ibrahim over dinner one night and outlined what we were looking for.

'Let me get Sean to show you three places tomorrow,' he enthused, his imposing frame and expressive manner making it sound irresistible. 'There's this beeeeaaauuutiful old bungalow, with three acres. Then there's an old tea estate, 60 acres, with these huuuuge trees, which also has a bungalow ...'

'Sixty acres?' I was surprised, since on current prices this should have been way out of our budget.

'Yes,' Ibrahim said with a laugh. 'Amazing, isn't it? Incredible views and a river that runs along one side.' It was sounding more appealing by the second.

'How far away is it?'

'Twenty kilometres, which takes about half an hour.'

'Sounds great. And the other place?'

'The other place is an old house at Kataluwa, the other side of Koggala Lake, which has a lot of potential.'

The following morning, Sean picked Yvette and me up from the Fort and we started out, full of anticipation.

'Where first, Sean?' I asked.

'First, the old bungalow, then the 60 acres, then back down to Koggala.'

We dipped off the coast road outside Galle and followed the Udugama Road north. Soon we started to climb and small tea estates replaced alluvial stretches of paddy. The vegetation became more diverse and, as the road wound further north into low country hills, the landscape took on a new dimension. Sinuous terraces of manicured tea receded round small interlocking valleys, shaded on two levels by huge spreading *albizzias* above and the leguminous nitrogen-fixing *gliricidas* below, their rapidly growing branches fanning out from coppiced trunks and catching the light like giant green feathers. We passed citrus orchards, patches of cinnamon, then a stretch of rainforest reservation at Kottawa, the dense jungle and majestic trees creating a darkened tunnel above the tarmac.

'That's the road up to the 60-acre property,' Sean said as we swung round a right-hand bend at the top of one incline.

'Looks intriguing,' I said.

'It's very intriguing,' he confirmed.

A few minutes later, the road brought us to regimented plantations of rubber, then oil palm, both equally stunning. The leaf litter from the rubber created an almost autumnal temperate effect, the exact tessellated spacing of the pale grey trunks adding geometric precision to the vistas. The oil palms were vast, their drooping fronds almost prehistoric in appearance and the solid straight trunks draped with ferns, mosses and lichens, creating a land-that-time-forgot vision in which one might expect to encounter a dinosaur. The views had become increasingly exotic since we left the coast and, by the time we turned off the road to the bungalow at the crest of a long climb, my enthusiasm for the area was brimming over. As Yvette said later, I'd bought the bungalow in my mind before we'd even seen it.

I thought it was perfect. A narrow dirt track wound round the side of a hill, before revealing the bungalow, a spacious looking old house, perched on the summit of a hill, surrounded by mature trees with a band of tea planted below.

'There are three acres of tea, stretching from the house down to that path,' Sean said, as we approached the drive. 'The boundary at the back runs along there.' He pointed to a shallow depression, heavily overgrown, but which I immediately picked out as a potential forest garden.

We pulled up to the house and parked beside a shrine made of volcanic rock and housing images of Christ and the Virgin Mary. This flashed me back to south India, where I had seen numerous similar shrines along the Coromandel Coast, where St Francis Xavier had walked some 500 years before. I felt at home. As I closed the car door, a brahminy kite flew across the garden and landed on top of the dilapidated garage. I could not help but see this as portentous.

'I hope there's someone here,' Sean said, walking to the firmly closed door. 'I did ring to say we were coming.'

It was quickly apparent that nobody was about, so we snooped round the outside. The wooden ceiling of the decaying front verandah had collapsed in parts, revealing rusted corrugated iron. It would clearly need a new roof, but once replaced with traditional half-round tiles, it would look stunning. The walls were thick and solid and, through shuttered windows, we could just see huge, well-proportioned rooms inside. A central hall was spanned by a single arch and four bedrooms led off from the corners, each of which could enjoy an attached bathroom. The rear verandah was linked by a covered walkway down to the kitchen annex. The views from the kitchen were superb, as they would be from almost anywhere in the house after some judicious thinning of the surrounding trees. With an added mezzanine level, the house could have a full 360-degree panorama of hills and valleys.

I could see that Yvette did not share my enthusiasm. Yes, it was too far away to live in with two small children. Yes, it was rather like our house in Wales. But, as a retreat for a writer, or for those seeking seclusion, tranquillity, stunning views and great bird-watching, it was hard to beat. In typically impetuous style, I had fallen in love with the first thing we saw.

We set off south to 'the 60 acres', turning up the track we had seen earlier. Sean shifted into four-wheel drive and we bumped slowly over cobbled stones up the side of a ridge. The best views we had seen all day opened up to our right, stretching towards the coast. Range upon range of hills receded into bluish haze and we could just make out the orange robes of a huge Buddha statue on the summit of a nearby hill. Brightly coloured parakeets flew between the splaying upper branches of *albizzias*, almost level with the car, thus giving us the impression of being suspended in the tree canopy as we climbed higher up the access road.

We swung round a bend at the crest of the ridge and parked between the old planter's bungalow and a tatty decaying shed, once used to weigh the tea. Towering above us were two African tulip trees, the bell-shaped orange flowers littering the ground around the bases of magnificent mottled trunks. A small rose apple stood in the shade of gnarled old mangos, the pink pear-shaped fruit dangling from branches like lurid Christmas decorations. A giant squirrel, with long bushy black tail, was scurrying high in the mango trees, feasting on neglected fruit.

Beyond that, it was difficult to see very much. One path led out from the weighing shed and we were able to walk about 50 metres along one terrace before the undergrowth became impenetrable. Another path, on a lower terrace, overlooked a bowl-shaped area, but the jungle was so dense it was hard to see where the boundaries lay. I could just get glimpses of stonework terraces, which looked monumental, but our overall impression was very limited.

'How do you get to the river?' I asked Sean.

'I will have to check with Ibrahim, but I think you follow this path. He came some time ago, so it may have been less overgrown then.'

'How long since it's been a working estate?' I wondered.

'Must be at least 10 years.'

'And how long has it been for sale?'

'Oh, for some time I think. A man from Singapore nearly bought it last year, but the deal fell through.'

'It's a large chunk of land.'

'And a good price,' Sean added.

'That's true. But a huge project.'

That evening, I spoke to Ibrahim on the phone. 'I'm very keen on the bungalow,' I said. 'Unfortunately, we couldn't get inside. Could we arrange another visit and make sure the owners are there?'

'Of course Rory,' he replied with his genial lilt. 'What about "the 60 acres"?'

'It's interesting, but difficult for us to really get an impression. How did you get down to the river?'

'Oh, it's quite difficult, but you can drive round there to see it. You can also follow those paths to the top of the ridge. You saw the stone terraces? They go all the way to the top. Absolutely amazing.'

This certainly sounded exciting.

'Maybe I'll take another look when we go to the bungalow again. By the way, do you know what the bungalow's called?'

'Yes, Rory. It's called Indian Walk.'

'I don't believe it.'

'Why's that?'

'Some years ago I spent six months walking through India, which sort of changed my life. I can't help thinking that place is meant for me.'

I put down the phone, convinced I had found my dream house. The pain of selling the house in Wales suddenly dissipated, since I had now seen something that resonated with me even more.

Yvette however, was far from convinced.

My enthusiasm for Indian Walk only increased with the second and third visits. The solid stone walls, the elegant proportions of the rooms, the mature fruit trees, the dingle-like depression behind the house, all combined to make it seem ideal. The similarities with our house in Wales were almost spooky, although the 'dingle' in Wales had been filled with decades of farmer's detritus: old cars, tractors, fridges, cans of sheep dip, batteries, corrugated iron, all piled into one heaving toxic dump that, through sheer inaccessibility, had proved impossible to clear.

With each visit to Indian Walk, I stopped at 'the 60 acres', since we passed right by. Each time, I was able to expand my knowledge of the place. We were shown to a series of stone-walled wells down in the bowl, each brimming with crystal clear water and surrounded by iridescent dragonflies and speckled butterflies dancing above pink and lilac flowers. The area had the qualities of a secret garden, waiting to be revealed. On the side of the ridge overlooking the bowl, a small spring issued from a crack between two massive boulders. Chandana, the current 'watcher' on the land and the only person employed by the owners, said that the spring did not run the whole year round, but was used to gravity-feed the bungalow for much of the time.

Sean and I beat a path through the undergrowth to finally get down to the river, a magical stream about five metres wide, bouncing its way between boulders, creating a series of natural pools. Studying the map later, I traced the source all the way back to Indian

Walk, then the course it took south to become the *Polwatta Ganga*, which flows into Weligama Bay.

On another occasion, we hacked our way to the top of the ridge with an old man called Peter, who had been the caretaker of the land many years before and clearly knew every square inch. With his wiry frizzy hair, high forehead and elfin stature, he had the appearance of a mad professor crossed with a wild man of the woods. On his left leg he bore the scars from a shotgun trap, many of which are placed in the neglected jungle areas to poach wild boar. In some parts of the country, more people die from accidents like these than from the dreaded dengue fever.

Despite being so overgrown, it was possible to catch glimpses of the views in all directions, stretching north towards Sinharaja rainforest and south to the coast. As Ibrahim had said, the old paths and stone terraces wound all the way to the top of the ridge. The terraces had been done with such precision that hardly a stone had been dislodged in the century or so since their construction. The paths were largely obscured by encroaching jungle, and neglected tea bushes had grown into straggly beanpoles more than five metres tall. Massive boulder formations dominated the ridge on the north side, some towering over the jungle canopy below. I could immediately see their potential as sites for low-impact houses. We found evidence of wild boars rooting around, scratching the surface of the soil with their feet to dig out tubers. I took tentative steps through fallen branches, wondering if the trip wire for a shotgun trap was lurking around every corner. On each of these expeditions, we returned to the bungalow drenched in sweat, but elated by what we had found.

As we started off back down to Galle, I looked back at the ridge. On previous visits, I had not fully appreciated the sheer scale of the place. Looking from the south, the ridge was vast and densely forested. It was the highest point in the area. I studied the old 1930s survey map that Ibrahim had given me and began to see how little of the land we had been able to get to.

'You know Sean, we've only seen such a small part of the total area. Maybe about 20 per cent.' Sean could see that my interest had been sparked, but was now wondering how many more treks through the jungle he was going to have to make before securing a sale.

Never in my wildest dreams had I imagined buying such a huge bit of land. It did strike me however, that in terms of a project I had long dreamt about, it had massive potential. Since the land had not been touched for so long, we could safely assume that no chemical sprays or fertilizers had been used for at least 10 years. In terms of an enterprise seeking organic certification, this was very appealing.

According to Peter, much of the tea, especially in the lower areas, could be easily brought back into production, having been plucked intermittently over the years by those living on the boundary. The bowl seemed to be peppered with wells, all with good water. Since topsoil would have been washed down from the surrounding ridge over millennia, it also seemed safe to assume that this area would be fertile and ideal for growing a wide range of crops. I suspected that the area might be protected by some sort of microclimate and started to imagine a tropical forest garden filling the whole bowl, an organic edible landscape filled with a cornucopia of fruit, vegetables, herbs, spices, shrubs and tubers.

My vision for a more permanent version of Colin's Village of Hope began to resurface. I knew it was not a practical place to live here full-time, at least initially, but in terms of what we could afford, and in relation to what else was on offer, it seemed like an incredible deal. The same sum of money could barely buy a shoebox in the Fort, or a scrap of land on the beach. It might be enough for a small house inland, but nothing so big and with such potential. In the longer term, this area would be spared the onslaught of development that would come with the 'super highway' and along the coast in general. The road that wound up to Udugama was not a main artery to anywhere, looping round and returning south at the bottom of Sinharaja rainforest. It was hard to imagine that it would ever get much busier. Even if we bought the land and did nothing with it for 10, 20 years, if ever, on the land value alone it still seemed like a good investment. There was always the option of dividing it up and selling portions off, while keeping a good plot for ourselves to build on whenever we chose.

In terms of a property for Sholto and Xan, I also felt that something of this nature was hard to beat – a large chunk of land, heavily forested, high in biodiversity, with excellent water sources, fabulous views, a bordering river and what appeared to be kilometres of stone terracing – a feat of engineering that would be out of the question nowadays. The natural resources available, and the potential for harnessing them in interesting ways, left my mind spinning. Harvesting rainwater off huge expanses of rock, running micro-hydro schemes for electricity, building with stone and compressed mud brick, incorporating the huge boulder formations within the structures, digging out the marshland at the bottom of the bowl and forming a series of aquaculture ponds. I started to see the Web of Hope ecological learning centre as a tangible reality. The more I explored the possibilities, the more difficult it became to ignore.

I was however, most in love with Indian Walk and, for a time, even considered buying both properties. This would have stretched us financially and left little money for building and renovation. I decided to go ahead with Indian Walk either way, telling Ibrahim to instruct lawyers and get the ball rolling. All the time, rumblings about changes in the law continued and I felt compelled to get at least something sorted out before that happened. A day was fixed to meet Mohammed, one of the most respected lawyers in the Fort area. I enjoyed his laconic manner and felt confident about his thorough approach.

But the affair started to drag. First, the owners seemed incapable of presenting the full title deeds to the property. Then the price doubled. Then Ibrahim informed me that someone else was making an offer. My interest had started to wane and I decided to make one last visit, this time accompanied by Ragi, an architect friend we had first met in Colombo the previous year. Like Yvette, Ragi did not really share my enthusiasm and, after walking round the property with him, I realized that renovations would cost far more than I had imagined.

On the way back to Galle, we stopped at 'the 60 acres' again and walked along a lower part of the ridge that stretched out from behind the bungalow and which we had hitherto overlooked. Here, Ragi's interest was piqued. It was spectacular. This lower section of the ridge was secluded from the rest of the land, with sheer drops on each side. In terms of views, it provided the best of both worlds – the expansive view to the south and the more enclosed view over the bowl to the north. In terms of design, it would allow interesting possibilities, such as using cross-ventilation to create 'passive cooling', thus saving the energy needed for air-conditioning.

For Ragi and now Yvette, it was a no-brainer. Why on earth buy three acres and a ruined bungalow when you could buy 60 acres for little more, where you would be 20 minutes closer to Galle, have infinitely better views and much better potential for many projects?

I had to agree, but it was also very daunting. I had grown up in an environment where I had seen what can happen when a project of this scale takes over. When my parents bought their house in Surrey in the late 1950s, it was a derelict farmhouse, surrounded by 16 acres of swampy land. The house had not been lived in for 30 years and the garden was a tangle of six-foot brambles and nettles.

As the years went by, the garden evolved and expanded. By the time I was born, it had grown to about 60 acres. Several lakes had been dug to drain the surrounding land. Formal lawns and flowerbeds near the house opened onto networks of grass paths, flanked by azaleas, magnolias, rhododendrons and clumps of bamboo. Amazonian *gunaras* flourished in the boggy conditions, their giant rhubarb leaves sometimes spanning more than six feet. Massive weeping willows spilled languidly into the lakes, draped over stone fountains and sculptures moved by my father with an array of ingenious contraptions from old country houses being demolished. Every weekend was like a military exercise, working out ways to suspend arched steel girders over expanses of water and create bridges, or float a gazebo out to an island on vast chunks of polystyrene.

Hugo, Adam and I grew up wielding chainsaws, driving dumper trucks, building bonfires, clearing the land and, bit by bit, expanding the reaches of the garden. It was rewarding work but the catalogue of accidents that it caused was never ending. Hugo dug the bucket of a digger into the back of Adam's cranium, leading to a dozen stitches. I cracked my head open on the dumper truck fuel tank when Hugo crashed into a tree. Hugo stuck his foot into a lawn mower and almost removed all his toes. Adam nearly had both legs broken while sitting on the front of a tractor as my father drove into a pile of logs. I came close to severing my foot with a chainsaw and blew myself clean off the ground by pouring petrol onto the dying embers of a bonfire.

Rarely was there any respite from these activities. I remember my father driving the dumper truck over a bonfire one Christmas Day, trying to deposit the pile of branches he was dragging behind him on top of the flames. His plan backfired, as the dumper lodged itself on a huge burning root. He could move neither forward nor back. Flames licked up around the diesel fuel tank. The tyres started melting. My mother was screaming at him to get off, but he wouldn't budge. Adam and I ran off and, returning with fire extinguishers, managed to douse the flames before the dumper exploded.

As the years went by, the project grew to the current 160 acres. More than a dozen lakes were built, along with a series of eccentric follies, including 'the hermit hut' and 'the potting shed', which is in fact a small chapel and will be my father's mausoleum. The garden was filled with classical statues, urns and obelisks, all strategically sited at the end of expansive vistas. The tree planting never ceased and, by the time we had all left school, my brothers and I must have gone at least some of the way towards offsetting a lifetime of carbon emissions. My father now claims to have as many species of tree and plant as any arboretum in the country.

Although I am full of admiration for what he has achieved, I have also witnessed the pain that can arise when a passion borders on obsession. As I grappled with the concept of buying 'the 60 acres' in Sri Lanka, I could not help but see the similarities. Was I chasing after the same dream? Was I just following the same path as my father?

15 May 2004. Galle.

A survey of the 60 acres is being conducted by Mr Ambawatte. It has taken 12 days so far, partly hampered by the rain. Today he plans to locate the boundaries in the more remote sections. I decide to join him to see where exactly the perimeters lie. In some areas, this is far from straightforward. The steep, almost vertical drops at the northeast edge, which enclose a stone walled gully and some of the most luxuriant rainforest vegetation, is especially impenetrable.

Mr Ambawatte proves to be meticulous and intrepid. I follow tentatively behind him and his three helpers as they thrash through thick jungle with machetes, carrying a selection of poles, tape measures and metal bars. Having a severe allergy to bees and wasps, I keep my eyes peeled for nests we have been warned about, including an especially aggressive type of hornet. I clutch the pouch around my waist, double-checking that I am carrying the out-of-date adrenalin injection, my only lifeline in the event of a sting.

As we reach the bottom of the gully, Mr Ambawatte turns in his stride and points to a shotgun trap just a metre away. It consists of a steel tripwire and an old sawn-off musket, loaded with large chunks of lead.

'I hope that's not on this land, is it Mr Ambawatte?' I ask nervously. He checks his paperwork, his bulging gooseberry eyes threatening to pop from their sockets at any moment.

'No. This is our boundary here.' He points to a section of stone terrace, covered in luxuriant ferns.

I am astounded by the way in which Mr Ambawatte constantly locates various key points. After wading through 50 metres of thick jungle, he stops, points at the trunk of a jak fruit tree, then directs his team to slash back the undergrowth and scratch the surface of the soil exactly 2 metres away. Almost invariably, this reveals a small concrete footing, signalling the apex of a boundary. Only twice do they have to search a second time. Then, an old battered tape measure is wound out from its ancient leather casing and one of the men blunders off through the jungle for anything up to a hundred metres, before locating the next landmark, which may be a tree, a large boulder, a well or section of stone culvert.

It's hard work, and not without its dangers. In addition to wild hornets and shotgun traps, there is the omnipresent threat of snakes. As I soon discover, the snakes most feared in Sri Lanka are not the huge pythons, or even cobras, but the small vipers, some of which are not much larger than worms, but highly venomous. As we stumble up the steep bank of an invasive cane-like grass, my snake paranoia reaches a new high and not without reason. I am told that this is the preferred habitat for small vipers. When we finally make it back to the security of a path, I find it hard to hide my relief.

I am however, extremely glad to have taken part, since I now have a fairly comprehensive impression of the land. What is apparent is that quite substantial parts of it are only accessible with considerable effort. This increases the appeal for me, since it means these areas have never been turned over to cultivation, have a high degree of endemic biodiversity as a result and no doubt provide habitat for a host of interesting wildlife. The notion that one might be buying so much virtually untouched, almost virgin habitat, in addition to everything else, is a further attraction. I know now that if we do move ahead with the project, we will leave whole areas untouched, making sure that we preserve large sections of the land as a biodiversity refuge.

It is hard to define exactly when the decision was made. A critical threshold was passed on one of my many visits, when all the attributes had so stacked up that the decision became irresistible.

At the same time, I needed to confirm that the land was truly as exceptional as I believed. So, I made a number of other trips to small working estates. Although I saw several stunning places, none of them quite matched up to 'the 60 acres', either in potential or in price. Thometotam, the original Tamil name for the estate, became the focus of my attention.

However, I was adamant that I would not forge ahead without Yvette's full consent. So I waited. We were both agreed that it was an unfeasible place for us to live in with two small children, but we were also both aware that we may never stumble across such an opportunity again. Purely as an investment, Yvette thought it made sense. The only thing holding us back was the fact that once we had bought it, we would still not have a place to live in. Finding a suitable home was clearly a priority, so we set to work.

I lost count of the number of houses we saw over those few weeks. We went out trawling with Sean, with tuk-tuk drivers, the owners of antique shops, in fact just about anybody who could show us 'a big old house with lots of space, a bit of land and close to Galle'.

'There is this huge old house,' Ibrahim said one day. 'But they don't want to sell it, only rent it.'

This was an option we had not considered, but in view of changing property laws and escalating prices, it suddenly seemed worth pursuing.

'OK,' we said. 'Let's take a look.'

Inland Hills is a rambling old colonial *walawwa* in Karapitiya, a suburb north of Galle and home to the main hospital, the university medical faculty and numerous doctors. It was not an area we would have otherwise considered, being a bit out on a limb compared with other areas occupied by the foreign community, but was close to Sholto's school and only 10 minutes' drive from the Fort. It was also an easy drive out to Thometotam, about 20 kilometres away. Geographically, this would suit us well.

We dipped off the main junction, between the university building and a Buddhist temple, into Inland Hills Road. After snaking round a couple of bends, Sean turned into a muddy entrance between two crumbling stone pillars. Tall trees and thick green foliage hung over the start of a long sweeping drive, the pale lilac flowers of a *thunbergia* scattered on the ground. The track wound up the side of a hill, past moss and fern covered banks, revealing a sprawling old house amid densely planted and mature trees. Our immediate impression was of the roof, now devoid of tiles and recently covered with cement sheets. It was hardly attractive.

We were greeted by the owner, Shanta, a large teddy bear of a man who came to the door dressed in a green sarong, his substantial girth on full display. He introduced us to his wife, Ravanni, and we followed them inside from the enormous verandah. The cavernous hallway was dimly lit, the black-painted cement floors and dark mahogany furniture accentuating the oppressive atmosphere. Most of the windowpanes in the bedrooms were also painted black and I reflected on this bizarre preference for living in the dark that seems to typify so many Sri Lankan houses. Since darkness is a huge attractor for mosquitoes, it seems to defy logic.

We wandered through the three rooms that opened off either side of the hall, each with its own decaying bathroom and scary plumbing. The hall led through to a 'pantry kitchen', with glass-fronted units displaying gaudy plates and frilly coloured glasses. This space too, had been enclosed and darkened with concrete walls, but would once have been an open living area, the old columns still visible within the block-work. Leading off the side were two storerooms, with split stable doors, and a large kitchen with an open hearth and chimney at the end. The kitchen was suffused with the smell of rancid coconut oil. A corridor down one side opened into a series of connected rooms, once the servants' quarters.

Most of the garden had reverted to semi-jungle. We could just see down to the well and the pump house, an ugly, awkward brick shed covered with cement sheeting. The three acres that surrounded the house dropped down to the boundary on all sides, the house itself positioned almost exactly in the middle of the land and on the crest of the hill. In terms of rising sea levels at least, we would be safe for some years. A few vistas opened up through the trees, revealing roofs of neighbouring houses and the university building beyond. These were not too easy on the eye, but could be overcome with strategic planting.

I could see that Yvette was intrigued.

'What do you reckon?' I asked her as we wandered round the garden.

'I think it could be wonderful,' she replied. 'It's the only place we've seen with big space. I think it could make a fantastic family home.'

The faded grandeur, the scale and sense of space, the potential for a lovely garden, all seemed to resonate well with what she was after. I was less convinced, since at the time we were contemplating a lease of only two or three years. The scale of the renovation required just to make the house habitable, let alone aesthetically pleasing, was financially implausible.

The proximity of the hospital also made me uneasy. We might never be far from medical help in an emergency but, by all accounts, this was not a hospital one ever wanted to find oneself in anyway. In case of anything critical, we would always sprint for Colombo. Then there was dengue. If a bad outbreak should occur, surely the hospital would be full of cases and the local mosquitoes all become carriers? Likewise filaria, Japanese encephalitis and all the other delights we have to be thankful to mosquitoes for. Was this really a sensible place for small children? (In fact, dengue is only carried by a certain type of mosquito, *aedes aegyptii*, which can only travel a short distance, bites during the day and is easily recognized by its banded legs.)

We left Inland Hills intrigued, but not seeing it as a viable option. Two weeks later, our thinking changed.

'Why not see if we can negotiate a longer lease, like 10 years?' Yvette suggested. 'Then the renovation might make sense? We could maintain the right to sublet and make some money back by renting it out as a villa during the season.'

This seemed like a very good idea. My only doubt was whether the size of the house was too compromising to my ecological conscience, in terms of things like energy and water use, especially if we put in a swimming pool, almost a prerequisite if we were to look for holiday rentals, since the house was several kilometres from a decent beach.

At the same time, part of my mantra with the Web of Hope had been to challenge the assumption that sustainable living was inevitably linked with deprivation and denial. I believe this is one of the main obstacles preventing people embracing the transition to sustainable lifestyles – the ingrained notion that we cannot live both comfortably and within the parameters of sustainability. In fact, through a combination of intelligent design, materials and technologies, sustainable living can actually be more comfortable than the levels we currently take for granted. Take air conditioning: an utterly inefficient piece of technology that requires vast amounts of energy, makes people ill and hermetically seals us off from fresh air. Contrast the sensation of stuffed up sinuses and dried out skin that AC encourages, with the cooling breezes created by fans, wind funnels and evaporative cooling devices.

At Inland Hills, we could avoid AC entirely, since the house was well suited for passive cooling, especially if we opened up the old verandah as the main living space. We would no doubt still need electric fans, but used judiciously this need not be a heavy load, especially compared with AC. Removing the asbestos ceiling in the hallway and main bedrooms would not only rid the house of a major toxin, but also increase the height and thereby the airflow. Solar hot water tanks would further reduce our energy load and, if affordable, we could install photovoltaic panels for at least part of our other electrical demands. This would be a major investment, but we could make it a condition of the lease to take them with us when we left. The abundant roof space could be used to harvest huge amounts of rainwater and recharge the aquifer supplying the well, making the house totally self-reliant in terms of water, even with a swimming pool. Sure, the Footprint involved with laying concrete for a pool might appear excessive, but minimal compared with what we might have used building a house.

I started to see an interesting challenge. Could we renovate a big old house and still bring our Footprint in line? By growing much of what we ate, both here and at 'the 60 acres', reducing our travel, especially by plane, being self-reliant for water and at least some of our energy requirements, I felt sure this must be possible.

And so we returned to Inland Hills for another look.

This time Ravanni presented a typed sheet, outlining the history of the house. I skimmed through it, reading sections out loud as Yvette wandered through the rooms. The house had been built in the 1860s by the Ephraims, a Dutch burgher family and original owner-managers of the NOH, the New Oriental Hotel that is now Amangalla. One descendant, the notorious Nesta Brohier, who died in 1995 at a ripe old age and held sway over the hotel during its heyday, had grown up here. Something of a local legend, Nesta had presided over the crumbling remains of her palatial hotel with a retinue of equally eccentric staff and her legacy remains in a catalogue of colourful stories that makes *Fawlty Towers* seem positively tame. An old acquaintance of Nesta's told me how, when a guest complained about not having hot water in his room, she had merely replied, 'Oh, well, that's funny. *I* have hot water.' And that was that.

Shanta's father had bought Inland Hills in the 1950s, when he had been a prominent local businessman and politician who famously beat the incumbent prime minister out of his own seat. When the Fort was evacuated during the Second World War, 200 pupils from Southlands Girls College moved in and the bedrooms were used as dormitories.

Looking at the house as a possible home for the next 10 years showed everything in a new light. I started to fantasize, seeing the 30-metre hallway and verandah as a perfect excuse for buying a skateboard, no doubt the first sign of a brewing midlife crisis. I could visualize an organically shaped pool, blending into decking at the back of the house. For two small children, it all started to seem perfect – enough room for them to run around and make mischief, while leaving enough space for me to have a quiet office and Yvette to have a studio.

By six o'clock that evening, we had a deal. A lease on the house for 10 years, which reflected the costs we expected to incur and allowed us to sublet. A few days later, I gave Ibrahim the go-ahead on Thometotam and a date was set with Mohammed. Suddenly, it was all happening.

Chapter Six

The Flamingo Effect

Capitalism is the extraordinary belief that the nastiest of men for the nastiest of motives will somehow work for the benefit of all.

John Maynard Keynes

The only stumbling block with Thometotam was what to do about Chandana, the watcher employed by the owners, who lived in the only other house on the land with his wife and three children. Without exception, advice from others was the same: we should insist that he vacates the house as a condition of the sale. 'You'll never get rid of him otherwise'; 'you'll end up with a five year court case'; 'you have no idea what kind of a man he is'.

All this may be true, I thought, but we would need to employ someone to keep an eye on things there. Why not give him the benefit of the doubt and see how it works out? Besides, he has a family. Where else would he go?

In a bid to resolve this outstanding issue, a meeting was called in Mohammed's office, with Chandana, Ibrahim and Mr Dahanayake, the owner's representative. We collected Mr Dahanayake, an elderly man with wild, ranting eyes, dressed in white sarong and shirt, from his house. He climbed into the back of Ibrahim's spanking new

Pajero and instantly began spitting great gobs of blood-red betel juice out of the window. I saw Ibrahim look nervously at his upholstery. From this moment on, Mr Dahanayake hardly paused for breath, talking in Sinhala at top speed. Ibrahim listened patiently as yet more betel-stained saliva was projected from the rear window.

Once in Mohammed's office, Mr Dahanayake continued to dominate proceedings, gesticulating at Chandana and frothing with a torrent of betel-fuelled verbosity. This was broken only by brief mutterings from Mohammed and Chandana, who looked petrified. Finally, I had to interject.

'Excuse me,' I leaned forward in my chair. 'But could someone give us an idea of what's being said here?'

Mohammed put his palms together and placed his elbows on the desk before him, then in sombre tones presented a summary. 'He's telling us that this man is no good. That he is a thief. That he must be got rid off. But the man is refusing to leave.'

'Why are they employing him then?' Mohammed shrugged. 'So, what do you suggest we do?' I asked.

'Either you offer him something to go, or you employ him,' he replied.

'But surely the problem lies with the vendor? It should be their responsibility to offer us vacant possession of the land.'

'They won't do it,' Mohammed said with certainty. As Yvette and I were beginning to appreciate, what we perceive as rationale and logic often have little to do with the situation.

Ibrahim offered his help. 'Let me have a word with the fellow,' he said, guiding Chandana and Mr Dahanayake out of the office.

While they were gone, I conferred with Yvette and Mohammed.

'Look, we're going to have to employ someone up there to keep an eye on things. Why not this man? Could we draft some form of agreement, in which we agree to employ him as a watcher? For the time being, he can remain in that house. If we need to use it, however, and if he remains in our employment, we will shift him to another house on the property. If we decide to terminate his employment however, he will have to vacate the house and we'll offer him three months' salary, or whatever is appropriate in these situations.'

Mohammed listened patiently, then offered his thoughts. 'I think you should get him out. He's a shifty and cunning fellow. I wouldn't trust him.'

'But how do we know that?' Yvette said. 'He looks terrified that he's about to be forced onto the street.'

'I will talk to him again,' Mohammed said.

Five minutes later, the others returned, but without a resolution.

Mohammed, doing his best to prevent yet more invective from Mr Dahanayake, explained my offer to Chandana, who shook his head glumly. I could not decide whether he looked shifty or just worried, since his eyes looked in opposing directions.

'An impossible man,' Mohammed concluded, leaning back in his chair. 'He will be nothing but trouble for you. He won't even accept your offer, which is more than reasonable.'

The meeting came to a close.

The following week, we tried again. Word came from Ibrahim that Chandana would agree to our offer. Once again, we assembled in Mohammed's office.

An agreement letter had been prepared in Sinhala, which was spelt out to Chandana. Again, he refused to sign.

'An impossible fellow,' Mohammed repeated, shaking his head.

Eventually, after another 30-minute tirade from Mr Dahanayake, Chandana conceded. The agreement was signed and, the following day, a time was set for the transfer of the property.

The owner of the property, a widow, was an elegant, mild mannered lady accompanied by her two sons. It seemed they owned another estate, which was managed by one son, but Thometotam had been neglected since the death of her husband and her other son had gone to work in Colombo.

Once again, Mr Dahanayake was present, fired up on betel and needing to be almost physically restrained from launching into yet further complications. There were accusations about neighbours cutting down jak trees on the property, others taking cinnamon, plucking tea, or asserting rights to certain wells. Mohammed held up his hand to try and call a halt to the verbiage.

'I think that's enough, Mr Dahanayake,' he said, shaking his head.

As we continued with the formalities however, Mr Dahanayake could not contain himself, now insisting that the title deeds should not be handed over until after we had been to the bank and handed over the cash.

'Is that normal?' I asked Mohammed.

'Of course not.' I could see that he was starting to lose patience. 'Never in my 30 years of practice has anyone made such a demand.'

I was also getting to the end of the line and insisted that the transaction was conducted as planned, or we would leave. This had the desired impact. Mr Dahanayake fell silent, the paperwork was signed and we all adjourned to the bank, where we handed large bundles of 1,000-rupee notes to Mr Dahanayake in a brown paper bag. His eyes lit up and we parted cordially. The deal was done.

In retrospect, we sailed through the purchase of this land with relative ease, especially compared with the challenges and difficulties faced by others we knew. For this fact alone, I was grateful, since my patience with bureaucratic hurdles is limited at the best of times.

Nailing down the terms of the lease with Shanta was more protracted, as more details had to be defined. We needed full clarification about what we could or could not do to the house, in terms of knocking down a wall here, or building one there. If we installed solar technology, could it be specified that we could take it with us when the lease expired? What about the garden? Could we replant as we wanted, or remove some of the trees that shrouded the immediate garden in semi-permanent darkness?

As far as Shanta and his family were concerned, they were happy for us to do whatever we wanted to both the house and the garden. After copies of the lease had been passed back and forth between lawyers a few times, we had an accepted document and scheduled a date and time to meet at Inland Hills for the signing.

Then, at the eleventh hour, Sean called with a request from Shanta. 'The land around the house comes to something like 3 acres and 56 perches. Shanta is requesting that he keeps those 56 perches back for himself, so that he has the option of building a small house one day.'

I conferred with Yvette. We were both feeling sorry for Shanta and his family. They had clearly fallen on hard times and were doing what they could to educate their two children abroad. Their son was going to university in Melbourne, Australia, and their daughter to Liverpool in England. We felt uncomfortable about displacing them from the family home but, at the same time, relieved that we seemed to be doing them a favour. They had been trying to rent the house for three years before we had appeared. Shanta even wept in front of me on two occasions, an expression of his gratitude for finally making it possible for them to educate their children as they had always dreamed. For us, having just moved away from the UK, this was not without its ironies.

In light of all this, it seemed hard to refuse their request. We would still maintain the three acres of garden around the house and a small portion would be carved off in one corner. I arranged for Mr Ambawatte 'to do the needful', providing a full survey of the land and the subdivided plot, from which the lawyers could establish new boundaries.

We all assembled at Inland Hills one Thursday evening, formally seated at a large mahogany table in the dim light of the hallway. Shanta's lawyer read through the terms of the lease, in painfully pedantic detail. As we signed at dusk, squadrons of oversized mosquitoes appeared from every corner.

Following my meeting with Michael Baldwin and his board, the Marion Institute had agreed to fund the next incarnation of Web of Hope's website, asking us to join them at the Bioneers Conference in San Rafael, California, that October, for the official launch.

Following my presentation earlier in the year, Michael had introduced me to the 'dynamic duo' who had recently overhauled the Marion site, suggesting that they might be people we could work with. Steve was a stocky young graphic designer from Nevada with an unusual sense of irony; Jonathan, a lanky hyperactive English copywriter, whose jerking movements and premature baldness reminded me of Stan Laurel.

After a series of conference calls, and a short visit to England by Steve and Jonathan to meet Tim and the team at Bath University, where the site would be hosted, we agreed to convene in Sri Lanka for two weeks in July. This brainstorm period would be used to rebirth the Web of Hope, creating the new image we hoped to launch at Bioneers.

I pulled into Colombo's Bandaranaike airport to collect them, finding only Tim and Steve. Jonathan's passport had been stolen at Heathrow. He would join us as soon as he could. Despite this hiccup, we decided to stick to our plans – to spend three nights at Ulpotha, before heading down to Galle.

We drove through a relentless pounding rainstorm, the surrounding landscape partially obscured, as if viewed through old panes of leaded glass. Steve sat in the back, seemingly in awe of all that surrounded him, occasionally bursting into effusive rhapsody about his first tropical experience.

'You know guys, I have never seen anything remotely like this in my life.'

By the time we reached Ulpotha three hours later, Steve's transition from Las Vegas to a mud village in rural Sri Lanka had reached its zenith. For the next two days, he wandered around like a zombie, his mood no doubt accentuated by quite abysmal jetlag but his jaw dropping open with each new wave of alien sensation. This started within minutes of our arrival, when we were shown to the 'triple hut' – a rambling extended version of the regular mud and thatch huts, with three inter-connected rooms constructed over boulders. We wandered down paths, surrounded by butterflies, birdsong and monkeys playing in the trees above. For all of us used to the Industrial Age, Ulpotha always induces a sense of displacement. To start with, the lack of electricity creates an immediate shift in perspective. Unaccustomed to the soft light of oil lamps, we fumbled about with our luggage, trying to make some sense of the home we would share for three days.

Steve then wandered through to the bathroom, and encountered a two-foot snake rippling across the floor. A torrent of expletives and a rapid exit ensued. We adjourned for dinner in the *ambalama*, an open-sided pavilion with raised ledge seating around the perimeter, joining a dozen-strong group, staying at Ulpotha for a two-week course in yoga dance. Bandara, the cook, had artfully arranged an array of curries in terracotta bowls, laid out on one woven reed mat that covered almost the entire floor. Alongside traditional vegetables, like drumstick, bitter gourd and *gotu-kola*, there were bowls brimming with plump whole grains of a rare red rice, clay tubs of buffalo curd, jugs of fresh wood-apple juice and flasks of tea made from ayurvedic herbs. Steve ate silently for about 30 seconds, his deadpan face staring straight into the middle distance, his jaws chomping slower and slower with each mastication.

'How's the food, Steve?' I asked with a grin.

'Man,' he said, breaking his gaze and turning towards me. 'In the last 10 seconds I've experienced about five billion new taste sensations.'

Tim was less effusive, more British, but equally blown away by the bare beauty and natural simplicity of life at Ulpotha. To begin with, it proved hard for us to do anything constructive. We lay on the mud floor of our hut, gazing up at the intricacies of the woven thatch, or the mesmerizing colours of giant passing butterflies. To alleviate any sense of guilt about not working, we spent several hours thinking of new names for the Web of Hope, a title that has invited some criticism from precisely the sort of people we were trying to engage with.

'It's too fluffy, mate,' some of my friends would say. 'You sound like born-again Christians,' said others.

This was not the response we were trying for. We thought we were hip and cool already, providing the perfect image for those mainstream people wanting to get more involved with issues like climate change, biodiversity loss and the impact of corporate globalization. Clearly, we had to think again.

'The Butterfly Project?' I offered, as one fluttered by.

'Hmmmm.' Tim was unconvinced.

'I like it,' Steve countered. 'It ties in with popular culture 'cos of the recent movie, which is part of what we are looking for.'

'And there's the chaos theory connection,' I added.

'Sure,' Tim conceded, 'but it's a bit too obvious. Old hat.'

The following day, I recalled a story first told to me by one of Michael's board members, while I was presenting my case for the name 'Project Flamingo'. An ecologist studying migrating flamingos on Kenya's Lake Naivasha noticed an interesting phenomenon. Every year, when the time came for migration, a few flamingos started the process by taking off from the lake. Since none of the others took any notice, they soon turned round and came back. The next day they tried again. This time a few others straggled along with them but again, the vast majority carried on as usual, so the pioneers returned to the lake. This trend continued for a few days. Each time a few more birds joined in but, since the thousands of others still took no notice, the migration plan was aborted. Finally, one day, the same few birds took off again. This time however, the tiny increment to their number was enough to tip the balance. The whole flock took flight and the migration began.

Various terms have been developed to describe this process – 'critical mass', 'the tipping point', 'the hundredth monkey'. Chaos theory talks about the 'butterfly effect', suggesting that a butterfly flapping its wings in Sumatra can start a tornado in Idaho. The insight is that tiny incremental changes within the dynamics of a complex system can lead to very dramatic effects further down the line. If we apply this concept to our current predicament, it gives rise to a sense of great empowerment. Rather than dismissing a small action – 'what difference will it make?' – or the role of the individual –

'what can I do about it?' – we see that change is always propelled by the individual, or that a small action can be an instrumental part of the significant changes that arise through complex processes. Seen from that perspective, we *are* the ones with the power – the power to cast ripples into the pond and become active nodes within a global network; the power to make positive change 'go viral'; the power to help build the sort of world we want for our children.

The others liked it and it passed onto the list of possibilities.

The majority of our two-week brainstorm was spent at the Lime House in Talpe, 8 kilometres east of Galle. This lovely old *walawwa* was rented by our friends Alex and Miss Pam, a Scottish schoolteacher educating local ex-pat children. They had gone back to the UK for a few weeks and offered us the space in their absence.

Days were spent hanging poster-sized sheets of paper up on the walls, covered with hieroglyphic ramblings about 'how to save the world'. The result was the decision to launch Project Flamingo, a seven-year campaign designed to run until what New Agers believe will be the end of the world in 2012, the end date of the Mayan calendar. In distinction from the Web of Hope, Project Flamingo would offer a variety of specific practical 'toolkits' to Web of Hope users, a series of hands-on guidelines for 'getting involved' and 'making a difference', ranging from composting advice to local food initiatives, from using an alternative currency to starting a wind power cooperative. It was more dynamic, interactive and prescriptive than the website, aiming to respond directly to that universal cry: 'but what should we actually *do*?'

In addition, we wanted to promote the concept of 'Hopesters', a word coined to give some identity to Web of Hope members. Some months later, the *Sunday Times* style section would seize on the term, describing Hopesters as 'Hipsters with a conscience – so very now', which suggested that we might have at least succeeded there.

When the time came for Steve to leave, two weeks later, I had to talk him down from the ledge outside Giles's flat, from where he was watching the sun rise over Colombo, then convince him that it was time to catch his plane. I sensed then that he would be back before too long.

The lease on Inland Hills was scheduled to start on 1 August, but because of the renovation it needed, we would remain in the Fort until after our planned trip to the UK, which we expected to last for at least six weeks from late September, when I would attend the Bioneers Conference. We also planned to load our remaining worldly possessions into a container and ship them out to Sri Lanka. All being well, we would move into Inland Hills when we returned in early November.

There was a lot to do. Not only did we have to redesign the house, negotiate with builders, choose materials and fittings, but we also had to find someone to manage the project while we were gone. We retained a few pieces of Shanta's furniture, and the rest was loaded onto a truck for delivery to their new home in Colombo. We arrived one morning to watch it disappear down the driveway, the overhanging branches brushing across chairs, tables, lamps and flowerpots perilously roped to the top. It was hard to believe that the 120 kilometres to Colombo could possibly be negotiated without at least some of these items being dispensed to the tarmac.

While trying to calculate the potential for harvesting rainwater, I estimated that the roof of the house must be in the region of 10,000 square feet. Not only was that a lot of second-hand tiles to find – in the end, about 70,000 – but an indication of just how much else there was to do in terms of plumbing, wiring and painting, let alone the 'knocking through here', 'building up here' and 'opening out there'. Inevitably, the more we looked at it, the more the scale of the project expanded. We had a figure in mind of what we felt was reasonable to spend, which we had both mentally doubled since 'it always takes twice as long and costs twice as much as you think'. We were however, anxious not to exceed that.

A routine of daily visits began, sometimes to meet contractors, or just to walk through and change our minds about everything we had agreed the day before. Some decisions were straightforward: removing old asbestos sheets which formed the suspended ceiling in the hall and two main bedrooms; knocking down the block walls enclosing the living space at the back of the house; removing black paint from the window panes.

Other decisions were more difficult. Could we remove black paint from old cement floors without them shattering? Should we remove the cement sheets from the verandahs, to expose the tiles in the traditional manner? Were we going to embark on the expense and impact of building a swimming pool? In the end, we had to look at the project as not just a home for ourselves, but also as a home to rent. Being more than four kilometres inland and at least 20 minutes' drive from the nearest decent beach, there was a strong argument that the house would be infinitely more desirable with a pool.

This was the sort of decision that I tussled with the most. Where do you draw the line between the interests of your family and your convictions? If making the house attractive for the rental market depended on having a pool, it clearly made sense to put one in. If the cost of doing so was no more than what we might make from a few weeks' rent, then it seemed mad not to.

A similar dilemma had emerged with transport. Shuttling about in tuk-tuks with two small children was proving exhausting. Also, it was hard to think of ways in which the boys could be exposed to greater levels of pollution, as fumes were almost permanently pumped through the cabs by the traffic. Tuk-tuks were also inherently dangerous. The tiny turning circle afforded by the single front wheel allows for instant pirouettes in the middle of the road. Since most drivers seem determined never to look at oncoming traffic, one is frequently exposed to a broadside impact from other vehicles. Every time Sholto went off to school in one, I felt nervous, almost irresponsible for letting him travel like that.

There was of course the option of buying a tuk-tuk ourselves, relying on our own driving skills to reduce the dangers. Various friends had done so and, for buzzing around in Galle or along the coast, it seemed like a sensible option. But our land was 20 kilometres from Galle, up long, twisting hills and quite a grind for a daily commute by tuk-tuk. Ideally, we would move Sholto and Xan around strapped into car seats. Not an option in a tuk-tuk. Even taking a trip to Colombo in a hired van was a challenge, since the seat belts were never compatible with the car seat design and we would turn round to see both children cartwheel onto their sides as we slid round corners.

I rarely had much faith in van drivers either. Once I had been forced to take the wheel myself, after our young driver had his wing mirror clipped by a passing truck. He stopped dead in his tracks in the middle of the fast lane and sat there, speechless and terrified, as maniac buses shot past us on the inside, their horns blaring and we in the back, shouting at him to move over.

Our thoughts turned to a car. I nurtured the romantic notion of buying an old 70s diesel Mercedes, of which there were many on the roads. Then we could make biodiesel and, to some extent, be 'carbon neutral' with our driving. I started scouring the classifieds in the Sunday newspapers, arranging to see a 'white Mercedes 200D in mint condition' when next in Colombo. Although I was ready for an interesting interpretation of 'mint condition', nothing could have prepared me for this. The car was a wreck. The front bumper was tied on with orange string and a strip of clear plastic used in place of the fuel cap. The whole interior stank of diesel. I could see tarmac through the rusted foot-well on the passenger side and the seats were in tatters. Out of curiosity, I asked to see under the bonnet, only to be greeted by a spray of oil from the blackened head gasket.

I reviewed my plans, looking at converting pick-ups to biodiesel. My enquiries invariably met with blank stares. After much meandering, I concluded that, in terms of safety for the kids, along with access to the land and coping with Sri Lankan roads, I could see few better options than a Subaru. Ever since owning them in Wales, I had been impressed with their engineering and reliability. I knew that would make me 'just another environmentalist in a four-wheel drive', but much of the travelling we had to do on the island would require that. With a catalytic converter and relatively clean engine, I knew that it would not compare unfavourably with a two-stroke tuk-tuk in an emissions test. (A few months later, this was confirmed when I found that a two-stroke tuk-tuk is roughly 200 times more polluting per kilometre than our car.) Compared with other four-wheel-drives, and anything else available in the country, the Forester was also relatively compact and fuel-efficient. If there had been a hybrid, or a hydrogen fuel-cell alternative, we would have pursued it, but this decision, like building a swimming pool, was for me a typical example of the compromises we are all forced to make.

Less than a week after signing the lease, we arrived at Inland Hills to find Shanta conducting excavations on the plot of land where he 'might build a small house one day'. The whole bank was being removed along our boundary, leaving a precipitous drop of 5 metres.

A few days later, the foundations were being laid. Shanta then proudly produced some architect's drawings, depicting a vast two-storeyed, six-bedroom concrete mansion.

'I thought you said you *might, one day, in a few years*, build a *small* house there, Shanta,' I said, trying to conceal my irritation. He smiled sheepishly.

'It's not really what you led us to believe, is it?' I continued.

We parted in awkward silence.

Next week, the walls went up. All of this before we had even employed a builder for our own project. Then, just as suddenly, work ground to a halt. To this day, the bare concrete block walls remain, now covered in creepers, with unwieldy lengths of rebar poking up through and swaying in the breeze.

We received a letter from Shanta. He had decided not to build the house. Clearly he had run out of money. Would we like to lease the 56 perches back from him – for 10 times what we had paid for the lease on the house and three acre garden for 10 years? I assumed he had his numbers wrong, having added an extra zero to the figure. But no. That was the offer which, needless to say, we rejected.

Work began at the land the week after we bought it. Chandana, joined by Peter, the former caretaker of the land, and his son Sunil, started clearing paths up the ridge and down to the river. As this work progressed, they revealed more and more stone terracing, almost all of it in perfect condition.

On each visit I made, the workforce expanded, as local men and women presented themselves, no doubt having heard about the mad *sudu mahataya* (white boss) who had taken over the estate. By the time we left for England four months later, we had taken on nearly 20 people.

During this time, I was unable to visit much more than once a week, when I would pay the week's wages and give them ideas about what to tackle the following week. Soon we had a network of paths covering most of the land and started clearing the bowl, revealing more terraces, stone wells and patches of tea to be brought back into production. Plucking started on a few acres in mid August, the 'green leaf' being sold direct to a local factory.

Before the clearing progressed too far, I knew it was important to conduct some sort of ecological study of the area, highlighting rare trees, shrubs, plants, ferns, or any habitat that might be important for rare birds, mammals or reptiles. With this in mind, I went to meet Robin who runs Rainforest Rescue International, the only environmental NGO in the south of the country. RRI had been started by Dr Ranil Senanayake, a rainforest guru whose name I had been hearing for years.

Robin was one of the original team to conceive the Eden Project in Cornwall and was curator of the 'tropical biome', one of the cathedral-sized geodesic structures erected in a disused Cornish clay pit. For the past year or more, he had been living with his family in Galle. RRI's main focus was to establish a 'biodiversity corridor' between Sinharaja and Kanneliya rainforests, connecting these two remaining reservations in the southwest of the island by pieces of land planted with rainforest species designed to accelerate diversification of the area.

By the time I made my way over to RRI's offices, I had already met Robin a couple of times. Blond, in his early 40s, his Dutch origins were barely discernible beneath his fluent English. He had boundless enthusiasm and passion for his subject. His knowledge was extensive, reeling off endless facts about the properties of certain plants as he bounced around the room, or up and down in his chair.

He invited me into his house and brewed a cup of coffee so strong it should have been illegal. Under high caffeine stimulation, he raced upstairs to the office, with me jittering along behind. Here I was introduced to Ajanta, a softly spoken bearded man in his mid-40s who was the leading local ecologist working with RRI. I described the land and some of my intentions – the concept of a forest garden, bringing back some of the tea, preserving large areas as biodiversity refuge, developing the potential for ecotourism and the ultimate aim of an ecological learning centre inspired by Colin's Village of Hope. Clearly, there were numerous parallels with RRI. Ajanta had even been working on a forest garden certification scheme for the country.

They both agreed that some sort of study needed to be conducted before any major clearing disturbed important areas. Ajanta had a week or so in which to do it, so I agreed then and there that we should forge ahead. Together we travelled to Thometotam, Robin brimming with information about *robusta*, as opposed to *arabica* coffee; the use of lesser *galangal* as a ground cover crop; the medicinal properties of various ayurvedic plants, like *weni-vel*; using the fibrous parts of the drumstick tree pod for purifying water. By the time we reached the bungalow, my head was spinning.

Robin raced up and down the few cleared paths, pointing out rare and useful plants, as well as those he considered worthless, like the slender but invasive *allstonia* trees, first seeded by the Forestry Department as a building material. Ajanta moved more slowly and methodically, but proved equally illuminating, pointing to patches of jungle with high diversity, or rare ferns and areas likely to provide habitat for various animals.

'I know we have wild boars here, Ajanta,' I said. 'But what else do you think we might have? Lots of snakes?'

'Snakes definitely,' he replied. 'Pythons, cobras, vipers ...' He reeled them off in measured deadpan tones.

'Anything else?' I wondered, sounding hopeful.

'Oh yes. Almost certainly pangolins, monkeys, giant squirrels. I'll put it all into my report.'

Although I had heard of pangolins, I had to admit that I could not picture them. Only some months later, when we gave Sholto some BBC documentaries to wean him off *Scooby-Doo* and *Sponge-Bob*, did we really appreciate the almost surreal nature of this rare nocturnal anteater, which moves around on its haunches like an armour-plated wallaby.

When Ajanta's vegetation map and report were completed later that year, the existing diversity of the land was revealed to be even more exciting than we had first imagined, recording indicator species of primary rainforest, important rainforest floral species like bird nest fern and Poson orchid, four endemic bird species and two endemic monkeys, the toque macaque and western purple faced leaf monkey. In addition to the indigenous giant squirrel, other mammals and reptiles included wild boar, pangolin, porcupine, ringed tail civet, python and cobra. All trees and plants of value had been meticulously highlighted with strips of coloured ribbon, or small dots of orange paint.

In light of Ajanta's report, I decided that one overarching cri-terion for developing the land was that these species be left intact and their habitat be preserved. He suggested that we interplant key areas with some climax and sub-climax species, specific rainforest trees and plants which would further accelerate diversification of the land. In terms of core principles for the project, the foundations were being laid.

Inland Hills was still a priority but, since I was working against the clock to write material for the launch of Project Flamingo and our new website at the Bioneers Conference in San Francisco in October, Yvette assumed the role of project manager, working with David and Ollie, a father-and-son team restoring houses for foreigners in Sri Lanka.

Once again, we seemed to be racing against deadlines and the stress levels mounted. I had rented a room in the Fort as an office, finding it almost impossible to work at home with two small children. Yvette was tearing around, finding doors and windows in reclamation yards in Bentota, choosing taps and shower fittings in Colombo, finding a good *terrazzo* specialist in the Galle area.

Then there was the question of what to do with the land, now abbreviated from Thometotam to TT, while we were gone. Who could we entrust to watch over things for several weeks?

Ibrahim's cousin Inti, who had some experience on tea and rubber estates, had been tempted down from Kandy to provide an added service for people like ourselves buying land with areas of cinnamon, rubber or tea that might need managing. I liked Inti at once. A well-educated Muslim like Ibrahim, he spoke fluent Tamil, Sinhala and English. With his rounded features, big smile and soft, unassuming manner, he was refreshingly straightforward and trustworthy.

Inti accompanied me on a few trips to TT, helping to translate and resolve a variety of issues. A neighbour, Chandrasekera, had laid a pipe from his house, half a kilometre away, to one of the wells in the middle of our land. Since there were several other wells closer to his house, this appeared to be little more than brazen provocation.

'This is very typical, Rory,' Inti assured me. 'When an estate like this changes hands, there are always people trying to take advantage.'

I could see that we had to tread very carefully. Quite understandably, our neighbours had treated the estate as common land for the past 10 years, helping themselves to the wells, cutting cinnamon, plucking tea, collecting mangoes and removing stone for building their houses. If there had been 60 acres of abandoned land next to our house in Wales, I might well have viewed it in the same way.

It was going to be hard to establish new parameters. Some of what they had been doing counted in our favour, like plucking areas of the tea and thereby, to some degree at least, keeping it maintained. However, if we allowed one family access to one of the best wells on the property, there was no knowing where it would end. The situation was only resolved when we dug them another well at our expense.

The main issue in this regard however, was that a path across the property had been used by people of surrounding villages as a footpath to the road. When we cleared this properly, it became a thoroughfare. Mopeds, tuk-tuks, cyclists, all came and went as they pleased. The notion that this was private land and now under new ownership cut no ice at all. Certain rights had been established over the last 10 years.

As a solution, I proposed to build a new road along the northern boundary, connecting all their houses with the main road. This road would be wide enough for four-wheeled access to all their houses, which had hitherto been denied them. (The previous owners had placed boulders across the main terrace path to prevent access.) This idea was greeted with considerable enthusiasm by the community and seemed like an excellent start to building good relations. It also turned out that the previous owners had been ordered by the courts to build just such a road, but had never done so. As the months passed, it became increasingly apparent that they had not been well liked in the area. Here was an opportunity for us to do better.

So, as if we did not have enough going on already, I put wheels in motion to build about 750 metres of road. This would involve blasting a few boulders and removing a number of trees. I asked Giles for advice and he arranged a meeting with Mr Gamage, a contractor from Weligama who had recently built a road for another client with an inaccessible hilltop.

Mr Gamage was having breakfast when I arrived, so I waited on his porch, flicking through the newspapers. A fleet of battered bulldozers, trucks and diggers were lined up in the yard behind his house, looking rusty and forlorn. A few months later, when the tsunami struck, this machinery played an essential role in clearing the damage.

We drove on beautiful but tortuous back roads from Weligama, through Yakkalamulla to TT. Mr Gamage walked with us along the boundary, noting various trees and boulders, confirming the exact route for the road. He quoted a price, which seemed much higher than Giles had suggested. Negotiations began and continued for days. When we finally settled on a figure, Inti and I met Mr Gamage and his operator at the land.

We arrived to find a village confrontation in full swing. Mr Gamage stood at the periphery, his machinery blocked by a mob of angry men and women. The police were there. Even the local GA (Government Agent) had been summoned from Yakkalamulla. Tempers ran high as Inti tactfully enquired about the cause of the problem.

'It's Chandrasekera again,' he reported. The man who had laid the pipe to our well. 'He's claiming that he owns that small piece of land where you want the road to start.'

97

'But that's impossible,' I said. 'That's reservation. I have the survey to prove it. It's also the route specified by the court order.'

'He says it's his land.' Inti smiled with resignation.

We talked with the GA. She also knew that it could not be Chandrasekera's land and said that he had already been ordered to remove the foundations for a house he had started to build there. Despite this, she seemed reluctant to step in and resolve the issue.

'Why not put the road here, on your land?' she asked.

I explained that, if we did that, the road would go straight up a steep incline, be prone to bad erosion and difficult for most vehicles to use. If the road had a switchback lower down, by cutting into the reservation, these issues would be overcome. Besides, I had already given my land for the rest of the road, rather than placing it within the reservation, where all my neighbours had encroached illegally and were now cultivating tea. Surely this was more than reasonable, especially since I was paying for it all?

Once again, neither the law, nor my understanding of what was logical, seemed of any relevance. As would so often be the case, I relented, to avoid stalemate and get on with the job in hand. Even so, this was far from the end of it. Some protested that the road, at 3 metres wide, was too narrow.

'What are they planning to drive up here,' I asked Inti. 'A tank?'

Some even expected tarmac to be laid, again at my expense. I began to see that, what you think is showing generosity or kindness, can often be taken for weakness.

Mr Ambawatte's survey had marked an area at the bottom of the bowl as *deniya*, meaning marsh, or wetland. Although such areas can be ecologically sensitive, providing rare habitat for migrating birds and various amphibians, I could not resist the temptation to dig a small lake and create a 'natural swimming pool'. Once again, I felt my father at my shoulder. The intention was to create a balanced ecosystem, introducing various species to form a cyclical food chain, from the phytoplankton through to the indigenous fish, or even freshwater crustaceans, like crayfish.

For some years now, this had been one of my main fantasies – to build a freshwater pool suitable for swimming but without resorting to chemicals to control bacteria. I knew it could be done, since permaculturists from subtropical Australia to tropical Bali and the temperate UK had all been experimenting with the concept for some years. The core principles are the same. If the ecosystem is properly balanced, the water will remain clear and relatively safe. With the right combination of micro-organisms, oxygenating plants and those that soak up nutrients from the water (like water hyacinth), along with fish and crustaceans at the top of the food chain, it should be possible to preserve these conditions in perpetuity.

Various modifications have been made to improve this model: using surface skimmers to remove floating leaves and debris; drawing water down through gravel and circulating it back into the top of the pool to control algae; using sprinklers just above the surface of the water to increase oxygenation; planting vegetation at the edges of the pool and then screening it off from the central swimming area with chicken wire stapled to a wooden fence below the surface.

I was pondering these possibilities while I watched Mr Gamage's machine lay waste to our boundary. It was disturbing to see how much damage one of these things could inflict on the landscape in a matter of hours and I wondered how many important plants and animal habitats had been eradicated in the process. We were, however, taking two or three days to build a road, an operation that would have taken months by hand.

Only then did it occur to me that we could dig out the lake at the same time, saving a great deal of money in the process, since a large part of the cost was in transporting the heavy machinery. I had to think fast though, since the road was nearly finished and we were due to leave for the UK at the end of that week. I cut some *gliricidia* poles nearby, then started marking out where I envisaged the bank, creating a figure-of-eight shape with one side left straight, following the line of an existing stone terrace. Inti and Chandana looked at me as though I was possessed.

The lake was excavated over the next two days, digging down to bare rock between two and three metres below ground level. The dark black slurry was removed, piled onto the banks, then graded down to the edges, the water draining back into the lake. By the end of the week, this had filled with more than a metre of chestnut brown water, which cleared as the sediment settled. By the time we returned from the UK two months later, the water was more than two metres deep and crystal clear to a depth of one metre.

Even after just six months, England was like another planet. Cars actually stayed in their designated lanes, gave way at junctions and even stopped at traffic lights. I had to consciously curb my rapidly deteriorating driving habits. A visit to the supermarket was jaw-dropping, especially when we were presented with a total at the checkout. London was something else again. Forced to drive on occasion, to accumulate the list of essentials we deemed necessary for our return to Sri Lanka, we fought endless battles with congestion charge machines and traffic wardens. Life seemed so regimented. Very rapidly, I remembered why we had left.

For the first three weeks, I was working flat out with Steve to pull to-gether all the elements required for the website launch. This involved a lot of late nights and many frustrations but we pulled it off. The site went live the day before the Bioneers Conference started.

I flew to San Francisco with Matt, a young researcher who had joined the Web of Hope team a few months earlier. California was even more of a contrast to Sri Lanka than London. The sheer speed and scale were so dissociated from the natural rhythms of life that it was disconcerting. The conference itself was an antidote to this apparent excess, pulling in key speakers from around the world, all of whom were an inspiration. Paul Hawken, the visionary eco-economist, made a closing speech that brought home the sheer breadth and diversity of the global movement, leaving many in tears. His talk highlighted the degree to which people all over the planet were becoming engaged and working for common goals. Referring to ecological solutions like biological medicine and renewable energy, in contrast to Big Pharma and the oil industry, he concluded: 'This shit works. Their shit doesn't.'

After my return from the US in late October, Yvette and I had three days to prepare for the final packing of a 20-foot container. Box after box was filled with books, records, kitchen utensils, glasses, paintings, photos and all of Yvette's pottery. Then there was the furniture, the garden tools, a chainsaw, the 'infernal machine' bush-cutter, and Yvette's kiln, a vast nine cubic feet gas-fired contraption that takes six men to lift.

Things started to go awry from the moment the container arrived. Some months before my brother Adam had moved to Australia and also shipped a container. Consequently, we understood that the lorry would have the necessary turning circle in the yard at my father's house to drop the container off and turn round. In Adam's case, this had not been a problem, so I merrily instructed the driver to come on up the drive and turn into the yard behind the garage, where it would be easy for us to load up and leave enough room for him drop off the container.

'It's fine,' I assured him. 'We did exactly this some months back. No problem.'

For the next three hours, the driver cursed me louder and ever more vehemently as he tried in vain to turn his lorry round and get out of my father's garage yard. Jumping up and down from the cab to assess new and different angles, he turned an explosive beetroot red as the hydraulic brakes heaved his lorry from side to side like some giant beached whale.

'I'll never get out,' he said finally. 'I'm stuck. Can't go forward, can't go back.'

'I don't understand it,' I kept saying, trying desperately to calm the situation. 'It's been done before.'

'So it's my fault, is it?'

'No, no, no.' Back pedal, back pedal. 'Must have been a different type of lorry, or something.'

As the light started to fade, we finally hit on a route winding out from the top of the yard and down the drive of another house. The only problem was getting through a rather narrow gate, but he squeezed through with millimetres to spare, leaving the container parked in the middle of a neighbour's drive. He finally steamed off more than four hours after his arrival, leaving three men from the shipping company to help us load up.

Rather than being parked right outside the garage with all our neatly stacked boxes, the container was now a good two hundred metres away. It was also dark. And it was starting to rain. Plans for a meticulous inventory itemizing the contents of more than 200 numbered boxes as they were loaded into the container, were quickly abandoned. Chaos ensued. We were still unsure that we could even fit this urban skyline of cardboard into one container, so we decided to start with all the most important items. Trying to direct this with three men eager to get home was a losing battle. Packaged paintings were stacked between hi-fi boxes and loose spades; cane-work sofas put upside down over dining room chairs; a chainsaw and the 'infernal machine' bush cutter propped up on clothes stands.

Then we realized there was loads of room. This was the point at which it all went haywire. Our friend Gabi was looking after Sholto and Xan. She suggested calling her sons to help. Soon there was a conveyor belt of four of us, filling boxes as fast as they could be carried away with all the items we had imagined leaving behind. More glasses, vases, picnic hampers, lengths of hosepipe. Then there was the kiln, which we had wanted to load first but now left about 12 square feet of floor-space for at the front of the container. This operation passed off with much grunting and heaving, but thankfully without injury. I nestled an old stone statue of the Buddha, which had been in the garden in Wales, into the base of the kiln. I was still throwing mops and brooms in over the top of this random pyramid as they were trying to close and bolt the doors.

As the container disappeared down our neighbour's drive, I felt an acute sense of relief, combined with anxious dread. Had I emptied the chainsaw and 'infernal machine' of fuel? Would they spontaneously combust in the middle of the Suez Canal? Would all the plastic bubble-wrap melt onto precious furniture and ruin it? Had we secured everything well enough? How much would break in transit? And just what would Sri Lanka's customs make of it all at the other end?

It had been raining almost constantly in Sri Lanka for the two months we were away. On days like these, people often forsake work and stay at home. Progress at Inland Hills had suffered as a result and it was apparent that moving in by mid November was out of the question. When we did move in, in mid December, it was to a house with two partially finished bedrooms and one functioning bathroom. There was no kitchen. The pool was still a quagmire of mud, brick and cement. There were builders everywhere – carpenters, masons, plumbers, electricians and a team of old men scratching paint off doors and windows with shards of glass.

All of this was presided over by 'Uncle', the contractor's father, a small, bony but dignified old man who had taken on the mantle of 'watcher' and was obviously under the impression that he was here to stay. He kept asking us about 'my room', which we had deemed to be our storeroom but over which he clearly had other designs. Uncle arranged tea and meals for all the builders during the day, then fell fast asleep every night on our prized antique *kohumba* (neem) bed with a skin full of arak and his head pressed firmly against the blaring white noise of his transistor radio.

I doubt any intruder would have been too overwhelmed by the appearance of this comatose five-foot septuagenarian, but his presence became a sort of comfort during these early days. By the time he finally packed his bags and left, he had become such a fixture around the house that we were sad to see him go.

The container arrived at Colombo docks in late November. After being notified by the shipper, I set off to try to extract our worldly possessions from customs. I approached this with trepidation, expecting protracted duels with ascending levels of officialdom.

The first complication was to secure a bank guarantee. This needed the company rubber stamp, which I had left in Galle, and the company seal, which was in the hands of our accountant, who had left to visit his daughter in Australia. The rubber stamp was ferried from Galle by the swimming pool contractor later that night. I managed to persuade the bank to waive the requirement of the seal. We were back on track.

Then we discovered that this was the one day in the year when the entire customs personnel changed over. They were all taking the day off and having 'a little party'. Reluctant to wait another 24 hours while clocking up storage charges, I asked the shipper to intervene. For a small fee, he thought it might be possible to extricate one customs officer from the arak-soaked proceedings. Later that afternoon, our container was delivered into a secured inspection bay and the locks removed. Then I remembered the Buddha statue, which would be the first thing to greet the eyes of the inspecting officer. This made me nervous, since fundamentalist sentiments had recently clamped down on the use of Buddhist effigies in secular settings, such as hotel foyers and private houses. Would we fall at the first hurdle?

The customs officer proved most accommodating. The first few items were removed and I explained about the kiln and how it was used. Having assured him that there were no cars, motorcycles or new electrical goods on board, he asked his men to bolt the doors back. We shared a cup of tea in his office as we went through the formalities of the paperwork. I told him about TT and discovered that he too had a small tea estate. From then on, it was plain sailing. He returned to his party and I left for Galle with the container following behind.

The lorry driver did not even attempt to negotiate the drive up to Inland Hills, so everything was unloaded at the crack of dawn and ferried up to the house in the equivalent of a Luton van. This took about half a dozen trips. As we stacked boxes and furniture into the guest bedroom, I surveyed the damage. Remarkably, all seemed to be in one piece.

We moved in to Inland Hills on 15 December. As we climbed into bed for the first time in our new home, fireflies flashed and danced through the rafters above the mosquito net, like little green sentinels keeping watch over us.

For the next 10 days, we slept and ate in our bedroom, living on 'hoppers', little rice flour pancakes delivered by Uncle from local stalls. Bit by bit, we made sense of the chaos, redistributing boxes through the length of the hallway, ready to be unpacked and installed in their appropriate rooms. Builders were gradually chased out of various rooms and some semblance of a functioning kitchen took shape around a two-ring gas burner and our fridge from the UK. My mother was due to arrive on the 28th, on her way back from Australia, so the pressure was on to have as much done as possible.

On Christmas Day, we left the muddle behind us and took off to the beach to meet friends. The weather had just changed, the tail end of the monsoon lifting to reveal crisp light, blue skies and turquoise sea. For the first time, the stresses of recent months all made sense. We were here. We had a house to live in. We'd done it.

By 10 o'clock the next morning, almost the entire coastline of the country was completely unrecognizable. The perimeter of the 'emerald island encircled by the sapphire wave' had been reduced to an apocalyptic disaster zone. Mangled metal and concrete debris mingled with dead bodies, toxic chemicals and asbestos dust.

In an instant, paradise had been poisoned.

Part Two

After the Wave

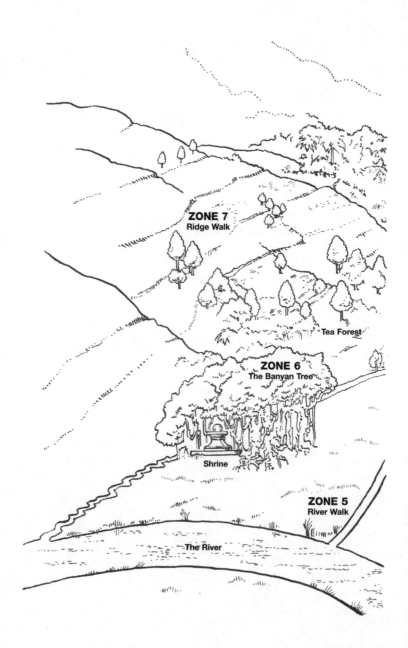

Chapter Seven

Rainbow Warriors

Another world is not only possible. It's on its way.
On quiet days, I can hear her breathing.

Arundhati Roy

There is an ancient prophecy among the indigenous tribes of the Americas that there will come a time when the world has been so plundered by greed that 'the earth will be ravaged of its resources, the sea blackened, the streams poisoned, the deer dropping dead in their tracks'. In response to this, a new tribe will emerge, the Warriors of the Rainbow, who would teach humanity once again how to live in harmony with natural processes. This prophecy provided the name for the most famous Greenpeace boat, *Rainbow Warrior*, which fought battles around the world against, among other things, the atmospheric testing of nuclear weapons.

I recently discovered that a similar prophecy exists in the East. It arose within Tibetan Buddhism in the eighth century and tells of a time when the world is threatened by dark forces and technologies of immense destruction. One of two opposing powers will be in the Western hemisphere and the other in the middle of Eurasia. Then a third power emerges, the Warriors of Shambala, whose aim is to defuse the tensions that threaten the stability of the planet. Rather than fighting, this tribe uses the powers of compassion and insight to infiltrate the opposing forces. Rather like Trojan horses, they work from the inside to dismantle the problem, taking control, shifting direction. Their mission is to reveal Shambala, another world that lies beyond.

It's easy to dismiss such stories as flaky New Age claptrap. Maybe that's all they will prove to be. Personally, I don't think that matters since, for me, they offer a sense of hope in dark times. And, as prominent Canadian activist and author Maude Barlow says, 'Hope is a moral imperative.' The alternative is cynicism, apathy, despair.

'Either we have hope within us or we do not,' Czech President and poet Vaclav Havel said in 1990. 'Hope is an orientation of the spirit, an orientation of the heart. It transcends the world that is immediately experienced and is anchored somewhere beyond its horizons. Hope is definitely not the same thing as optimism. It is not the conviction that something will turn out well, but the certainty that something makes sense regardless of how it turns out. It is hope, above all, which gives the strength to live and continually try new things.'

To my mind, this distinction that Havel makes between hope and optimism goes to the heart of the matter. Optimism is a projection into the future, a conceptualization about how we would like things to be. Hope is about the present moment, about pure intention, about working for something simply because it is good, with no attachment to the result of our actions.

I believe hope, this simple four-letter word as Colin once described it, resonates within us more powerfully now than at any stage in human history; that it has become the human quality most essential to our future well-being as a species because, without hope, none of us would even believe in the possibility of a different world, let alone work towards it.

We need hope to go viral. Although we tend to associate viruses with death and disease, there is much we can learn from the effective way nature spreads infection. Similarly, the efficiency of a terrorist network has much to teach us about building our own positive network of ideas, about consolidating the work of activists from around the globe, accelerating the move towards critical mass. Robert F. Kennedy said that 'each time a man stands up for an ideal, or acts to improve the life of others, or strikes out against injustice, he sends a tiny ripple of hope, and those ripples, crossing each other from a million different centres of energy, build a current which can sweep down the mightiest walls of oppression and resistance'.

When we feel helpless in the face of the enormity of the issues confronting us, these words remind us of how powerful we can be when united, when we keep casting those ripples of hope into the pond. The manipulation of fear has done much to undermine these ripples, but the only antidote to fear is hope.

The country was now faced with a massive reconstruction effort. At the same time, I was now faced with building my own dream over the coming year, casting my own ripple of hope into the collective pool.

Chapter Eight

Project Galle

31 December 2004. Galle.

Within hours of forming, Project Galle 2005 has attracted an eclectic spectrum of voluntary aid workers from the local population. Over the following few months, the office at 71 Pedlar Street would become the centre for a diverse collection of people from around the world, some offering specialized skills – as builders, doctors or IT experts – others just wanting to help in any way they could.

There's Mave, the Irish sheep farmer, with an inexhaustible vocabulary of swear words, who starts running the supplies warehouse in the Walker's building in the Fort, struggling to keep an inventory of stuff arriving from all over the globe; Alex, who has hardly slept in days and Becky, who has been living with him at the Lime House, start setting up an office. Eduard is soon saddled with the unenviable role of finance manager; Eric, a Zimbabwean farmer, is made head of field operations, overseeing the delivery of aid to 94 registered camps in the Galle area; Eric Coleman takes the helm, along with Ollie, who project managed Inland Hills for us. Both will play a pivotal role in holding the ship together during the coming months. Keith has been working round the clock in his badly hit neighbourhood, Dewatte, using his submersible pump to dredge wells that have become salinated and directing JCBs to remove debris from the roads and dig out drains. Ivan, who has been working with Giles on the property scene, now adopts Unawatuna as his focus, providing families with home starter packs consisting of gas burners, pots, pans and cooking utensils. Jeff, a Scot who had been living in Thailand, joins Mave in the warehouse, losing several kilos over the next few days because of the suffocating heat inside an old building that has no ventilation and is suffused with the stench of bat shit. He maintains this role for the rest of the year, much relieved when the warehouse is moved to a large airy hangar near Boosa, a few kilometres north of Galle.

Thrown into the mix are local van drivers and officials, delivering aid to the camps and helping as translators, along with a contingent of Nepalese Gurkhas, who seem to have appeared from nowhere. Two young Belgian doctors are making whirlwind tours of the camps, patching up septic wounds, assessing sanitation and keeping a watchful eye out for the first sign of epidemics. The house we had first rented in the Fort, on Pedlar Street, is taken over as accommodation for this swelling crowd, where Woody cooks all day to the strains of Creedence Clearwater Revival, until she breaks her ankle in an attempt to pinch the backside of a US marine.

I am helping to get the office together when two muscular, shaven-headed Russians appear at the door in a van stacked with supplies that they have just driven down from Colombo. A human chain quickly forms, unloading bags of rice, lentils, bottled water, milk powder, antibiotics, bandages. The two Russians, who could have been dancers in a Madonna stage show, pass a video camera between them, capturing the moment, then produce a bottle of whisky to share with us as we all celebrate our strangest New Year ever.

It's a gruelling time for all concerned. Smokers are immediately on double rations and a few cold beers are almost mandatory in the evening to take the edge off the stress. I recall needing at least two large scotches every evening, just to feel normal.

My mother, who had been due to arrive on 28 December, postpones her trip until 2 January. After a few days in Dambulla with her, we all drove back to Galle. It was the first time since the tsunami that I had driven the coast road in daylight and seen the extent of the devastation. I expected to see convoys of UN cars, Red Cross trucks and the presence of the major aid organizations. Apart from a World Vision Land Cruiser, I saw not a single vehicle. Entering Hikkaduwa, less than 20 kilometres north of Galle, the landscape was hardly recognizable. Old women sat on piles of rubble, surrounded by the pathetic remains of their homes. It was hard not to weep.

The WoH team in the UK had already launched an online appeal, using our charitable status to collect the tax deductible Gift Aid from every donation. These funds would then be directed to Project Galle, Friends of the South and Giles and Viren's Lanka Real Aid. The evening meetings of Project Galle were an inspiration and I was constantly amazed by the degree of commitment. A small group of highly motivated people, dismissed by some as little more than gin-soaked, neocolonial lotus-eaters, had rapidly mobilized themselves as the most effective aid organization working on the south coast. When the 'big boys' did finally appear – the large NGOs and aid organizations – they all came knocking at Project Galle's door for the information they needed, since the local knowledge it had accumulated was second to none.

Our impression of the official aid effort was far from flattering. There were rumours of five-star hotels in Colombo being block booked by senior aid workers, some of whom were spotted playing golf while drawing daily salaries which would feed a thousand people a day. A visit by US secretary of state, Colin Powell, turned out to be little more than a photo-op, and Project Galle was asked to provide the props necessary to the US media. Some weeks later, UN workers were seen pasting UN stickers to houses built by Project Galle and taking photographs.

Geoffrey Dobbs, the hotelier, would swing by the Project on occasion, between trips tearing up and down the coast from Galle to Weligama in his green Mini-Moke. Geoffrey had launched Adopt Sri Lanka, another online appeal aimed at twinning villages and schools in the UK with those affected in Sri Lanka. This generated huge amounts of funding over the course of the year, topping $3,000,000. Having been saved by a fisherman in Weligama Bay, Geoffrey paid special attention to the Weligama fishing fleet, flying back to London and launching the 'Fish and Ships' appeal at the House of Commons with Foreign Minister Jack Straw in attendance. It was hard not to be impressed by his sheer hard work.

With all this good work going on, it was also a time of craziness. There were rumours of a second tsunami, which caused widespread panic at times. People filled the roads as they dashed to collect children from school. Traffic poured into the Fort, as people sought higher ground. Some even jumped from moving buses.

There were also the conspiracy theories. Some people talked of secret 'tectonic weapons' developed by the US, using ultra-low frequency sound waves to trigger earthquakes in seismically active places. Many wondered why it was that, within hours of the tsunami, US troops and ships were heading for oil-rich Aceh, where Exxon-Mobil had already been drilling? An American friend of ours who led a UN team defusing landmines in the northeast of the island reported that all staff at the US embassy had been told to take a break over the Christmas period, because the civil war was about to re-erupt, according to officials. I could not help thinking that this seemed rather odd, since there was little indication of this at the time. There were also the inevitable UFO sightings near Aceh just before the tsunami, an area now viewed as the new Bermuda Triangle.

Although I was keen to involve myself as much as possible with Project Galle and the immediate aid effort, I soon hit a wall, overwhelmed by the projects already demanding my attention. Our house was still a work in progress, our lives entangled with an endless procession of carpenters, masons, electricians and painters, many of whom were sleeping in the garage. All of them needed constant supervision. Privacy had become an even scarcer luxury than normal.

Sholto and Xan were unsettled by the frantic energy that surrounded them and neither Yvette nor I could find the time we'd have liked to spend with them. Thankfully, we had been joined by Priya, a radiant Sinhalese woman in her 50s, who had previously worked in Kuwait but now moved in with us full-time. She took the boys under her wing.

Then there was TT, with more than 20 people to manage, plus WoH commitments, writing newsletters and responding to a daily barrage of e-mails as our requests for volunteers and advice were passed around the planet.

Eventually, the combined pressure took its toll. I found myself literally grinding to a halt, laid low by a virus and confined to bed for a few days with chronic back pain. Inti went with me to see an ayurvedic doctor near Imaduwa, where I promptly fell out of the car and onto the ground. The doctor dispensed his magic potions from a small cubby hole, concealed by a tattered curtain. After waiting in line behind a motley crew of ailing, injured people, I was ushered inside. His frenzied eyes seemed to stare into the middle distance, a quality I have observed in people who seem to have a shamanic ability to diagnose an imbalance within people and their environment. Colin Campbell, the white *sangoma* from Botswana who threw the bones for us, possessed this slightly disarming characteristic. As did Tennekoon.

The doctor, who spoke not a word of English, took my right wrist and checked the many different pulses recognized by traditional modalities like ayurveda and Tibetan medicine. Then he delved behind him and produced a small paper sachet filled with tiny black pellets, like miniature rabbit droppings. I was to dissolve these in hot water twice a day, and drink this with two tablespoons of a black syrup, which he dispensed in a recycled glass bottle. Then he grabbed a small sheet of paper, scribbled down a list of about 20 ingredients in Sinhala and dispatched me to the ayurvedic apothecary in Imaduwa. His fee for all this was 50 rupees, less than 30 pence.

At the apothecary, an old man with smooth mahogany skin and white silk hair studied the sheet of paper, then coiled four sheets of newspaper into cones and placed them in a wrought iron stand. Then, from the boxes of dried roots, twigs, leaves and spices arranged neatly in front of him, he started to assemble the ingredients for a *cassia*, which I had to boil down into a condensed, foul-tasting concoction.

Back at home, Priya followed the instructions in detail and presented me with a small cup of astringent liquid the colour of strong black tea. I bolted it down and, within two hours, was completely cured.

Chapter Nine

Samakanda

On my many journeys from Inland Hills to TT, I passed an intriguing permaculture-style experiment at the roadside and watched it evolve over several weeks. Three concentric rings of black dustbin bags had been stacked into three levels and filled with coir coconut fibre, fine soil and rich compost. A cone of thin poles radiated out from this central tower like the spokes of an inverted umbrella, each connecting with vertical poles at a 2-metre radius. These were firmly planted into old fertilizer bags, also filled with a coir, soil and compost potting mixture. Within a few weeks, this compact latticework structure was obscured by a profusion of different vegetables, all grown together and trained up the ingenious trellis. Cassava, or manioc, stood next to bitter gourd and snake gourd hanging from the poles; wing beans crept through this edible green canopy and pumpkins trailed off to the sides, crawling over the ground like invasive triffids.

Driving along the road one day with Inti on board, I could resist no longer. I had to stop and investigate. The work had been done by Asanka, a young farmer who lived within the bare walls of a modern concrete house he was building into the bank below the roadside. Asanka came from a long line of traditional farmers, claimed to farm organically, had recently won an award for a small biogas system he had designed and was being featured in a series of national television programmes. He was clearly intelligent, knowledgeable and capable, but there was an element of self-importance that I found disconcerting. However, he was keen to volunteer his skills and contacts for our project, offering to provide us with young fruit tree saplings, tea bushes and 'anything that will grow in Sri Lanka'.

'It's most important that these have all been organically raised,' I stressed to Inti, who was translating. 'One day we may want to apply for organic certification, so if there are any traces of urea, or chemical fertilizers, we will be compromised. Please make sure he understands the full implications of this.'

Inti relayed this point to Asanka, who gave his complete assurance that this would be the case.

'No problem,' he said, wobbling his head from side to side. 'No chemicals.'

One result of the tsunami was to intensify my desire to put various food-producing systems in place at TT. At the same time, I could see huge opportunities to try a wide variety of ideas and technologies from the WoH database, from harvesting rainwater to building with stabilized soil blocks, from microcredit schemes to community composting projects.

Slowly, these disparate plans began to crystallize into a more coherent vision, combining the tropical forest garden and the ecotourism elements with an emphasis on ecological education, running workshops and courses for local farmers as well as students from overseas. Recalling Thomas Berry's theories about changing the direction of our educational institutions, I coined the term 'bioversity' to describe a living biological university with a floating population of 'students' passing through. The bowl would be developed as the 'campus'.

We also needed a new name for the land. Thometotam is a Tamil word and, since those working there were all Sinhalese, it did not seem appropriate. To begin with, I settled on Samagama, meaning 'peaceful village' in Sinhala, but this changed to Samakanda, meaning 'peaceful hill'.

Asanka sourced and delivered 1,500 fruit trees at the end of January. An intensive tree-planting programme was soon under way at Samakanda, intercropping the bowl with mangos, bananas, papayas, mangosteens, rambutans, oranges, limes, avocados, cloves and pepper vines trailed up the trunks of *gliricidias*.

Since our own composting systems were not yet running efficiently enough to produce all we needed, I also ordered 500 kilos of 'organic compost' from Asanka. It was then that I first realized Asanka and I had very different ideas about the meaning of organic. I found scraps of old polythene and even dead batteries in some of the bags. When I asked for some of these to be replaced, my request caused offence.

'But these batteries contain heavy metals, Asanka,' I said. 'This is not organic. It is poison for the soil and the food.' He looked offended but finally relented, producing fruity-smelling, high quality compost the next week. However, I could tell that his feathers had been ruffled and that we would have to tread carefully in the future. I had the feeling that he was going to prove unpredictable.

Over the previous few months, I had been in touch with Sebastian, a friend of a friend from New York who runs In Pursuit of Tea, a company specializing in niche-market gourmet teas, many of them organic and all sourced from small-scale producers in obscure parts of Asia, from Bhutan and Sikkim to Korea and Mongolia. He was planning his first trip to Sri Lanka and, undeterred by the tsunami, arrived with his girlfriend Yishane, a travel writer.

They arrived in Galle at the end of January, having travelled down from the tea country in the middle of the island with two friends. Sebastian proved an inspiration from the start, opening up the world of tea to us and revealing the steep learning curve that lay ahead. Tea tasting started at breakfast, with Sebastian producing one bizarre product after another. Yvette and I quickly began to appreciate that we were dealing with a subject as complex and involved as wine. We had a lot to learn. There was Puer leaf, aged and fermented for up to a hundred years in large flat cakes that looked like cow pats; jasmine pearls, little scented hand-rolled pellets of green leaf; a tea called Nantou Oolong from Taiwan, that tasted like drinking flowers. It was all an education: discovering the correct temperature of water for certain teas, exactly how long the leaves should be steeped and the appropriate time of day each should be drunk.

Our education continued at Samakanda, where Sebastian leapt from bush to bush like a sprightly mountain goat, enthusing about the endless possibilities at our disposal. 'You could make a white tea from your silver tips, then use your green leaf combined with rice to make something like a Gen Mai Cha, the Japanese green tea which is mixed with roasted brown rice to soften the tannins. Just start playing around, do some experiments.'

By the end of our walk, he had plucked a variety of different blends, some of which he air-dried in his mosquito net back at the house, allowing the rest to wilt slowly in a wok over a low flame and producing the classic Chinese style of green tea. The next day, we were trying our own teas for the first time, marvelling at the relative ease and simplicity with which they had been prepared. Yvette was soon hooked, drying different batches in different ways and making a successful experiment with the white tea flowers. The tea bush is in fact a type of camellia, *camellia siniensis*, and the delicate flower is not dissimilar to its more ornamental cousins.

Our first attempts at producing green leaf tea proved very tannic, a taste favoured in the Middle East, which is where most of the tea grown at these elevations ends up. Despite this, and the fact that most brews ended up a strange psychedelic pink, we were enthralled with our efforts.

'It's really rather good,' I kept saying.

Sebastian was less convinced, but unerringly polite.

'It certainly has potential,' he offered.

'Gen Mai Cha has always been my favourite type of green tea'. I had been drinking it for years, and, at the time, it was the only kind of tea that I enjoyed. 'Maybe what you were suggesting makes sense, to try and balance the tannins. I've been thinking about growing some rice at the bottom of the bowl. Maybe we should look into that a bit more?'

'Sure,' he agreed. 'Sounds like a plan.'

Sebastian's visit coincided with an invitation from Shanta, our landlord at Inland Hills, to join him at Galle Cricket Club. Anxious to smooth over any issues surrounding the construction of his new house, I accepted, taking Inti with me to help with translation.

We arrived at 11 in the morning and were shown upstairs to the club house, a stark concrete cubicle with a bar in the corner, presided over by a scruffy old man with bloodshot eyes and betel-stained mouth.

'Beer?' Shanta offered.

'Bit early for me,' I replied, but I could see this was irrelevant. Four bottles of super-strong Sri Lankan beer were soon sitting on the table before us. I surveyed the scene. After the tsunami, the Galle cricket ground had provided one of the iconic images for the media, the pitch strewn with mangled cars, buses and fishing boats, inter-locked with fallen grandstands. The remnants of this carnage could still be seen one month on, now stacked into a neat pile of scrap metal at one side, while groundsmen busied themselves with laying new turf.

The scorching sun was high in the sky above the Fort. The reflected light forced me to hide behind my sunglasses and seek refreshment in a second bottle of Black Knight Super Deluxe. It was soon evident that Shanta was more interested in angling for funds to resurrect the Cricket Club than discussing the extension of our lease. Since I failed to share the national obsession for the game, his offer of becoming a member did little to entice me, but I agreed to see what we could do.

By the time Inti and I left, an hour and a half and many beers later, I was half-drunk and nursing a pounding headache. By the late afternoon, I had retreated to bed with sunstroke. My whole body broke out in a rash and I was overcome with lethargy. I took five days to recover.

It was in this debilitating condition that I first took Sebastian, Yishane and their friends to Samakanda. To make matters worse, I was greeted with a long list of complaints from the work force and our neighbours. The road was not wide enough. The signs I had made were inappropriate. Another family wanted a well.

Then there were the letters – lengthy, ponderous missives, penned in archaic English by a local scribe, whose services were now enlisted on a regular basis by people levelling endless accusations against each other. The stonemason Piyadasa accused Peter of stealing tea, cin-namon and jak trees. Peter accused Piyadasa of brewing *kasippu* on the land and poaching wild boar. Peter and Piyadasa both accused Chandana of embezzling money from tea. Everyone accused everyone else of being 'a cunning fellow' and wanting to cheat me. Suddenly, it all got too much. I lost it.

'Look,' I remonstrated. 'I've built you a road at my expense and all you do is complain. I've given you some of my land, so that this can be done. Some of you are living illegally in the reservation zone, where the road should have gone, but I did not want to upset you. I'm paying you all nearly double what you would be paid elsewhere. I've dug new wells for you. I don't need to do all this. I could put a 15-foot wall around the whole property and never employ any of you again. Is this what you want?'

With his inimitable tact, Inti tried to convey the essence of what I had said. But, as I would slowly begin to learn, this is not the way to operate in Sri Lanka. I had raised my voice. I had lost my temper. Hence, regardless of what I was saying, I had also lost face.

Chapter Ten

The Banyan Tree

3 February 2005. Galle.

The days are hot and dry. Whenever I drive through town, or along the coast road, diggers, trucks and bulldozers can still be seen clearing piles of tsunami debris. Great clouds of dust billow in the sea breeze, drifting across the road to create an almost permanent sepia haze. This is the dust of shattered bricks, concrete blocks, old tiles and, most alarmingly, asbestos sheets. The dangers are far from over. Workers in machines wear simple protective masks. Others wear scarves tied over their heads. Parents in tuk-tuks cup their right hands over children's faces. Sholto and Xan sit in the back of the car, protected by closed windows and air conditioning. I feel guilt and relief at the same time.

I know we all wonder what we are doing here at some stage. The essential part of the tropical dream that brought so many people to live and work here, that coastline of swaying palms, turquoise bays and golden sands, has been reduced to a sad strip of demolished houses, blocked waterways, piles of rubble and toxic dust. Snorkelling now truly offers another world, the detritus of terrestrial life merged with the marine – everything from asbestos shards, window frames, doors, saris and household chemicals now lodged within damaged coral reefs.

On the very first day we had arrived in Galle to live, Yvette and I took a walk around the Fort. Dutch colonial architecture predominates throughout the compressed grid of narrow streets. Peering through verandahs with elegant wooden pillars, or simple tapering columns, we caught glimpses of the courtyards beyond, some shaded by frangipanis or breadfruit trees. Judging the dimensions from the street, many of these houses had the space-expanding qualities of Dr Who's Tardis, opening into gracious living areas.

We noticed few changes in the year since we had last been in Galle. There was a new hotel on Church Street, a couple of new tourist shops, renovations in full swing on a few houses recently purchased by foreigners. Otherwise it retained the same time-warp charm, like a condensed version of Cochin, or the old part of Pondicherry, in south India.

Cows wandered between piles of garbage, families walked the ramparts, schoolchildren in pristine white uniforms filled the streets twice a day, young boys flew kites and their elder brothers played cricket on the street. Vehicles came and went, but the Fort was spared the full-on cacophony and chaos of the town. Life was sedate, enclosed, almost cocooned from the outside world. Entering by either gate, the transition was always the same, like leaving Sri Lanka and entering a parallel world. It was the same sensation as crossing the canal into the French colonial part of Pondicherry. The decibels dropped, the throngs of people dissipated, the energy slowed down. Walking and cycling became the best mode of transport.

Wandering back from lunch, I followed Yvette into a small boutique selling souvenirs. A lean, dark figure stepped out from the shadows at the back of the shop, his presence like an apparition. There was a calm brooding intensity in his eyes, enhanced by his high forehead and long wiry hair. He stepped furtively around the room, smil-

128

ing. I found this rather disconcerting, so looked for something to buy, settling on a packet of incense. From the small exchange that followed, I could tell that he spoke fluent English.

'I like your shop.' I offered, for the sake of saying something.

'Thank you,' he replied, with a beguiling smile. 'Are you here on holiday?'

'No, we're actually in the process of moving here,' I replied.

'Yeeees,' he hissed, still smiling sweetly. 'Are you going to live in the Fort?'

'We've rented a house here for six months but we'll probably look for something outside, a little bit inland.'

'Yeeees.' The hiss was soft, genial, mesmerizing.

'You speak very good English. Did you live abroad?'

'Yeeees.' He looked up intently. 'I was in Australia for 26 years.'

'Oh, right. Whereabouts in Australia?'

'Sydney, most of the time.'

We stood on the threshold of his shop and he lit a cigarette.

'You like music?' he asked suddenly.

'Sure,' I replied. 'It's a big part of my life.'

'Me too. I used to DJ a bit when I came back, in Hikkaduwa, Colombo . . .'

'Great. What sort of thing?' I was intrigued.

'Oh, a real mixture. Right now I'm really into Nick Cave and Leonard Cohen.' That figures, I thought to myself. 'Mike Scott, you know, from the Waterboys?' He drew deeply on his cigarette.

'Yeah, I do. Like him a lot,' I said.

'Me too.'

Yvette was already down the street, looking in other windows.

'Well, nice to meet you,' I said. 'No doubt we'll see you around.'

'Yeeees. What's your name?'

'Rory,' I replied. 'And yours?'

'Vimal.'

I felt his piercing gaze on my back as I walked off down the street.

As it happened, we had seen surprisingly little of Vimal over the following year, beyond the occasional meeting in the street. With his German wife and two beautiful children, the family appeared to be the perfect unit, but kept their distance from the foreign community. Despite his disconcerting manner, we warmed to them all. Yvette and I would often say to each other that we should make more effort to see them.

Then, about six weeks after the tsunami, I received a call.

'Hi, Rory, it's Vimal.' The mellifluous but disarming tone of his voice was instantly recognizable.

'Hi, Vimal. How's things?'

'Good, thank you. I was just wondering, Rory, could I speak with you about something? You see, since the tsunami, I have been trying to do some things in the Fort, like clearing up the rubbish. And the beaches too. I've got a few people together and we've been putting out proper garbage cans, picking up all the plastic.'

'That's wonderful. Good for you.'

'Yeeees. And I was speaking to Pam, you know the teacher.'

'Sure.'

'And she was saying about you being involved with the environment.'

'Right.'

'Well, I really want to do something now, after the tsunami, to try and educate people about all this, about the garbage, the plastic.'

'Great. It's really needed.'

'Yeeees. I was just wondering if I could come and speak to you

130

about it and whether you could help me to make some posters, or some leaflets, to make people more aware of this issue?'

'Sure. That would be great. It's one of many things I would like to do but never seem to find the time. Why don't you come over and we'll talk about it?'

Later that day, Vimal appeared at our house, surprising us by walking up the drive and materializing from the bushes beside the pool. This seemed to be his preferred method of making any entry – silently, stealthily, surreptitiously. I could never quite fathom whether this was a sign of humility and shyness, or an indication of something deeper, maintaining a sort of voyeuristic distance from the world around him.

He talked in more detail about what he had been doing and I congratulated him on taking such initiative. He mentioned that he had approached people in the Fort for more money to develop the project, but nobody seemed interested. In retrospect, he was clearly pitching for money from me but, in my naivety, I didn't notice. Instead, I genuinely wanted to provide him with some educational materials, giving him copies of basic composting and waste separation advice that I had drawn up for Project Galle and those working in Unawatuna.

'If you could translate these into Sinhalese, that would be a good start,' I suggested. 'Then they could be printed up and distributed.'

'Yeeees.' He peered down through reading glasses, scanning the key points.

'Also, we're having this guy called Max Lindegger to stay. He's one of the top permaculture designers in the world and comes from Crystal Waters, an award-winning eco-village in Australia. He's been working with an NGO here on some tsunami projects and is now coming to advise us on the project we are developing on our land. Perhaps you would like to meet him?'

'Yeeees.' As always, his answer was affirmative but also ambivalent.

I collected Max from Hikkaduwa the next day, where he had been advising Sarvodaya, a local NGO, on some housing projects. He was a tall, lean figure, with fair skin, reddish hair and beard. His accent was hard to place, but sounded like Afrikaans, the language spoken by Boers in South Africa. In fact, Max hails from Switzerland but had been living in Australia for the past 30 years. With a background as a civil engineer, he found himself attracted to the common sense of permaculture early in its evolution. His expertise now ranged from rainwater harvesting to sustainable agriculture; from renewable energy to biological sewage treatment.

As we drove south along the coast road, I apologized for my increasingly Sri Lankan driving habits, then asked Max about the work he had been doing with Sarvodaya.

'As you said in that first e-mail you sent me, I think we all saw some huge opportunities to get some appropriate building ideas into the reconstruction effort,' Max said, staring nervously at the road. 'Sarvodaya are certainly trying, by avoiding asbestos for example. I've also just been advising them on some rammed-earth houses up near Kalutara.'

'That's great to hear,' I said. 'But as you must have already seen, this kind of building is very much the exception. Most people want what they see as a *modern* house, built with *modern* materials – so a concrete box with asbestos sheets on the roof. It's hard to persuade them otherwise, since anything built with mud, like rammed earth or compressed mud brick, is seen as a regression to what they hope to leave behind. It becomes just another example of people from the Western world trying to sell them a different package from before. Same as us now turning round and telling them to stop burning fossil fuels.'

Max shook his head. 'Education is the key.'

I told him more about the Web of Hope, our educational pro-grammes in the UK, the Samakanda Bio-versity and other ideas we wanted to develop in Sri Lanka.

'There's also this guy called Vimal, who you'll meet later. He's asked me to help him with some basic awareness campaign, which has been a bit of a catalyst for me to get going on these issues.'

Vimal joined us for lunch at Inland Hills and we discussed some ideas in more detail – waste separation, recycling, community com-posting initiatives.

'I'm taking Max up to look round our bit of land,' I said to Vimal after we had finished eating. 'Would you like to join us?'

'OK,' he smiled.

As I talked with Max and set out my ideas, Vimal walked quietly behind us, occasionally commenting on a view, a tree or a distinc-tive rock. I could see that he was surprised and intrigued by the land.

Max's advice was practical and down-to-earth. He was the first to challenge my ambitious plans for placing the 'pods' (the name I had given to our low-impact eco-lodges) on the top of the main ridge and suggested bringing them down to the cleared terraces of the bowl. Sure, the views from the top were spectacular, but access was hard, especially for the elderly. Some people would immediately be excluded. At the same time, clearing sites at the top would dis-turb more of the natural habitat for the rare mammals we wanted to protect and be much more difficult to supply with water, with-out using a lot of energy to pump. If we placed the houses lower down, cantilevered out from the line of terraces that marks the tran-sition from cleared tea to untouched jungle, we would have the best of both worlds: privacy and seclusion from the working land, while being fully immersed within it. If we could harvest and store rainwater further up the ridge, we would have an ideal system, being able to direct water to wherever we wanted on the land without using pumps.

Water samples from seven of the wells had already been tested and found to be potable. Max and I now made a rudimentary study of the levels, using a stone tied to a length of rope. It was the height of the dry season and we found more than three metres of water in the main well. The others at the bottom of the bowl all hit bedrock about a metre below the surface, but nevertheless contained about a metre of fresh water. This all looked promising although, as Max pointed out, we would need to calculate the flow rates and compare them with our demands before drawing final conclusions.

Max's suggestion about placing the pods within the bowl would satisfy my passion for incorporating rammed earth into the construction, but maybe just for attached bathroom blocks at the back. Existing stone terraces could be built into retaining walls to create the platforms, but walls and roofs might be most practically made from lightweight materials with low thermal mass and which encouraged cross-ventilation – sliding panels made from woven rattan, or bamboo; *cadjan* palm frond thatch; wooden decking on balconies, with gaps between the boards. The challenge would be to make the pods as cool as possible, while retaining privacy, good views and easy access. A formula was starting to appear.

As we drove back down to Galle, I could see that Vimal could no longer contain his enthusiasm. I knew what was coming.

'You've really found yourself a piece of paradise there, Rory,' he said, leaning forward from the back seat.

'We've been very lucky.'

'Yeeees. You know, I could really help you up there. I've done a lot of designing before, for restaurants in Hikkaduwa, an ayurvedic place near Galle, all with natural materials. If you like, I could give you some ideas and see what you think?'

'Sure,' I replied. 'Let's get together and talk about it.'

Thus it was that Vimal entered our lives.

In a sense, he seemed to have appeared at the right time. Inti's wife had recently given birth to a baby girl and the family had moved back to Kandy. I needed someone to take over his role as translator and to help with administration. Vimal clearly had a creative streak, an understanding of the whole concept and an aesthetic sense that could be conveyed to the others. It made sense to take him on. Yet I was worried. I could not quite put my finger on why. I spoke with friends, all of whom said the same: 'Be careful'. When I asked why, nobody could offer a clear answer. There was nothing specific, just a sense of discomfort.

Miss Pam, who knew Vimal and his family well, was the exception.

'I think this would be a huge break for him, Rory,' she said. 'He has his problems, like the rest of us, but he's bored running that shop. He needs to do something more creative. I think it would be wonderful if you could help him out. It would be good for the whole family.'

So, partly out of necessity, partly out of compassion, I offered Vimal a role as 'creative designer'. The day after Max left for Colombo, the two of us drove up to the land and went for a walk.

We were 30 metres up the path to the ridge when we spotted a small viper, only eight inches long but highly venomous. I was surprised to see Vimal pick up a rock and hurl it at the snake, missing by a few inches. I could not help thinking of Colin Campbell, the shaman from Botswana, and a story he had once told me, about observing the signs around us. This was the first snake I had seen on the land. To date, it is the only viper I have ever seen there.

There was no shortage of ideas for Samakanda but it was too early to implement most of them. Vimal wanted to start a restaurant, build a recording studio, open a library. I was more concerned with laying the foundations for the forest garden in the bowl, clearing the terraces, preparing to plant tea during the next rains, putting in the paddy fields. We chose a location for a simple open-sided hut, halfway down the crest of the main ridge. I was happy to see what Vimal would come up with, using just the materials and labour at his disposal.

Sunil and Sarath, sons of the old caretaker Peter, took on the role of carpenters, helped by Vijaysekara and Amarajeeva. Amarajeeva had the most complete knowledge of working with traditional materials, like the woven *bata-kola* thatch we decided to use and which we expected to last much longer than *cadjan*. A seven-sided structure took shape around a raised wooden platform, with 'round wood' columns and rafters made from debarked poles. The *bata-kola*, which resembles bamboo leaf, was pleated together into splaying spiky fans and tied to the roof, crowning the hut with a punk haircut. Other poles were debarked and sanded to create a bench along the back, with panoramic views towards the coast in the south, over the bowl and up to Sinharaja rainforest to the north. It was simple but effective.

It soon became clear that Vimal and I were working from opposite ends of the spectrum. He was dismissive of architects and the notion that we needed to employ anyone else. Why not just forge ahead with what we had there? Part of me agreed. We had all the stone, timber and mud to build an entire village. With the traditional skills of men like Amarajeeva, we could circumvent much of the need for other specialists. It was very appealing.

Impetuous as I may be, what was holding me back was the realization that this was not the time to launch into more building projects of any significance. We were still trying to finish Inland Hills. At Samakanda, we had 12,000 holes to dig for new tea bushes. There were paths to clear, areas to open up, terraces to repair, paddy fields to prepare. Besides, we were still in a period of observation and planning. There were so many potential sites for houses, for a restaurant, for a yoga hall. The options were bewildering to say the least. I changed my mind every day. As soon as I reached some decision, someone would suggest an alternative and plans would change again.

Also, I was still grappling with the overall concept. Did we plan to live there ourselves and, if so, where would we put our house? How much could we ourselves invest in the project? Were we going to look for other investors? There was the option of developing some sort of time-share scheme, selling leases on plots, building low-impact ecological houses which could be rented to anyone attending courses or yoga retreats. This seemed the most obvious way to make the project economically sustainable.

One thing I was sure of was that when we did build, we had to make sure we had crafted a basic design that met certain criteria. It had to be cheap and easy to build, requiring minimal specialized knowledge, but it also had to be very comfortable. I was looking for a marriage between simplicity and sophistication, blending mud floors and sparse furnishings with fine bed linen, top quality mosquito nets and well-designed bathrooms. The pods had to prove that sustainability, functionality, sophistication and comfort can all harmonize.

So intelligent design, like passive cooling and low thermal mass, would render air conditioning and, hopefully, electric fans, unnecessary. The use of locally sourced materials, as many as possible taken from the land itself, would ensure a low Footprint. Ideally, water would be captured from the roof, although using natural materials like *cadjan*, this is difficult without resorting to plastic membranes. Solar panels would produce the energy needed for a few electric lights and recharging laptops, phones and digital cameras. Biological waste treatment could deal with the sewage. The Biolytix cell, developed in Australia and introduced to me by Max, is a sealed unit that can be buried underground, like a conventional septic tank, but it processes all compostable kitchen waste, grey-water and sewage into crystal clear nutrient-enriched irrigation water. The aim therefore, was to design a small house that, like a tree, harnesses or produces more energy and water than it consumes.

I was due to fly back to London for a week in the middle of March for a Web of Hope fundraising event and also to collect video equipment I had bought to start documenting our work at Samakanda.

Before flying, I was making daily trips to the land. A series of terraced paddy fields were being constructed in the bowl, between the lake and the cottage, the house occupied by Chandana's family. The terraces, which had been rebuilt, would be planted up with rare red rice seed donated by Ulpotha when the rains appeared in April. The work was done quickly and with sensitivity to the surrounding landscape, proving that much could be done without my interference. The aesthetic sense of those doing the work was faultless and, over the coming months, I would often marvel at how much their taste matched mine, and without my input. They just did it and did it beautifully.

On each side of the paddy fields, Asoka and Mangala had started to prepare vegetable beds, ready to be planted up with seeds ordered from Max's contacts at Crystal Waters. By the time I returned from England at the end of the month, these were already filled with the first leaves of rocket, basil and a variety of lettuces. The beds had been artfully arranged, although I would later insist that those running perpendicular to the contours needed to be turned through 90 degrees, since heavy rains had started to erode the topsoil and deposit nutrients in the lake – exactly what we wanted to avoid.

Just before leaving for Colombo to catch the plane, I got a call from Vimal.

'Rory, you won't believe what we discovered today.' He sounded unusually upbeat. 'Up by Romeyel's house, in the middle of the jungle, these huge banyan trees. And all around, massive boulders and some caves. It's incredible. Honestly. I think it's the most amazing thing I've ever seen in this country, or anywhere.'

I was sceptical.

'Seriously. Do you mind if we start clearing around there? It's a bit difficult to get in there now. Then, when you get back, there will be a proper path and you can come and take a look.'

'Sure. Go ahead. Just be careful that they don't get carried away. I'd hate to lose any important plants or trees.'

'Of course. I'll make sure of that.'

As ever, the transition back to London was surreal. Fortunately, I arrived at the same time as the first burst of spring. The skies were clear and the blossoms starting to appear.

It was of course a frantic week, with back-to-back meetings and final preparations for our fundraising event at a nightclub in north

London. I collected the film equipment, then spent every available minute racing around with a long shopping list from Yvette, stocking up with items ranging from Ecover products to Angostura bitters, homeopathic remedies and citricidal grapefruit seed extract, an amazing weapon for the incessant battle with tropical parasites taking up residence in our guts. When I arrived at Heathrow to fly back, I found that my luggage was some 35 kilos overweight, largely due to the camera equipment.

Eager to see the area around the banyan trees and to start using the camera, I drove up to Samakanda on the first morning back. Vimal guided me down the path they had cleared from Romeyel's house, at the tip of our northeastern boundary, which opened into a clearing around the base of one banyan. It was indeed an impressive tree, the vast canopy sheltering a writhing mass of roots and branches, lashing over boulders like the tentacles of a giant squid.

'And this is just one of them.' The excitement was evident in his voice. 'There's another over there, another up there.' He pointed through the jungle. 'And you won't believe it Rory, but there are some caves down there and what looks like a place where people gathered for rituals of some kind.'

I followed him down a stone drainage gully, dropping past huge boulders, the surfaces covered with striations and rounded, sculpted depressions. 'These almost look hand carved, Vimal. What do you think?'

'I don't know. Maybe they were used for trapping water?'

'That could be it. They look like strange shapes to have appeared through natural processes.'

We clambered down rocks, pausing to look at a so-called sleeping viper that Sunil had just uncovered beneath a thick mat of rotting leaves.

'A sleeping viper?' I asked.

'Yeeees. They look dead but if they bite you, they send you to sleep.'

'How long for, I wonder?' Nobody knew.

Winding round the base of two vast overhanging rocks, separated by a vertical split three feet wide, we emerged in a small clearing of maybe 10 feet square. Five rocks arranged in a semicircle provided seating in front of a boulder, about five feet high and eight feet wide. Positioned at the bottom of this, directly in the middle, lay a stubby stone phallus, 18 inches tall, 12 inches wide.

'A Shiva lingam,' I said, hardly believing my eyes. 'And the large boulder is the yoni, representing the feminine energy, the Shakti.'

'Yeeees,' Vimal purred, crouching on his haunches beside me.

'I wonder how old this is,' I said. 'Presumably there were no Hindus here before it became a tea estate a hundred years ago, when the Tamils arrived in the area. But the banyan looks much older than that – 300 years or so. Maybe it's animistic? Some non-Hindu cultures dating back thousands of years worshipped shapes like these. Maybe this was a gathering place for indigenous people from long before?'

'Yeeees.'

'Amazing though. Our very own temple, complete with lingam!' I felt as though I was walking through the final pages of Conrad's *Heart of Darkness*. The horror hung around us in the jungle, but here was the light within. All of this, on our own land, I thought to myself. It seemed too good to be true.

'I've been hearing some interesting stories about this place,' Vimal said in a beguiling way.

'Oh yeah? Such as?'

'Amarajeeva, who you know lives just over there, says he has seen a green light shooting into the jungle right here, like green lightning.'

I laughed. 'What was he on?'

'Well, you know Amarajeeva. He's a strange man. Piyadasa says there's a cave, somewhere over there, just off your land, that can take 500 people inside it.'

'Five hundred?' I stammered. 'It must be the size of a cathedral. Still, even if that's exaggerated by a factor of 10, it's still a big cave! Do you know where it is exactly?'

'It's very difficult to reach. But we should try.'

Later I realized that this shrine and the banyan tree lay in a direct line above a grotto, which I had passed many times on the path down to the river. The boulders there were about 15 feet tall, covered in ferns, lichens and moss, huddling together like a protective barrier. Every time I walked into the space between them, I felt the atmosphere change. A green effulgent light seemed to emanate from the rocks, like a calm breeze wafting over the path. And it wasn't just me. I began to notice a similar shift in perception would often happen to others when they entered this spot. Reactions ranged from 'Whoa, what was that?' to 'Wow, there's some juice here.'

In India, a spot like this is known as a *tirtha*, or bridge, and refers to the transition into sacred space and time at a certain location. These are present all over the globe of course and I remember having similar reactions to certain places in Wales, where the roots of old oaks merged with slate, stone and springs to create natural shrines that appear to be charged with some special quality. The idea of 'ley lines' connecting ancient sacred sites across the British Isles has been used to describe this. Some say that when a ley line intersects with a watercourse these sites manifest a sort of natural energy grid. Whatever the explanation, there was a presence at this spot.

I spent the rest of the day filming, heaving the camera, tripod and sound equipment up and down the ridge, in and out of the bowl, sweating like a fiend and trying to film myself presenting various pieces to camera for my attempt at a 'pilot' programme, which I might use to attract interest from broadcasters. This was a steep learning curve and the broadcast-quality equipment was fraught with complications.

For the moment, I was looking for only a few minutes of material, which could be added to our website, or used in a promotional DVD. Since the land was changing so dramatically and so quickly, I really wanted to capture these early moments, choosing key positions from which to shoot establishing shots to contrast with others taken from exactly the same position over the ensuing months and years, creating a sort of time-lapse tapestry of the land's evolution, from ruined tea estate to diversified forest garden and tropical rainforest.

I kept removing my feet, head or even my entire upper body from the frame, ending up with shots of my knees set to a monologue of ramblings about the banyan tree, or a headless torso pontificating about forest gardens and natural swimming pools. Once I failed to appear in the shot completely. My white shirt gave off terrible glare, so I changed to grey. This gradually turned to black as the sweat poured and I stumbled up and down stone drains. Then there was the kit itself. Either I had left one of the radio mikes switched off, or forgotten to remove a lens filter, so I ended up miming to the sound of the wind, or merging into the darkness. Some shots took more than a dozen takes and were still a disaster.

Fortunately, my cinematography improved as I became more familiar with the equipment over the following days.

Chapter Eleven

Arugam Bay

25 April 2005. Galle.

I received a call from Dr Ranil Senanayake, Chairman of Rainforest Rescue International (RRI), and we arranged to meet for lunch at Inland Hills so that we could discuss our respective projects. I had heard a lot about Ranil, from Robin and others working in this field. He was constantly on the move, from his current home in Ecuador to Costa Rica, Sri Lanka, Vietnam, the Philippines, in fact any spot on the globe with remaining rainforest, juggling numerous projects in each place, from conservation to cooperative enterprises, launching rainforest and forest garden products to support indigenous communities. By all accounts, he was a fount of knowledge and a whirlwind of energy and enthusiasm. This was soon confirmed.

Ranil arrived at Inland Hills and I was immediately struck by his vitality. He looked 20 years younger than his 65. Tall and broad, with a close-cropped beard and playful gleam in his eyes, he instantly held Yvette and me spellbound. Rather like Colin, his grasp of his subject left my head spinning, as he launched from one fascinating topic to another, reeling off names of rainforest trees, plants, butterflies and amphibians faster than I could write them down. I outlined my ideas for managing the water at Samakanda, trying to harvest rainfall from huge rocks on the ridge, and he confirmed that we were thinking along the right lines.

'Yes, traditional terracing and drainage on tea estates is a very efficient way of preventing erosion and draining the land,' he said. 'But that is not the way water would naturally pass through the landscape. If you can superimpose another system onto what you have there, one that is organic, rather than running in straight lines, you will then kick-start a variety of other ecosystems. If you study the contours, you can develop an idea of how the water would naturally flow through the land.'

'That sounds like a good example of bio-mimicry,' I said. 'Using nature as the inspiration for designing a model with systemic benefits.'

'Exactly. That's what my concept of analog forestry is about. If we look at what the inherent energy of the landscape is, then we can work alongside that, strategically planting edible, medicinal or other useful plants. As you know, that's the fundamental problem with modern agriculture and monocultures. It's the antithesis of what natural systems are trying to do – to keep diversifying – and that's why we resort to an arsenal of chemicals and high-energy inputs.'

'All in the name of efficiency,' I added.

'That's right,' said Ranil, his eyebrows arching.

6 May 2005. Galle.

I spend the day interviewing families who will be moved into one of Project Galle's housing schemes. Their stories are harrowing. Fifty-three-year-old Sityapathina lost eight family members in the tsunami, including her husband, brother, sister and two of her grandchildren. Titus, a mason in his mid-40s, lost his wife when she was locked in the house where she worked and told to look after it as her employers ran for safety. Vithanaga Sriyawatha lost his one-year-old son and has been living in a tent for five months.

Others were lucky in comparison. Naziem was picked up by the wave at Katugoda petrol station and carried a quarter of a mile before finding that a concrete wall had toppled onto his daughter near their home. She survived, but he lost his house, his job, his savings. As part of their Livelihoods programme, Project Galle have given him some scales and he is now working again as a scrap-metal collector. Saribdeen told me how he had watched the water start to seep around his feet in his house before finding himself up a coconut tree with his wife and two children. He is now working as a labourer for Project Galle and being paid.

Regardless of their age, or the degree of suffering, I am constantly amazed by how these people recount their experiences. Compared with the public grieving we witness in the West, they appear so collected, so accepting. It would be easy to ascribe this to an ingrained Buddhist fatalism, but many that I spoke with were Muslim. It is, I believe, more about an entirely different way of looking at the world, a deeply conditioned set of beliefs that transcend mere religious labels and is symptomatic of the East-West divide. The concept of karma is accepted without question. At Seenigama for example, just north of Hikkaduwa, the community believes that the tsunami hit them with such severity as punishment for destroying the reef by dynamite fishing. Ecologically of course, this is true to some extent, but interesting to see how it has been construed as a reason for discontinuing the destruction.

All along the coast, churches, temples and shrines of every faith were left remarkably unscathed. Inevitably, this is widely interpreted as a sign of divine intervention. A small shrine to the Hindu goddess Kali, which few even knew existed on the Galle harbour road, was left exposed but intact, as though the tsunami had intentionally revealed her to the outside world by removing the external wall. Most of these religious buildings, many of them hundreds of years old, were of course built on solid foundations and with robust materials. Many examples like this could be observed all around the country.

What I find most disturbing is to hear just how many of Colombo's 'polite society' see the tsunami not only as divine intervention, but as a blessing, an act of God designed to rid their shores of the fishing communities that they hold in such disdain.

11 May 2005. Samakanda.

I am starting to get nervous. Vimal keeps taking on more workers without consulting me. There are now nearly 30 people on the payroll. This is starting to clock up to a serious sum every week and I have had to put my foot down. No more people. Work is proceeding at an incredible pace as a result, but we simply cannot sustain this level of investment much longer.

The issue of how much to pay is pushing me into a difficult space. I have discovered that the Government sets a standard rate for workers on tea estates, which is 238 rupees ($2.38) a day for men and an even more meagre 165 rupees for women. This seems positively insulting and, from the start, I have insisted on paying at least 300 rupees a day for both the men and the women. I have since raised this to 350, encouraging yet more workers to come knocking on the door. This has now proved destabilizing and local tea estate owners are up in arms, complaining that they are losing their workers to our project. I am now in a difficult position and reluctant to bring the figures back in line.

Then there is the complication of payments to the Employees

Trust Fund and Employees Provident Fund, involving nightmarish amounts of paperwork and dealing with an antiquated bureaucracy – another relic of colonialism.

Although I am delighted to be offering work to so many people from the local community, most of whom were previously unemployed, and to be in a position to pay them comparatively well, I still feel uncomfortable. Am I engaged in precisely the sort of activity to which I have been so opposed? Is this just another form of 'neo-colonial globalization', exploiting cheap labour just repackaged in the worthy language of 'eco-speak'? These are hard questions and they weigh heavily on me.

How do we improve livelihoods most effectively? Of course, paying people well, looking after them during times of medical need, giving loans to build or extend their houses, all of this must be a step in the right direction. But I know this is not enough. We need to encourage self-reliance, offer other incentives. Our workshop programme will go some way towards this, offering advice on harvesting rainwater, composting, forest gardening. I have given a small loan to Vijaysekara to start a project cultivating edible mushrooms, which will give him an additional source of income. I am encouraging Sunil, Sarath and any others to make coconut wood products such as bowls and spoons, or small wooden pendants, which they can sell to people passing through. These feel like the sort of enterprises to encourage, some of which we could expand into larger cooperatives over time. The WoH database includes a number of schemes that might serve as role models, most of which help to keep money circulating within the local economy rather than losing it to the global casino.

5 June 2005. Arugam Bay.

I drive to the east coast with Giles and Vimal. Some of the first houses built by Giles and Viren's organization, Lanka Real Aid, are to be handed over to the tenants, as well as a fleet of fishing boats. These projects have both been supported by the WoH appeal and I plan to film the ceremony. I have asked Vimal to accompany us, so that he can see the Galapita eco-lodge on our way back, a stunning example of how to use natural materials intelligently.

We are bowling along at breakneck speed, with Giles at the wheel. I am sliding from side to side on the back seat, struggling to avoid injury.

'I must talk to you about something, Rory.' Vimal turns towards me from the passenger seat. 'It's about Chandana.'

'Fire away,' I say, bracing myself.

'You know he's very unpopular with the others working there, don't you?'

'Yes. I'm aware of that. Do you know why?'

'He's very rude to them. Always shouting, ordering them about. And he never does any work himself. He just walks around look-ing important in his baseball cap, carrying a mobile phone. He's useless.'

'I know, I know. What to do, though? It won't be easy to get rid of him, since he lives in that house. We would need to have some evi-dence that he's doing something wrong.'

'Well, that's what I wanted to discuss with you. Some of the work-ers are accusing him of all sorts of things.'

'Such as?'

'Oh, that he's cut down trees and sold the firewood to the factory.'

'Seriously? How much?

'Anil says more than one lakh.'

'A lakh?' I am astonished. 'That's 100,000 rupees, or $1,000. Do we have any proof?'

'Only what people are saying. They also say that he and his son-in-law have a scam going to embezzle money from the tea.'

'How could they be doing that?'

'Something to do with faking the receipts.'

'We need to look into all this as soon as we get back.'

The drive to the east coast is always a treat. A few kilometres out of Tangalle, the landscape changes abruptly. The luxuriant, almost oppressive tropical vegetation of the 'wet zone' suddenly gives way to open spaces and big skies, reminiscent of Africa. Miles of green paddy stretch to bluish hills in the distance and conditions become increasingly arid. We drive through the shaded avenues of *mara* trees lining the bund beside the huge lake at Tissamaharama, on past Kataragama, the most sacred site on the island and the destination for pilgrims of every faith, then the distinctive hills and stunning landscape which surround Buttala and Moneragala.

This is also the first time I have driven so far east along the coast since the tsunami. Once again, it is striking to see how differently parts have been affected, scenes of utter devastation contrasting with relative calm. Hambantota, a big town that received the brunt of the damage, is in shock. Arugam Bay is something else again.

6 June 2005. Arugam Bay.

Regarded internationally as a top surfing spot, Arugam Bay is famous for one of the longest surf breaks anywhere on the globe. The town is preparing for an international competition, bringing hot young surfing stars from as far afield as Cornwall and Australia.

As we drive through the small town that morning however, I wonder where they are all going to stay. Almost all the beachfront hotels, with their cabanas and restaurants, have been completely obliterated. Nothing remains of the Galaxy, where I stayed with my family last year, nor the Stardust, the restaurant next door, run by a Danish couple who had been here for years. Heavily pregnant Sri, an Anglo-Sri Lankan who runs the Galaxy with her Aussie surfer husband Wayne, describes how she ran from the coast and turned to see a huge concrete wall concertina behind her like a pack of cards. The two of them were washed up on high ground almost two kilometres inland. In some parts of the flat and barren east coast, the sea swept in more than four kilometres before retreating.

Our trip to Arugam coincided with the release of new Government plans for redeveloping the area. The Ministry of Tourism proposal involved requisitioning all the land along the coastal strip, offering little compensation to the thousands who depend on it for their livelihood. The entire zone would be developed for up-market tourism, transforming a sleepy haven for surfers and back-packers into a 'luxury destination'. There were even plans for a heliport, for all those cashed-up surfers who choose to travel in style. As someone remarked, the document looked like little more than a cut-and-paste report from some well-meaning NGO.

As expected, the plans have met with considerable local resistance. More than a thousand people had turned up to demonstrate that morning. The national and international media were there, but so were the army, with personnel carriers, armoured cars and bulldozers, preparing to flatten half of what remained of the town that morning. Tensions were running high and plumes of black smoke rose from burning tyres beside the road. Concrete pillars erected by Government surveyors were torn down. Thankfully the army held back and violence was avoided.

In the afternoon I filmed the handover of new fibreglass boats to delighted fishermen, then the first house from Lanka Real Aid's building programme. The land, on which about 120 houses were to be built, was beautifully situated, with views down to a lagoon. The houses, designed by Giles and Viren in conjunction with the Muslim community, were the best compromise I had seen between an aid organization's desire for ecologically appropriate materials and the local desire for concrete houses. Concrete has been minimized by using timber trellis-work for half-walls around the living quarters and the roof is covered with palm frond *cadjan*. At more than 400 square feet, the houses were also substantially larger than those these families would have had before.

'This could almost be a tourist attraction,' I say to Giles. 'A post-tsunami eco-village.'

Sadly, other NGOs have erected hideous corrugated iron boxes on plots within the same land, shiny metal bomb shelters which probably work well as sun ovens during the day but are incongruous and impractical alongside the muted colours and cool spaces of the LRA houses.

10 June 2005. Galle.

I spend the morning with my friend Keith, filming Project Galle's housing project near his home at Dewatta and which he has been working on. As he shows me round in his tuk-tuk, he reflects on the previous few months.

'You know, when this whole thing started with Project Galle, we all thought it would last about a month. We would do what we could, then hand it over to the big boys when they came in. But that never happened.'

Working with a group like Project Galle has been both an intensely rewarding experience and a steep learning curve, not least in terms of assimilating huge differences in social and cultural values.

'At the beginning,' Keith continues, 'the Sri Lankans I was working with all used to say "don't be hurry, Mr Keith". They all knew that this was going to take five years. We were all gung-ho at the start, saying "don't worry, we'll put it all back together in a year". But we were wrong.'

Yet Keith is less critical of the big NGOs than many other people I spoke with.

'When you see the hoops these guys have to jump through, the mountains of paperwork and bureaucracy, you can see why so little has happened. I think most of them decided very early on that their housing programmes wouldn't start until January 06. It's easy for us to criticize but we don't see the problems on their side.'

As we hit the coast road, Keith paints a vivid picture of how it looked in the days post-tsunami.

'We had JCBs down here clearing the rubble and rubbish. Soon there were 10-foot high piles stacked along the road reducing it to a single lane. Clearing the ditches and sewage system was absolutely critical to prevent disease, so we had a team of 20 Buddhists working here in a Muslim area alongside a Muslim team. We cleaned 164 wells in three weeks.'

We draw up beside some foundations, where a team of men are bailing black water from four-feet deep holes.

'Because of the high water table here, and being so close to the railway track, we've had to take serious measures to prevent subsidence,' Keith says. 'These holes are filled with steel cages, the water is pumped out and then we pour in concrete. This forms a reinforced concrete pad, to build the houses on. Each house has reinforced concrete corners. The theory is, if we have another tsunami, the walls will be knocked out but the main structure should remain.'

In addition to rebuilding 22 houses, partially rebuilding another 55 and a separate project to build 26 new homes funded by the Salvation Army, Keith's work extends to Project Galle's Livelihood's Programme, helping local residents to get back on their feet and start earning again.

'That shed over there is where we have provided a team of guys with a block-making machine. They're up and running now, totally self-reliant and running their own business. They're making blocks for us and other contractors too.'

And the project does not finish there. Keith outlines plans for landscaping the area, using RRI's expertise to provide fruit trees and kitchen gardens. As we wander back to his tuk-tuk, peeking in to some of the finished homes, I cannot help but be hugely impressed with what has been achieved. As Keith points out, this feeling is echoed by those from the UK who support the project.

'I brought Gordon here, Alex's mate who has been fund-raising for us in the UK. When he saw what had been done, I could see that he was close to tears.'

Chapter Twelve

Chandana

17 June 2005. Yakkallamulla.

I stand in the local police station, a few kilometres south of Samakanda, where I had spent most of the week. After hearing what Vimal had to say, I have no choice but to confront Chandana. I am determined to find out just how much money he may have embezzled from selling firewood, or fiddling tea invoices. Beyond hearsay, it is proving impossible to find any concrete evidence about the stolen firewood.

However, a quick visit to the tea factory gave us all the proof I thought we needed to ask him to leave. From the second month of plucking, he has been fabricating invoices, making the tea factory run two different accounts, one to the estate and one to a fictional name – K. Wilson.

'Who's K. Wilson?' I asked the factory owner's daughter, who administered the accounts.

She looked puzzled. 'That's you. Isn't it?'

'No, it's not, but now I see what Chandana's been doing. Handing over some of the revenue to me, under the estate name, and keeping a portion for himself, which you have filed as K. Wilson. Can I just flick through the accounts for the last few months, to see how much he actually owes us?'

In addition to an outstanding loan, I calculated that Chandana owes us at least 100,000 rupees, excluding what he may have raised from selling firewood. Armed with this information, I had come to the local police, expecting a cut-and-dry case.

I have been here every day for five days now and we are still seeking a resolution. In addition to proof of the theft, I have the original documents signed by Chandana when we had first purchased the property. Yet none of this seems to count for much. Vimal translates as the saga continues.

'They're telling him to go to the labour tribunal and make a case against you,' he says.

'You're joking. He's a thief. We know it. We have proof. As soon as they saw him, they said as much – they knew he was brewing *kasippu* up there and running illegal gambling.'

'I know. They just think you should give him some money to get rid of him. That's the way things are done.'

'But he owes us money, not the other way round.' It is hard to conceal my exasperation. At the same time, I am determined not to be saddled with a court case. If there is any bit of advice that has been drummed into us by our friends, one is universal: 'Don't ever go to court in this country. It will go on for years, cost you huge amounts of money and be a constant hassle in your life.'

As a result, I am hanging in there for a settlement. I am even prepared to waive the issue of the missing funds, so long as we avoid an intractable court battle that might end with us paying compensation just to be shot of it.

Finally, after five days of mounting evidence, I see no alternative but to make a case against him. Then, just as I sit down to inscribe my version of events into the police ledger, he retracts. Two days later, he and his family move from the cottage and take up residence a mile down the road. However, I know that this is not the last of Chandana.

As our trip to the east coast had shown, the diversity of Sri Lanka is astounding for such a small country, geographically, ethnically, culturally and biologically. Outside of the Amazon, the country is thought to have the highest degree of biodiversity on the planet.

We witness this every day. We go to sleep with fireflies flashing around the mosquito net, wake to the sound of monkeys in the trees outside. Weeks pass watching mud wasps build intricate nests on wooden screens beside our bed. The five-minute trip to school takes us down the canal, where Sholto and Xan might see three or four monitor lizards, six-foot prehistoric monsters lurching into the water like displaced dinosaurs. Iridescent kingfishers swoop over the pool by day, the dark shadows of bats by night. At dawn and dusk, the trees at Samakanda are laden with exotic birds, the air saturated with their combined song. The roadside bursts with tropical abundance, great plumes of colour cascading over fences and rooftops – bougainvillea, crotons, heliconias, ginger and canna lilies.

The other side of this is less comfortable to deal with. The fireflies may be there, but so are the mosquitoes – in abundance. The monkeys may be out there, but so are the snakes – also in abundance. One night, Yvette closed the bedroom door to the verandah. Only the next morning did we discover that in the process she had killed a snake, which now lay there with an angular kink in its lifeless body. The harmless rat snake is quite welcome, although when it first took up residence at my feet in the office I felt slightly uneasy. The nasty snakes are all there too and regularly encountered in the garden – kraits, vipers, cobras, even a six-foot python, about nine inches in diameter, which the gardener insisted on bashing with his spade.

Then there are the insects. These come in plagues. On one evening, it's giant flying beetles, the next cockroaches, or huge flying ants. There's an almost constant parade of big red stinging ants marching through parts of the house, climbing into beds and getting entangled in the mosquito nets. Huge black scorpions regularly drop into the pool, hide underneath cushions, or in shoes. Once removed from the pool, they appear to be dead, but soon rear their tails and scuttle away. Perhaps the most alarming though are the centipedes, descended from some of the oldest living species on the planet and one of the things that would survive a nuclear holocaust, along with scorpions and cockroaches. I have no problem with scorpions or cockroaches, however centipedes, which can grow up to several inches long, move like lightning and inflict an intensely painful and venomous sting. Eric, the Zimbabwean farmer working with Project Galle, told me how he had been bitten by snakes, scorpions and centipedes over years spent in the bush.

'Which was the worst?' I asked.

'The centipede – by far.'

2 July 2005. Samakanda.

With a shifting population of more than 30 men and women working at Samakanda, it is hard to keep track of all the comings and goings. There seem to be new faces on almost every visit I make. Although some come and go as they please, working maybe one or two days in a week, a core team is emerging, most of whom joined towards the beginning and are still with us.

Despite the language barrier, it is always a pleasure to see people like Vijaysekara, a wiry old man with permanent grey stubble and innocent eyes; Bandara, who has perhaps the greatest knowledge of traditional farming and works impossibly hard all day; bright and cheery Asoka, now taking charge of the vegetables, with his apprentice Mangala, a lanky, broad shouldered young man with a genial smile; Anil, an ex-soldier, now engaged as the watcher and taking over Chandana's role as foreman, keeping the 'check roll' and other books with his wife Inoka; Wilbert, with his handlebar moustaches and large floppy hat; Hemachandra, a permanent grin spreading across his drawn, tapering features; Amarajeeva, the 'jungle man', his wired, unblinking eyes constantly staring into the middle distance; Sunil and Sarath, Peter's sons, now working together on carpentry jobs, slowly at first but eager to improve their skills; the hulking young Kumara, who has the strength of a bulldozer and carries huge banana trees on his shoulders.

Without exception, the women are consistently charming. They find it impossible to suppress their giggles when I attempt any interaction in my faltering Sinhala. Peter's wife Somawathi has joined Asoka and Mangala on the vegetables, always smiling through betel-stained teeth; there's the tall and gracious Karunalatha; stern but solid Vineetha; the placid, innocence of Nandawathi.

There are a few troublemakers. The sullen Piyadasa, who leads the stonework team repairing the main terrace and lives on the boundary, looks every inch 'the cunning fellow' the others report him to be. He presides over Lal and Pemasiri, who have clearly come under his spell and are always demanding extra pay. With Chandana gone, these three have become the new source of agitation, seeing themselves as somehow separate and superior to the others, constantly complaining that their work is more arduous. On hearing that he has 'years of experience', I entrusted Pemasiri with my prized Husqvarna chainsaw, which my father gave me when we moved to Wales. He dismissed any advice I offered on maintaining the saw and sharpening the chain. Within weeks, it has been decimated: the bar is bent, mountings sheared, the handle broken. Despite being expressly asked not to, Lal seems intent on stirring up the local community over Chandana's various misdeeds. Ultimately, it's hard to see these three ever gelling with the others.

Inland Hills was now complete enough for us to consider a house-warming party and impromptu invitations were circulated for the first weekend in the month, just before my planned return to London for a week of meetings with publishers. Determined to turn the hallway into a dance floor, I was perched precariously on one of the painter's ladders, attaching Henri's ultraviolet light to one of the crossbeams with insulating tape. Suddenly I heard an ominous splash and a scream from Priya.

'Xan!'

I knew instantly that he had fallen in the pool. I slid down the ladder, dashed through the hall and launched myself off the steps, twisting my left foot in the process. Xan was thrashing around in the deep end, dipping below the surface. In retrospect, I should have run along the edge, but swam instead, reaching him just in time. I hauled his spluttering frame from the water and passed him up to Priya. After a good long scream, he settled down and five minutes later was fine.

My foot however, was not. The swelling stretched down the whole of one side and all around my ankle. After a few arak cocktails, I persuaded myself that all was well and proceeded to dance for most of the night. By the morning, my foot looked like the inspiration for a Francis Bacon painting, a lurid mix of purple, green and black, blended over a disfigured limb.

'You really ought to have an x-ray,' Yvette kept saying. 'It might be broken.'

'Do you think so? Surely I wouldn't be able to wiggle my toes if it was?'

And so I left it.

The next day, Sholto developed a fever. A tiny nick in his knee, sustained in the park playground, had flared up. The pain extended right down his leg, his glands were up and he could hardly walk. For two days, Yvette tried a variety of homeopathic remedies, but Sholto's condition deteriorated.

'What do you think we should do?' Yvette said. 'Shall we take him to the doctor down the road?'

'Maybe we should, but we know what will happen. A course of super-strong antibiotics.'

'I know. But maybe we should get another opinion.'

'Sure. Let's see how he is the morning.'

We hardly slept. Sholto's fever was raging and he was in tremendous pain.

In the morning, one of the remedies kicked in and he started to recover. But this proved temporary. By the middle of the afternoon, he was even worse than before. We headed off to the doctor.

'Hmmmm. I think you should see a specialist,' she said. 'I would imagine that he needs to be admitted to hospital for a couple of days of intravenous antibiotics.'

'Really?' I thought that this sounded severe.

'There is always the possibility that the infection gets into the bone. The consequences could be dramatic.'

Only then did we appreciate just how serious the situation was. We raced around Galle's hospitals to find an orthopaedic surgeon. Sholto was now in agony, crying and screaming with pain. Yvette and I were alarmed, angry with ourselves for not having dealt properly with the situation earlier.

'Whatever happens, we're not admitting him to Karapitiya,' I said to Yvette.

'We'll have to head for the Apollo in Colombo,' she agreed. 'I'll start packing.'

'I'll see if I can change my flight from tomorrow to Monday,' I said.

Later that evening, we raced off for Colombo, Priya in the back seat trying to soothe Sholto on her lap, Xan sleeping in his car seat. I drove fast, spurred on by the agonized cries from the back. We arrived at the Apollo soon after midnight, whisking Sholto straight into emergency. An x-ray dispelled our worst fears. The infection had not hit the bone, yet. Strong intravenous antibiotics were deemed essential. We booked Sholto into a palatial room, the only one available, where he was connected up to a saline drip. His wretched condition was partially ameliorated by a 24-hour cartoon channel. I noticed that the antibiotics, the first he has ever had, had a discernible psychological effect on him. He talked even more incessantly than normal and hardly slept. Yvette and I struggled to stay awake and keep him company during the two nights we spent there.

Since we were now residing in a hospital, it seemed foolish not to get an x-ray of my foot. The swelling had largely subsided, so it did just fit inside a shoe, but it was still far from comfortable. I was however, surprised to find that there was a fracture in the bone below my outside toe. I took my x-ray to Dr Jayasinghe, the orthopaedic specialist. He held it up to the light.

'What on earth have you been doing?' he asked, astonished.

'What do you mean?' I was confused.

'When did you say this happened?'

'About a week ago.'

'A week?' He now thought I was insane. 'Did you go to see anybody about it?'

'No.'

'What about the pain? Didn't you take any painkillers or anything?'

'Not really. Just a few drinks the night after it happened. Why?'

'This should be very painful. You must have a very high pain threshold.'

'I don't think so. I'm a hypochondriac really.'

'Well, it needs to be put in plaster, otherwise those two bones will splay apart and never heal properly.'

'But I'm flying to London the day after tomorrow. Is it really necessary?'

'Look my friend,' he seemed to be losing patience. 'If we were in America or Europe, I would recommend a small pin being inserted, as well as a cast.'

'But can I fly with my foot in plaster?'

'You can, but we have to cut it down the side before you fly, in case of it swelling up in the cabin pressure. Then you'll have to have it done again in London.' This was all starting to sound very dull and far from what I had planned for the week ahead.

'I think I'll chance it,' I said. 'It seems to have got better in the last week anyway.'

'Well, it's up to you, but I think you're mad. You'll have to sign this, saying you refused my advice. I don't want to be sued.'

I signed the form and left.

Yvette was not impressed with my decision and soon I was back in Dr Jayasinghe's consulting room. An hour later, I was hobbling around the hospital on crutches, my leg in plaster to the knee, feeling very grumpy.

That night, Sholto and I made quite a pair, lying side by side, left legs raised in the air, watching *Scooby Doo*. By the following afternoon, the antibiotics had taken hold, Sholto's fever had disappeared and he was discharged.

It had been quite a week. Xan falling in the pool, my broken foot, Sholto's infection. Priya put these misfortunes down to black magic curses.

'Some Sri Lanka people like this,' she kept saying.

The upsides to my injury, whether caused by occult powers or not, were the perks lavished on me at the airport by Sri Lankan airlines. I was whisked through immigration in a wheelchair, rolled onto the hydraulic tailgate of an old truck to make a terrifying journey across the runway, then deposited unceremoniously into the plane. As the flight was overbooked, I had been upgraded to business class. Must do this more often, I said to myself, must keep the cast and crutches for future journeys.

Sprawled across my fully reclined leather aisle seat at the front of the plane, plotting my viewing schedule for the journey and perusing the menus, I was joined by a senior monk in robes. He settled in by the window and we exchanged pleasantries. Once airborne, I could not help but notice the surreptitious interest he expressed as Halle Berry cavorted in a leather catsuit on the screen before me.

A week later, I was back in Sri Lanka, buoyed up by the hope that I may have secured a publishing deal but conscious that my Footprint for the year had now gone through the roof. As they say in Lanka, 'What to do?'

Although Chandana had gone, there was still some instability at Samakanda. Vimal had taken to staying in the bungalow, needing some distance from his domestic situation. As a result, he was becoming more and more embroiled in the web of local drama as various characters plied him with arak every evening. He soon knew who was having an affair with who's wife and the intricacies of various local vendettas, some of which had been running for decades between families living within a stone's throw of each other. Every day, I would be greeted with yet another twisted story or complaint from someone. The local letter-writing scribe was hard at work, writing reams of soap opera-like scripts for my attention as the various factions plotted to incriminate the others. The degree to which this was disrupting the work was verging on the ridiculous and I had begun to feel reluctant about even visiting Samakanda. The project had become a drain on my energy and resources, and I was now approaching it with trepidation rather than my earlier passion and enthusiasm.

Despite the evidence against him, Chandana was trying to file a case against me through the labour tribunals for unfair dismissal. He kept a low profile locally but was busy stirring the others up against the project. I could sense that the triumvirate of Piyadasa, Lal and Pemasiri were party to this. Vimal was revelling in the intrigue, enjoying his role as mediator but adding fuel to the fire by allowing himself to be drawn ever deeper into petty local politics. Having thought we had removed the source of the troubles, it soon became apparent that this was just the start.

At the root of this ongoing dilemma, I felt that there was a need to change the structure to the organization. I disliked the notion of running things like a conventional tea estate, with all the archaic bureaucracy involved and the extent to which it smacked of colonialism. However, my attempts at doing things differently had so far backfired. Trying to change these traditional structures too quickly had proved destabilizing, but I was determined to keep trying, hoping to create some cooperative enterprises that would help to improve the livelihoods of those working for us.

Chapter Thirteen

Mr Pitchamurtu

One evening, Vimal went up to Samakanda, unannounced. He arrived to find Piyadasa having a party in the bungalow, my CD player cranked to the full and the discs scattered all over the floor amid a sea of empty arak bottles. It was difficult to work out quite what happened next but it resulted in a fight between Anil and Piyadasa. Vimal intervened and the three of them tumbled off the main terrace. They were all grazed and bruised, and Piyadasa narrowly avoided smashing his head open on a boulder.

This was a final straw. I was incensed that they were even in the bungalow, let alone mistreating my music. The first rice harvest loomed in three days and I wanted to celebrate this with the family, without a background of conflict. Because the party would take place outside the Cottage, the name I had given to the lower bungalow, I asked Anil and Inoka to move back to their own house, since they had taken up residence after Chandana's departure. This had been a huge mistake. With their new positions of responsibility, Anil and Inoka had assumed superiority over the others. I now realized that giving anyone from the community any role above others was doomed to failure. They had to be on an equal footing. I also realized that nobody should be allowed to live on the property itself, since this in itself gave an impression of seniority. Instead, I decided to start giving small parcels of land to those who lived near the boundary, had proved trustworthy and seemed deserving of a new or better house.

7 August 2005. Samakanda.

We arrive for the rice harvest around nine on a Saturday morning. Vimal has been drinking all night in Hikkaduwa and has not been to sleep. Anil and Inoka are up in arms about having to move from the Cottage, despite having being told that it was a temporary arrangement. I can see that they are blaming Vimal for having turned me against them, which is not true. Piyadasa is ranting about having been attacked by Anil. Amarajeeva is looking even more spun out than usual. The tension is high.

Then it snaps. Suddenly Vimal, Anil, Inoka and Piyadasa are all yelling and screaming at each other. Sholto and Xan stare in bewilderment. Their having to witness this madness provokes me to join in.

'Look. I am here with my family, trying to enjoy this place together for the first time. All I asked was that you respect that and leave us alone. Instead, you're all fighting.'

Everyone is silent. I turn to Vimal.

'We're going to walk to the banyan tree. Could you ask everyone to just leave. We'll come back in 10 minutes, eat our picnic and then head home.'

'OK, Rory. Sure. I'm sorry it's like this. It's all a mess.'

'I know. Let's all talk about it on Monday and work out what to do.'

We walk to the banyan tree shrine, light incense and pour milk over the lingam for the first time. Sholto and Xan chant their 'Hari Oms'. There is a moment of pure calm within the madness.

9 August 2005. Samakanda.

I receive a letter, signed by Sunil, levelling accusations against virtually the whole team. Asoka is accused of stealing seeds and vegetables, Anil of having parties in the bungalow, Piyadasa of brewing *kasippu* on the land, various people of poaching wild boars and porcupines. Stupidly, I confront the whole team with the contents, without telling them who wrote it. I doubt very much that it was actually Sunil but only later suspect that it has come from Chandana.

10 August 2005. Samakanda.

If the letter has come from Chandana, it has had the desired impact. All the men are now pissed off. A full-scale revolt is at hand.

'Who has written that letter?' They want to know. 'We'll kill him.'

As ever, the women are unperturbed. I try to pacify the situation.

'Let's forget the letter. I don't know who it's from anyway, or if any of it's true. Look, why doesn't everybody take the rest of the week off, spend some time at home with your families and we'll meet again on Monday morning and try to move forward?'

They all look bewildered, now suspecting that I will abandon them all and bring other workers in.

'Don't worry. Nobody's losing their job. We just need a few days to work this out.' I ask Vimal to convey this assurance to them but it cuts no ice.

For a moment, it looks like some of the men are going to get violent, moving aggressively towards us.

'Maybe it's time to leave, Vimal,' I say, moving towards the car.

'I think that's a good idea.'

By the time we reach the gate, the car is surrounded by more than 20 men, demanding to know who has written 'that letter'. Some have been drinking heavily, their bloodshot eyes and betel-stained mouths flaring with rage. I lock the car doors and windows, inching carefully through the crowd and down the drive.

'That was intense,' I say to Vimal, parking up when we reach the road.

'Yeeees. I was getting a bit worried back there.'

'The letter must have come from Chandana,' I turn to Vimal. 'Clearly, he is going to keep causing trouble as long as we fail to respond. I see no option but to file a case against him. Maybe when he's threatened with court, he will desist.'

'Yeeees.'

'Let's stop at the tea factory office and ask them to give us photocopies of those invoices as evidence against him.'

As we draw up at the tea factory's bungalow, Asanka appears on his motorbike. He wants a cheque for the outstanding balance on the tea bushes. I tell him that there were issues surrounding their organic status and I had sent six plants to a laboratory for testing. As soon as the results confirm that they are genuine, as he had promised, I will happily give him a cheque. If not, we would have to return them. This sends him ballistic. Once again, we are confronted with a screaming maniac.

'What's he saying?' I ask Vimal.

'That he's a devil when he gets angry, and that he wants to kill you.'

I doubted that Asanka would attempt to kill me, but I took extra care locking up the house that night. I knew that people were regularly murdered in this country over the pettiest of squabbles.

The confrontation with Asanka compounded the tension. Vimal was feeling even worse, since he had understood every threat made during the last few days, many of which he hadn't relayed to me to avoid worrying and depressing me even further. We had both received at least three death threats in the previous two days. Gradually, he retreated, finding the situation too overwhelming. I was at my lowest ebb, not knowing which way to turn. I felt like abandoning the project altogether, selling the land, moving on.

Then I remembered Mr Pitchamurtu.

A few weeks before, on the Sunday morning following Chandana's departure, an earnest middle-aged man had appeared at our house.

'I am sorry to be troubling your good self,' he said, looking serious. 'But I have come to understand that there is a vacancy for field officer at your Nakiyadeniya estate'.

'News travels fast,' I replied. He smiled a half smile, shifting his stern countenance momentarily, then continued. 'I have 33 years' experience on estates, up country and low country tea. Here are my references.' He handed me a sheet of paper with the names, addresses and telephone numbers of two superintendents at up country tea estates.

'Thank you Mr ... ?'

'Pitchamurtu.' A Tamil name, I thought to myself.

'Thank you, Mr Pitchamurtu, but we are trying with someone else at the moment and there is no vacancy.'

'Please take my details and call me if you change your mind.'

He handed me a small slip of paper, deftly torn from the pages of his notebook, inscribed with the neatest handwriting I had ever seen.

At the time, I did not think we would ever see each other again. Now he seemed to be the answer. I rushed to my desk, rifling through old business cards and scraps of paper accumulating in a drawer, looking for that beautiful handwriting. I had no recollection of having saved it, but there it was.

Mr Pitchamurtu arrived at Samakanda the following Monday morning, wearing perfectly pressed grey flannel shorts and a matching shirt. His leather boots were polished black mirrors, his features engraved with an austere determination. With Vimal translating, I talked to the assembled crowd, all gathered beside the cottage. Mr Pitchamurtu walked up and down behind me, scanning the faces before him.

'I know that there has been trouble over the last few weeks and that Chandana has had a lot to do with it,' I began. 'But please, let's put this all behind us now and move on. Mr Pitchamurtu is going to start work with us today. He's a field officer with many years of experience and I'm sure will do a wonderful job. Please work with him to resolve any outstanding issues. You've done amazing things here over these last months and it is sad that so much time is spent arguing. Can we all just try again to make this work?'

Heads nodded with approval and work began again. As the crowd dispersed, Vimal asked if he could take some time off. He needed a break from recent events.

'Of course,' I said. 'Take as long as you like.'

It was his last visit to Samakanda.

There were some obvious concerns about giving Mr Pitchamurtu the helm at Samakanda. Would the fact that he was Tamil upset the all-Sinhalese team? What kind of relations would develop between them? I was worried that his manner might prove too severe, too rigid and domineering.

These concerns rapidly dissolved. I soon began to appreciate that a developed sense of irony and humour lay beneath that earnest, furrowed brow. Within days, he had broken down any tension or suspicion among the others, laughing and joking with them while managing their days efficiently. Over the following weeks, he got to grips with the paperwork, starting proper accounts, sorting out the minefield of form-filling, making fastidious entries in the 'check roll'. All these jobs had been anathema to me and Vimal. Soon, the various ledgers became inscribed with Mr Pitchamurtu's elegant script.

Mr Pitchamurtu's talents did not stop at basic administration. I saw that he had a fine eye for aesthetics and, as the months passed, felt increasingly confident that I could leave him with a basic idea, from planting frangipanis around the lake to building a small hut, without needing to intervene. Through his own initiative, he sent passion fruit vines up into trees, or over trellis, creating shady stretches on the main terrace. He supervised Sunil and Sarath knocking up tables and benches for the bungalow and intercropped new tea bushes with mung beans and chickpeas. Hardly ever did I oppose any of his ideas. He was also eager to learn, borrowing books from me and reading up on some of the specialist herbs and vegetables that we were experimenting with. As a result, a loose, fluid structure began to evolve, taking on many of the characteristics that I had always hoped to encourage, various groups developing their own levels of autonomy and self-regulation, whether it was the vegetable team, 'the stone-wallers' or the women plucking tea.

After he had 'observed the workers' for a month, Mr Pitchamurtu made recommendations about who should remain as a core team, reducing the numbers to a much more manageable group of 15 men and 15 women. The vibe began to change. Letters, gripes and complaints disappeared. Days were structured, well coordinated and work continued at a tremendous pace. A system of advances and loans was put in place, allowing many families to improve or extend their houses. I provided Anil and Inoka with a piece of land at the new entrance and gave them materials for building a new house. All animosities disappeared and Anil now proved to be the most loyal and industrious man on the team, always eager to embrace any task and showing a rare degree of initiative. After a turbulent few weeks, we seemed to be back on track. Tea yields improved and the vegetables were thriving, leading to weekly circuits of the Galle area, delivering rocket, basil and other leaves to hotels, restaurants and shops. Sholto referred to this as 'the salad spin', sitting in the back seat, studiously noting down the quantities sold at each stop, a practice he called 'doing the governance'.

Part of what endeared Mr Pitchamurtu to me was his wonderful use of English and Victorian sense of propriety. People were either 'cunning fellows', or 'innocent chaps'. He was always ready 'to do the needful', filing the Employees Trust Fund payments on time, paying the electricity bill for the bungalow, sourcing secondhand roof tiles. Everyone was addressed as 'your good self' and he observed a great sense of protocol over every possible action, from applying the company stamp on a form to slicing open coconuts for visitors. Much to my embarrassment however, he insisted on calling me 'Sir', despite my protests. I felt blessed that he had appeared in our lives and I became re-enchanted with the project as a consequence.

One concern with Mr Pitchamurtu was his knees. Early on, I noticed that he seemed to be in some pain as we climbed steps between the terraces.

'Is there something the matter with your knees, Mr Pitchamurtu?' I asked.

'Yes, Sir. It seems there is some fluid, causing some pain.'

'Have you been to the doctor?'

'Yes, Sir, at Karapitiya. I have some medicine.'

'Has it helped?'

174

'To begin with it did, Sir. Now not so much. I seem to have some digestion problem now as well.'

'Probably from taking the medicine.'

'Yes, Sir. I think so.'

'Have you seen an ayurvedic doctor?'

'No, Sir.'

'There is a very good doctor at the Lighthouse Hotel. She's a homeopathic doctor, from South Africa. All the medicines are made from plants. Would you go and see her if I arranged it?'

'Yes, Sir. Thank you, Sir.'

'Mr Pitchamurtu.'

'Yes, Sir?'

'Please stop calling me Sir.'

'Sorry, Sir. But I have to address your good self in this way.'

And so Mr Pitchamurtu started his homeopathic treatment. Soon he was so impressed that he took along his wife who was seeking relief from shoulder pain. Although he professed a preference for ayurveda over 'Western medicine', Mr Pitchamurtu had, like most people we met, been brainwashed by the apparent miracles of pharmaceutical drugs. Most of the Sri Lankans we knew would rush to allopathic rather than ayurvedic doctors at the first sign of a sore throat or a headache. Having spent relatively large sums of money, they return home with brown paper bags filled with pills. Asked what the doctor had said was wrong with them, or what the pills were, they could rarely answer. The doctor was treated like a priest, whose conclusions were never questioned. Antibiotics were dished out like Smarties, causing a vicious spiral of ever-decreasing immunity and fuelling ever more virulent diseases.

Chapter Fourteen

Dark Days

9 October 2005. Xan's birthday.

A tuk-tuk arrives at the house, bearing a letter from Vimal. My heart sinks from the moment I start reading. Four pages later, I am speechless. It is largely a work of fiction, bitter and vitriolic. I am accused of 'stealing' all his ideas and held responsible for the collapse of his marriage. One groundless accusation is laid out after another, at the end of which he demands a cheque for 200,000 rupees, by return of post, by Monday morning – a physical impossibility anyway, given that it's Sunday – otherwise he will take me to court.

Take me to court over what exactly? Although I know this is just a pathetic grasp for money, I feel both saddened and betrayed. This is a man we had taken into our trust, assumed was our friend. We had lent him and his family our house when we went away. We shared a passion for music and literature, swapping books and CDs. We fed him, invited him to parties, his children over to swim. Contrary to his protestations, I had paid him well. Mr Pitchamurtu is doing 10 times as much work, 10 times more efficiently, for less than half of Vimal's salary. Whenever I offered him more money, he refused to take it. He keeps perfect accounts, knows about planting and plucking tea, building, carpentry, dealing with the Labour Office, tasks that Vimal had little experience of or the inclination to take on. Now he expects me to give him $2,000. I fail to see the logic.

The episode left me in tatters. I no longer felt that anybody could be trusted. I was suspicious of everyone. This is so antithetical to my normal outlook, believing people can be trusted until proved otherwise, that my whole world was turned upside down. I began to feel that I could not operate here, surrounded by webs of deceit, jealousy and lies. What was the point? Why bother? Life was too short. I could see no alternative but to abandon the project, sell the land, maybe leave the country altogether.

The second monsoon arrived. The days were dark. Rain fell in waterfalls. For the first time, I began to miss the simplicity of our life in Wales. I thought about walking the hills on a golden autumn day, foraging for wild mushrooms; about lying in front of the fire, on the felted rugs we had made together, sharing a bottle of red wine; about sitting at my desk in the straw-bale house, watching perfect rainbows spill into the valley below. That life suddenly seemed so secure, so cosy, so removed from the daily pressures in Sri Lanka. I began to withdraw, physically and mentally, retreating to our bedroom and reading incessantly as a distraction. Nothing else appealed. Samakanda had become a burden, a nightmare of my own making. I avoided going there as much as possible.

Everything became a struggle. For no apparent reason, a local accountant in Galle refused to hand back the paperwork we had given him to prepare the year's accounts, leaving us little time for us to submit them before the deadline. It took several visits to his office and numerous phone calls and letters, before we finally prised the documents back from him. I was also fighting a battle with a local bank, having withdrawn 40,000 rupees from an ATM and been presented with a receipt but no cash. This saga went on for months. I filled in a form, which was mislaid. I made visits to the bank. I called. Nothing happened. I am still waiting for my account to be credited.

Every day there was a new problem. The water pump broke down on a regular basis, leaving us without water for days at a time. The telephone line was severed by falling trees. Once repaired, the line was disconnected, despite the bill being paid. The roof sprang leaks in several places causing electric shocks every time we used the toaster. Sholto and Xan came down with one weird virus after another. Yvette had huge sandfly bites itching her to distraction for weeks at a time and fought a losing battle every night with the mosquitoes. I rubbed a hairy caterpillar into my stomach from a swimming towel, giving myself an intensely painful rash which took a month to dissipate. People were stealing our coconuts and avocadoes, or ripping us off on virtually every transaction we made, whether it was the garbage man or an official at the Labour Office, who expected me to give him a mobile phone in exchange for his cooperation.

For all its allure, the tropics has never been an easy place to live. The heat, the humidity, the mosquitoes, all can become overwhelming. At times, the sheer density of vegetative life, the world drowning in a green flood, starts to feel oppressive and claustrophobic. I sometimes feel so drenched by the abundance that a slow suffocation starts, eating away at my core. Impatience, frustration, exasperation, then anger all arise.

The damp, warm conditions give rise to ubiquitous parasitic life. Creepers throttle trunks and branches as they scramble for the light; epiphytes cling to decaying rotted stumps, new life swiftly erasing the old. This is true internally, too. The body is invaded by alien bacteria. Amoebas take up residence in your guts. Parasitic worms retreat into the liver, in defiance of antibiotics. These can be hard conditions to cure, one cleanse of the system dovetailing with the next encounter.

Some say it takes seven years to adjust. The bouts of prickly heat subside; the digestion deals with the frequent influx of ferocious chilli; the rivulets of sweat reduce to trickles. But the pervasive heady energy remains, coursing through the sap. It can be powerfully dark, intoxicating, irresistible, all at the same time. I can see why men have been driven mad. Kurtz and 'the horror' are everywhere.

Some say that by trying to avoid one danger, you merely step into another. In this context, the ironies of our move to Sri Lanka were stark. I had been fixated with climate change, had partly moved my family to the tropics as an insurance policy, looked at potential houses in the light of rising sea levels and had just written a book called *Rising Tides*. Within a week of moving into our house, the tsunami arrived.

As well as being an iridescent, seductive turquoise, the sea in south Sri Lanka can be powerful, dark and wild. The weather systems move north from Antarctica and pummel the coast with stormy rage. When he was Chile's ambassador to Sri Lanka in the 1930s, Pablo Neruda wrote some of his finest poetry, much of it absorbed with the waves of this hypnotic sea. I am sure that 'The Southern Ocean' was inspired by these waters, 'blue and blue, pierced by blues'.

Few times in recent history has the power of the sea been made so manifest as with the tsunami. Conventional earthquakes have killed similar numbers in single countries, but rarely has so much damage been inflicted so quickly and on such a scale by natural forces. The potential for nature to wreak such huge and instant destruction has rarely been made so poignant. The whole globe was touched by the tragedy, the aftermath, the breathtaking forces that were unleashed under water.

To some degree at least, the whole Sri Lankan nation was traumatized by the tsunami. Virtually everyone knew someone who had been affected directly. Among those that we knew, the psychological repercussions would surface for many months. There were recurring dreams about another wave, vast walls of dark blue water advancing on the beach. It was hard to look out to sea without this image surfacing in the back of your mind. Once in a while, I found myself scanning the horizon as Sholto and Xan swam beside me at the beach.

'What are you looking at, Daddy?' Sholto would ask.

'Oh, nothing really. Just looking out to sea.'

Although attracted to living near the coast due to apparently abundant seafood, we were often disappointed. Most of the fish are dark, oily and strong in taste. When we could find it, *mahi-mahi* was our preference but, like most fish these days, difficult to eat with a sound conscience. Since the flesh is soft, it tends to be ignored for local curries, flaking into pieces under intense cooking. The tiny *haal-massa*, like miniature whitebait, are plentiful and safe, compared with tuna and other big fish near the top of the food chain like seer, which have heavy metals, PCBs and other toxic compounds infused in their flesh, some in concentrations that can be 25 million times greater than when first released into the environment due to 'bio-accumulation'. In this regard the prawns and lobsters can be exceptionally bad, depending on where they are from. Some hail from polluted waters and the whole family was badly poisoned soon after we arrived.

Dark Days

There were times when it was hard to feel inspired about cooking and eating. Although I love a good 'rice and curry', it can soon become monotonous and the daily overdose of chilli and poor quality, rancid coconut oil, just too much for the body to sustain. Due to the general absence of refrigeration, or lack of awareness about using it correctly, fish and meat could be a gamble. Deliveries of frozen chickens could frequently be seen stacked on the pavement outside supermarkets, half-cooking in the blazing heat for a few hours, before being placed into freezers again. Large fish like tuna were often pulled in nets behind boats for two days before being landed, the fish bleeding internally and the flesh rotting. Then there is the practice of splashing buckets of water laced with formaldehyde over fish soon after they are caught, thereby maintaining the fresh look of bloody gills and translucent eyes.

It was often hard to know what we could eat with a sound conscience and in safety. The imported frozen chickens came from unspeakable factory farms in Thailand, Vietnam, even Brazil. The local chickens rarely appeared healthy or well-kept, the roadside cages looking like bird-flu incubators. Fish stocks around Sri Lanka, like everywhere else, are depleted and most of the species either dangerously toxic or on the endangered list. Beyond what we grew ourselves, it was hard to trace organic vegetables, the upcountry carrots, beets and cauliflowers all liberally dosed with the dodgiest of pesticides, banned in the developed world of course, but still manufactured and sold to poor countries. Although I love pasta and rocket salad, it was hard to eat twice a day for weeks on end. Despite being passionate about food, we frequently found ourselves doing the most extraordinary thing: just not eating. Summoning the energy at the end of the day, to try to be inventive within a kitchen devoid of exciting ingredients, often proved impossible.

Thankfully, the more we grew at Samakanda, the less challenging this became. We now had a steady supply of organic red rice, with enough surplus to sell or give to friends. Traditional Sri Lankan vegetables, like manioc and the wonderful wing bean, were plentiful and constant. The slightly slimy local spinach and *kankun* provided more than enough chlorophyll. Priya often made *kola-kanda* for breakfast, putting *gotu-kola* and other green herbs like *polpala*, a kidney diuretic, and *penela-wel*, a sort of ayurvedic Viagra, into a green rice congee. Bumper crops of different chillies were pickled in jars, or dried in the sun. Mung beans soaked and sprouted. Cloves and peppercorns were packed in jars.

Although Sholto was happy to eat some local dishes, like *pittu*, a steamed sausage of rice and *kurukkan* flour, Xan proved much more adventurous, having been exposed to the flavours from an earlier age. He enjoyed a little chilli and had an almost obsessive fixation with intensely bitter or sour local fruits: the extraordinary *billing*, dangling directly from the trunk like disfigured gherkins; the Sri Lankan olive, the *veralu*; or the pungent aroma and perfumed taste of *waraka*, ripe jak fruit, all tastes that I struggled to cultivate.

This diet was perhaps as healthy or more so than the greater variety we would have enjoyed in Britain. However, there were frequent cravings for the unobtainable, sometimes satiated by a quick trip to Colombo. Yvette missed a good burger. I wanted an endless Japanese banquet, eating huge seaweed salads to detox the heavy metals in my sushi.

10 November 2005. Galle.

Darkness continues. I constantly wonder why I am here, what I am doing, why I am pouring the only resources I have into such an ambitious and difficult project. Will anyone benefit from it? Is it just a deluded ego-trip? All motivation and enthusiasm has drained away. I feel stagnant, hollow, apathetic. I cannot think of a single thing that excites me, except reading. Life appears futile and banal. Mahinda and the JVP look set to win the presidential elections in a week's time, which may usher in changes in laws that affect our residency. The Tamil Tigers are revving up for war in the north. The media are in a frenzy over bird flu. The future looks bleak.

This is compounded by having a blazing row with a friend over dinner, who accused me of double standards, talking about ecological lifestyles but driving around in an air-conditioned car. In a sense, I know he is right, which inflames me even more. If I was really 'walking the talk', I would be living at Samakanda, taking the bus to Galle, never getting on a plane. He even thinks it hypocritical that I smoke cigarettes, since clearly the stereotypical 'greenie' should never be susceptible to such addictions. I become even more acutely aware of what are perceived to be inconsistencies.

At the same time, I have a defence. I have been planting trees all my life and will continue to do so. I am just doing what I can, within the limitations of my situation. Much as I admire people who can make the decision never to fly, abandon their cars, live so lightly on the earth that they remain within their share of Ecological Footprint, I also feel that, for many of us, this is virtually impossible. We are locked into a system that prevents us making many of the changes we may aspire to. Inflicting extreme eco-living on my children could be seen as a selfish imposition on their freedom. Keeping them from seeing their cousins and grandparents in the UK seems unfair to all concerned. Do we ban plastic toys, keep our children completely removed from television and computer games? These are difficult and complex questions.

Chapter Fifteen

Serendipity

The first major goal on my walk through India was the French colonial town of Pondicherry and ashram of Sri Aurobindo, a political activist turned mystic who died in 1950, having developed a convoluted philosophical system about the evolution of consciousness.

Pondicherry proved a disappointment. The solemn uniformity of the ashram felt stifling, even sinister. I found myself reading the teachings of Ramana Maharshi, a great saint who also died in 1950. He lived most of his life in Tiruvannamalai, a town about a hundred kilometres inland. Although I was interested to visit Ramana's ashram, I had not included it on my route.

Then I read about the festival of *Kartikai Deepam*, which happens every year in Tiruvannamalai and draws about a million people to walk round the sacred mountain of Arunachala while a huge cauldron of *ghee* burns on the summit like an erupting volcano. It certainly sounded dramatic. Since I was making radio recordings for BBC Radio Four, and had precious little material to date, the thought of taking part was appealing. An American 'ashramite' had encouraged me to go, saying that the festival started on the new moon – the following day. This put me in a quandary. Should I leap on a bus the following morning, thereby compromising my intentions to walk all the way, or stay put in Pondicherry as planned?

That evening, while mulling over this by Aurobindo's tomb, I met Martha, a Polish lady who had spent several years living in Ramana's ashram. With short, grey hair plastered to her skull, an elastic face and twitchy eyes, she must have been in her late 60s.

'This festival, *Kartikai Deepam*, is it on the new moon or the full moon?' I asked her.

'Oh, I think it's the new moon,' Martha said vaguely.

'That means it starts tomorrow. Is it worth me going?' I asked.

'Oh yes, you must go.' She looked at me intensely.

I left Martha and wandered back to the ashram guesthouse, torn between two options. Passing a newspaper stand, I stopped to look at the magazines for the first time since I had arrived in India two months previously. I pointed to one at random, an arts magazine hanging over some string at the back of the stall.

'I'll have that one, please.'

Back in my room, I sat down on the bed and the magazine fell open. What I saw made me laugh out loud; a double-page spread with pictures of Ramana Maharishi and the sacred mountain of Arunachala. The next morning, I jumped on a bus.

Martha proved to be wrong. The festival was not for another two weeks. However, so strong was the attraction when I reached Tiruvannamalai that I stayed for a month. I even considered abandoning the walk altogether, assuaging pangs of guilt by making the occasional ritual circuit of Arunachala. It took me three attempts to leave. The teachings that I encountered there have affected my life ever since, most notably by meeting Ramesh.

Later, listening to Ramesh unfold his radical teaching, I spent much of my time in discussion with Heiner, a German architect. Before he left, Heiner gave me a cassette of some ambient world music. I listened to it a few times but, once back home, it found itself confined to a cardboard box full of half-decomposing tapes that never saw the light of day.

Until, that is, nine years later, when Yvette and I unpacked the contents of our container in Sri Lanka. The cassettes seemed of little use, especially since we had no player in the house. We did however, have one in the car, so I put them aside.

I had received an e-mail from a German student called Daniel. He was doing a diploma in tourism and ecology and spending his internship in Sri Lanka. After three months at Arugam Bay on the east coast, he was now looking for work around Galle. Could we meet? I had received a few requests like this before, but never followed them through. This time, however, I felt compelled to do so.

Two days later, I was heading towards Unawatuna to pick up Daniel and Lisa, his girlfriend. Fumbling through the glove box for a cassette as I drove, I picked one out at random.

'Ah, that's the tape that Heiner gave me in Bombay,' I thought. 'Perfect.'

The following day, Daniel walked into my office, where he noticed a picture of Ramesh on the wall.

'Is that your father?' he asked.

'No, no,' I replied with a laugh.

'Your grandfather?'

'No. No. Just a wise old man who lives in Bombay.'

'Oh really. What's his name?' he asked, looking startled.

'Ramesh Balsekar.'

'I don't believe it,' his mouth fell open. 'Lisa's parents have been to see him. And their best friend is a man called Heiner, who sees him a lot.'

'I know Heiner,' I said. 'In fact, that tape I was playing in the car when we first met was given to me by Heiner, nine years ago.'

'I don't believe it. That's so weird.'

Variously known over the ages as Taprobane, Ratnapida, Zeloan, Zeilan, Seyllan, Ceilon, Ceylon and now Sri Lanka, the island was once also referred to as Serendib.

It may seem ludicrous to suggest that any part of the globe should have some propensity for a high incidence of such encounters, but that has certainly been the experience for us and many others that we know, whether they were born here, lived part of their lives here, or just recently arrived. Whether you call it mere coincidence, Jungian synchronicity, or divine serendipity, it is almost impossible to believe that the catalogue of such seemingly preordained events are the result of randomness. It's almost as if there is some pull, which spins people into each other's orbit and starts making connections, fusing nodes within networks like the synapses and neurons of one global brain.

This analogy has often been used to express the accelerated 'connectivity' which modern communications is bringing to the world, but there is also the sense that it also happens on a more subtle and intuitive level, which might relate to other fundamental energies and patterns which are not necessarily recognized by the prevailing scientific view. Like many others I know, I have experienced certain apparent coincidences, and been somehow drawn to certain places, which have then had a tremendous influence on my life. I often wonder if there truly is such a thing as 'coincidence'.

7 December 2005. Galle.

Relentless rains are now broken by spells of fine weather. My mood lifts. I remember why I am here and all the things I love about Sri Lanka. The smiling faces. The innocent joy of life. The radiance of a flamboyant bursting into flower. The charm and pace of Galle Fort. Flying kites with Sholto and Xan on the ramparts, as a crimson sun drops into the big blue behind us. Even the mundane tasks that can become so exasperating – trying to extract a parcel from the Post Office, queuing to pay the monthly bills – all take on a different air, revolving around the surreal exchange of archaic pleasantries and a lot of smiling. Impatience dissolves in acceptance. The energy shifts. The pendulum swings.

Daniel and Lisa were installed in the cottage for a three-month stint as our first student volunteers. I soon realized that fate could not have sent two more appropriate people to Samakanda at this time.

Living in very basic conditions at the start, with no electricity or running water, they took to the challenge immediately, soon creating a comfortable home. After a low ebb, my motivation for the project returned. I raced round shops in Galle to equip Daniel and Lisa with what was needed. Gas cooker and cylinder, hurricane lamps, the basics for a kitchen. Their arrival also coincided with a visit from Louis, a permaculturist working in the Maldives who had just attended Max's design course at Tanamanwila in the dry zone. As a consequence, we were able to walk round Samakanda together, discussing ideas that Daniel and Lisa could work on over the coming months.

The results were mostly successful. A banana and papaya spiral shower at the back of the cottage, with a moss and stone base surrounded by thick green foliage and fed by a bamboo pipe laid from tanks beside the spring, worked perfectly. We developed a new composting system, the three chambers built on a slope, the first easily fed from the path above, then turned into the second one below after a few weeks, the finished compost landing in the third and accessible for wheelbarrows in a small loading bay below. The area behind the Cottage was developed as a small kitchen garden, where ambitious attempts at growing tomatoes were compromised by poor drainage, but *kankun* and Ceylon spinach thrived. Lisa put love and attention into creating a small herb spiral over some boulders beside the Cottage, with three types of basil, flat-leaf parsley and ayurvedic herbs like *polpala*. Daniel maintained paths with 'the infernal machine' bush-cutter, achieving in hours what would take days with handheld slashers.

Their presence also prompted me to make some decisions. The recent election had created a limbo period, making me feel hesitant about proceeding. Now that Mahinda had won, we at least knew where we stood. Rumours abounded about changes in the law, but this was nothing new. Renovation to the bungalow was moving along and I ordered solar hot-water tanks for both buildings, as well as two small solar panels for the Cottage, providing enough power for 12 lights and to recharge a laptop or mobile phone. With a few additions to the Cottage, like kitchen units, and the bungalow completed in the New Year, we would soon have comfortable self-catering accommodation for 10 people – enough to run a course. The subsequent construction of the 'Pods' would increase that number.

With Daniel and Lisa in residence, the real purpose of Samakanda finally crystallized. I began to see my concept of the 'Bio-versity' come to life and the reciprocal exchanges start to flow, as they developed bonding relationships with Mr Pitchamurtu, Bandara, Vijeysekera, all of whom were soon learning from each other. Interesting people would turn up, offering thoughts and advice. Lisa cooked like a dream and I was now able to invite day visitors from the hotels in Galle, Olivia sending a steady stream of Aman guests. Soon there was a vitality to the project that had been lacking. For the first time, I saw the results of what it was we are trying to do.

Daniel and Lisa's final job was the construction of a wood-burning pizza oven. As with most projects, I announced that 'I have a book about it', which I gave to Daniel, along with various other instructions gleaned online. Over the next few days, an inner chamber of fire-bricks, mounted over a layer of crushed glass for insulation, took shape on a base of conventional brick pillars, then rendered with mud, like adobe.

Quite by chance, Rose Gray, my old boss from my days at the River Café and long-term supporter of WoH, passed through Galle with her husband David, at the same time as Daniel and Lisa were putting the finishing touches to the oven. After some involved discussions about flue dimensions and designs for the door, both agreed that the oven might just work, but reserved final judgement. Two weeks later, when the mud had dried, the first 'firing' was a huge success.

Rose and David were part of a now steady trickle of visitors to Samakanda. Some weeks I found myself taking people round every day and it was gratifying to have so much positive feedback. In the New Year, there was Greg Sams, whose last book, *Uncommon Sense*, had been compared with the classic anarchist writings of the Russian Prince Kropotkin. We had a lot to talk about, found multiple synergies within our work and soon became firm friends. Once again, I saw that it took someone like Greg, with no formal qualifications, to approach the subject with a fresh eye, thinking new and different thoughts.

This was equally true of Linda Garland, who had been resident in Bali for 30 years and was now regarded as one of the world authorities on the systemic benefits of bamboo. Known as the Bamboo

Queen, Linda was able to give chapter and verse on hundreds of different species, drawn from a total of some 1,500, specifying the particular attributes and applications for each one. Some were good for raising water tables and rehabilitating watersheds, some for sequestering pollutants, others for building, furniture, crafts, edible bamboo shoots, even bamboo beer, packed full of nutritious enzymes. We discussed drip irrigation systems using bamboo, planting a 'collar' of bamboo around the ridge, slightly tilted to the contours, thus harvesting more water and diverting it into the catchment area of the bowl. Linda talked about the high silicate content of bamboo, which lends it quartz-like qualities and the ability to harness and resonate 'positive energy', a claim borne out by trials in prisons. We discussed plans for a demonstration project at Samakanda, propagating various bamboos and running training workshops for the south of the island.

Like Greg, Linda had no formal qualifications, but was a fount of knowledge and vibrant wisdom, delightfully eccentric, passionate about her work – a true inspiration. One evening we met over dinner and I voiced my concerns about Samakanda, the gamble we were taking financially, the uncertainties of life in Sri Lanka.

'You know what,' she said, looking me in the eye. 'I saw a T-shirt the last time I was in New York, which relates to what you're saying. You know what it said? "If you're not on the edge, you're taking up too much room". Isn't that great? Look, if you're doing what you believe in, just hang in there. The integrity of your vision is all that counts.'

It had been a stressful two years since we first made the decision to come to Sri Lanka. Selling our house, moving to a new and different culture with two small children, the tsunami. Inevitably, this took a toll on our relationship. Unresolved issues came to the surface, demanding our attention. Ultimately however, this was positive, strengthening our relationship in the face of adversity. For the first time, Yvette and I were able to confront these issues head on, see them in a new light, tackle them in a different context from the milieu of our respective backgrounds. Through immersion in an alien culture, confronted with new challenges, I became more aware of my own shortcomings – my impatience, impetuous nature, what others perceive as arrogance. I doubt that these would have been made so manifest in the familiar dynamics of 'life back home'. Life has taken on a certain edge, but one that feels more alive as a result. There is an element of uncertainty and, as I write, the country slips ever further into civil war.

At the same time, in the last year since establishing Samakanda, we had come a significant step closer to 'living the dream'. The pros and cons will of course continue. War may start. Bird flu may become a global pandemic. 'Peak oil' and climate change may cause the end of what we perceive as 'civilization'. Nobody knows. But whatever does happen, I now know that we have at least tried to bring this dream to fruition. We have taken that first step.

Epilogue

Fireflies in the Rain

Walk on!
The Buddha's last words

15 March 2006. Samakanda.

It's exactly two years to the day since we first came to Sri Lanka. I am alone at Samakanda for the first time. No friends, no family, no Anil, no Mr Pitchamurtu. Tonight, I will spend my first night in the bungalow. I am walking along the main terrace path, my bare feet on the soft clover and cropped grass beneath. I stop, immersing every sense in the green thought that surrounds me.

Passion fruit vines spill down the stone terraces beside me, some trailing up coir string into old mango trees, others creeping over wooden pergolas that span the path. New tea bushes are inter-cropped with mung beans. Pineapples cling to rocky outcrops. Papaya trees, planted just over a year ago, are laden with clumps of pendulous green fruit. I can spot a wide variety of the sapling fruit trees we planted at the same time: mangos, rambutans, avocados, limes, wood apples. Pepper vines snake round the trunks of *gliri-cidias*, whose feathered branches filter the early evening sun and shimmer slightly in a gentle breeze. A few clove trees, a clump of bamboo, jak fruits dangling from overhanging branches.

I walk on to my favourite rock, and sit, suspended above the bowl. Kingfishers and parakeets swoop from splaying branches of *albizzias* over ripening golden paddy. A chameleon appears, frozen static at my side, then changes hues before darting into tea bushes below. A loud screeching. Two monkeys drop from the jungle behind me, chase each other across the bowl, bouncing off terraces, yelping as they cross the paddy and disappear across our boundary. Silence again, broken only by birdsong.

I turn to study the stone terrace behind me, the lichen, the moss, the tiny flowering plants clinging to the crevices. In the light, the stone takes on a green then purple luminescence. It too seems to be alive, breathing with the whole landscape. I become entranced by the soft green blanket of moss, clover and *gotu-kola* that surround the rock like a fitted carpet, finding its way down stone steps and into the bowl, one cascading chlorophyll wave, nourishing and protecting the soil beneath.

I walk on, past a fresh flush of unplucked tea and a series of boulders poised on terraces above, each like the head of a totemic animal – a whale here, then an elephant, a crocodile, even a walrus. The path breaks out of the shade. New cassava plants are thriving in rich coffee soil, along with daikon radish and a variety of chillies. The path splits at Kumara's new house and I drop down to the left, towards the river and back into the shade. Winding along the edge of the gully, the stonework here is even more alive, the luxuriant foliage above filled with more diversity: bird's nest ferns, cycads, *kittul* palms, banyans. The canopy of one huge banyan spans boulders and small caves. My feet press down on old jak fruit seeds and rotting leaves. The air is dark, humid, filled with insects. This feels like proper jungle. Brooding, dank, festering with life, death and 'the horror'.

I walk into the orbit of the grotto beneath the shrine, filled with ferns, creepers, lichens. The surface of the stone is green and, as always, the area seems bathed in a green diaphanous haze. Time stops. The world revolves. I stand, motionless, eyes closed, soaking into stone. Then on, up steep stone steps reclaimed from invasive roots and branches, deeper, further, higher. The path meanders between boulders, past a wild boar lair in a sheltered cave, up towards the main banyan tree. I dip down to one side, towards the huge overhanging rock that shelters the shrine. A river of leaf litter tumbles through the narrow canyon to one side, the giant dried leaves of wild bread-fruit scattered across the ground, curled at the sides but otherwise perfectly preserved.

I enter the space, taking a seat beside the lingam, the stubby phal-lic stone thrusting up from below like a tumescent tip of primal energy piercing the ground. I sit in the silence, eyes closed. The universe breathes. Each exhalation a miniature death, sending ripples through darkness tinged with the birth of light. How many have sat here before me? For how long have they gathered here?

Then I recall the words of a friend, when he first visited the shrine. 'Always remember to leave a stick when you come, propped up against the rock. That would be the tradition.'

'Why's that? To stop it falling down?' I'd laughed, thinking he was joking.

'Exactly!' Clearly he wasn't.

So, in accordance with his instructions, I search the ground for a suitable stick, finding one about three feet long. I stabbed one end into the ground, then jammed the other against the rock. The stick becomes a symbol, linking two different worlds.

The rain falls at dusk. Fireflies appear in the trees, tiny green beacons, flashing in the darkness. Their numbers grow. Soon, the jungle is pulsing with their presence. Amidst the horror, little seeds of light.

Afterword

18 October 2006. Galle.

It's about 7.45 am. Yvette and I leap out of bed to the sound of four massive explosions in quick succession. The windows are rattling. Sholto and Xan come running into our room, scared.

'Those were bombs,' I say to Yvette.

'Where?'

'Probably the naval barracks.'

Then machine gun fire breaks out.

'And those are machine guns,' I add. 'I don't believe it. Galle is under attack.'

I call Rob in the Fort.

'What the hell was that?' he says on answering.

'Sounds like bombs and guns to me. Can you tell where it's coming from? Could it be the naval base?'

'Sounds like it. I might walk up the Aman and see what's going on. I'll call you back.'

A flurry of text messages follow, to Henri, Keith and others we know closer to the action. The phone network is soon jammed. Then the helicopters come in. It all starts to seem rather familiar. *Apocalypse Now*, or just another day in paradise?

Notes from a Forest Garden

Tis true; there's magic in the web of it.
William Shakespeare

Early on in the evolution of the Web of Hope, I recognized that the 12 letters that spell T-H-E W-E-B O-F H-O-P-E could be used as the basic taxonomy for the database, with each letter corresponding to a different topic. T for Transport, H for Habitat, E for Energy, W for Water, E for Economics, B for Biodiversity, O for Organization, F for Food, H for Health, O for Oceans, P for Peace and E for Education. Just about anything we wanted to highlight could be shoehorned into one of these categories and used as a basic curriculum for Samakanda, our first Web of Hope Bio-versity.

The following essays introduce each of these 12 topics, highlighting some of the horrors of our current predicament, while presenting some of the initiatives, projects and technologies that give us cause for hope.

Transport

*The ability to accelerate a car that is low on
gasoline does not prove the tank is full.*

The authors of *Natural Capitalism*

Enhanced mobility has become a defining feature of the Industrial
Age. Like so many aspects of modern living, the possibilities of cheap
travel have become something we take so much for granted that
we regard it as a fundamental human right. And let's face it: cars and
airplanes are not going to disappear overnight, however catastrophic
their effect on climate change. In a sense, we are addicted to the
freedom provided by modern transport. At the same time, measures to curtail that freedom can surprise those most hardened to
their auto-addiction; many motorists now accept that London's
Congestion Charge has improved life in the city and the system is
set to be expanded and replicated elsewhere.

Most of us can offer all manner of excuses for not getting out of
our cars and onto two wheels, or using public transport. I certainly
can, and have already done so. The dismal state of the rail network
in the UK for example, and the sheer expense of travelling by train,
prohibits many from making the shift. In Sri Lanka, travelling by

bus is simply too terrifying to contemplate and, at peak times, trains can be human sardine tins. Our decision to buy a car was not one we took on lightly, but I saw no realistic alternative. In addition to all the other factors – two small children, the state of the roads, the safety issues – I frequently travel back from Samakanda with 20 kilos of fruit and vegetables on board, then sell these to hotels and restaurants in the Galle area. This would be challenging on a bicycle, or even a motorbike.

Where we lived in Wales was inadequately served by alternatives to the car. The distance to work engagements, or even shopping, was too daunting to contemplate on a bicycle. This can be one of the ironies of trying to live 'the good life'. One can be in an idyllic rural location, growing your own food and the rest of it, but if you are still dependent on a car, even for short trips to the local town, your Ecological Footprint may well be higher than those living the urban equivalent.

At the same time we know that our behaviour is bordering on the insane. Single occupancy of four-wheel-drive SUVs on crowded urban streets is simply not an intelligent way of moving about, travelling at an average of 8 miles an hour, doing 12 miles to the gallon and incubating road rage. We know that those on two wheels move around faster on urban journeys, the cyclists producing no pollution and improving their fitness at the same time. And research has shown that those of us enclosed in cars can be exposed to more pollution than cyclists or pedestrians.

It is of course a complex issue and there will always be those who simply cannot reduce their reliance on four wheels. Compared with the alternatives, the car is comfortable and convenient. Then there's the status symbol element – it's hard to imagine most senior executives trading their Jags and Mercs for mountain bikes. This may change of course. As climate change accelerates, it may become increasingly difficult for the current patterns to be morally justified. In the same way in which the Prius hybrid–electric car has become a Hollywood status symbol, so the current love for the SUV may diminish as social attitudes make them appear less desirable.

Although various alternatives to conventional internal combustion are appearing, from Electric Vehicles (EVs) to Liquid Petroleum Gas (LPG) and biodiesel, we must not forget that none of these are a final solution. If EVs are charged with electricity generated from fossil fuels, the problem is still there, just shifted to another area. Similarly, LPG is a fossil fuel, albeit a cleaner one. Even if powered by homemade biodiesel, there's still the embodied energy within the manufacturing of the car itself and the materials used, the equivalent of 10 years' average driving.

Even the Hypercar concept and hydrogen fuel cell, where the only emission is steam, fall short as a truly sustainable option, since we still have to manufacture the hydrogen from fossil fuels. Only when hydrogen is produced from purely renewable sources will we truly make the transition to a new era in energy and transport – and even the most optimistic projections suggest that could take decades.

In terms of climate change however, the trend towards cheaper air travel is of even more concern than our love affair with the car, the carbon dioxide emissions alone being 25 per cent higher per passenger mile. A return flight from London to Sri Lanka for example, generates as much CO_2 as driving 10,000 miles, more than many UK motorists travel in a year. In addition, other emissions at high altitude, like water vapour and nitrous oxides, compound the greenhouse effect and damage the ozone layer. In this area I am as guilty as anyone, and it could be argued that Samakanda will encourage some people to travel by plane, whether coming to attend courses or just passing through as tourists. Some of the people I know who travel the most are environmental campaigners, flying around the world to give speeches about climate change. The ironies are stark, the conclusions complex. If their work brings about the necessary changes, then presumably their accumulated Footprint can be justified. Similarly, I hope that the impact of air travel will be balanced to some extent by the Samakanda 'educational experience' and, in the future, by its 'deep green' carbon offset schemes, such as investing in renewable energy projects for the local community.

Many of the adjustments we need to make depend on a radical shift in our economic thinking. We are very good at putting a *price* on things, but continue to ignore the real *cost*. For example, there is no tax on aviation fuel. If taxed at the same rate as petrol, the average long haul flight would cost an extra £500.

Currently, all the social and environmental costs of our economic activities are excluded from the equation. The fossil fuel industry is effectively subsidized since, if the effects of the industry on human and planetary health, from asthma to global warming, were suddenly reflected in the price of petrol, most of us would abandon our cars overnight. Not to mention the military expense involved in keeping the black gold flowing. For every $50 spent by the US on a barrel of oil, $150 is spent on keeping shipping lanes open. If that cost alone were internalized, the price of US gas would treble.

It is hard to envisage a truly sustainable society emerging until fossil fuels are replaced with a new energy. Flying is the area in which many of us have the greatest impact on the biosphere, one long haul flight in the year doubling our Ecological Footprint. By refusing to fly this year, especially over long distances, the chances of cutting your Footprint to your fair share suddenly become tangible. In contrast, one long haul flight in the year will make that goal virtually impossible.

In energy terms, walking one mile in 20 minutes is the equivalent of running a mile in 10 minutes. This is the equivalent of swimming breaststroke for 10 minutes, playing football for 12 minutes, cycling for 16 minutes, or weight training for 17 minutes. Walking is an amazingly efficient way of exercising. Half an hour a day cuts the risk of heart disease by up to half and reduces the risk of some cancers, diabetes, obesity and osteoporosis. And it's free.

As I found in Africa, then India and more recently in Wales, walking not only makes sense for our physical health, but also for our mental and spiritual wellbeing. We all know how therapeutic the process of walking can be, whether confronted with some dilemma, searching for inspiration, or just seeking solace. As we travel, placing one foot in front of the other, an almost meditative state may emerge, connecting us with the earth and our surroundings.

In addition to the more obvious options – walking to work, or at least part of the journey – there are other elements that we can combine with walking to create systemic benefits. The Walking Bus concept for example, recently developed in the UK, takes children to school with at least one adult at the front and rear, acting as 'drivers' and 'conductors'. Children are steered safely to school and back on foot, picking up and dropping off passengers at organized 'bus stops' along the way. The Walking Bus reduces CO_2 emissions and exposure to pollution, and it allows children to chat with each other on the way to school, develops their road-safety awareness, provides invigorating morning exercise and brings them to the classroom more settled, attentive and ready to learn. In addition, the Walking

Bus reduces rush hour traffic, some 20 per cent of which is formed by the school run. According to pupils questioned in a survey, walking to school was more fun than driving, due to opportunities for chatting with friends, getting fresh air, taking exercise and spending more time with their parents. Oh yes, and going to sweet shops along the way.

As an 'intermediate technology', the bicycle is hard to beat. Its basic design has hardly changed in a hundred years. This surely tells us something – bicycles not only work, but work really well.

For millions of people, the bicycle is a passport to mobility and, as such, to greater freedom and independence. In a poor country like Sri Lanka, journeys previously considered too daunting by foot, or not adequately served by other forms of transport, not only become possible but, beyond the initial cost of the bike, can be made virtually for free. (Strictly speaking, we have to consider the extra calories required to pump those pedals, which as Colin observed, if composed of high Footprint energy bars for example, can actually be quite high.)

Anyone who has ever ridden a bike can attest to the liberating feeling. As children, our bikes become our first vehicles, opening up new adventures and explorations. As adults, we enjoy sailing through urban traffic and the sense of reconnection when we ride down empty rural lanes.

The multiple systemic benefits that this appropriate transport technology brings, from your health to your wallet to the state of the planet, are a testament to its efficiency. It is estimated that cycling 20 miles a week reduces the risk of heart disease to less than half that for non-cyclists; during rush-hour, a bicycle is about twice as fast as a car; bicycles require no road tax, no insurance, no licensing, no breakdown recovery services, and above all no fuel bills – except of course the calories you burn off while pumping those pedals.

As an example of a public transport system that people choose to use in preference to the car, the city of Curitiba in Brazil is a role model all urban planners could emulate. Despite a population of more than 2 million people and 500,000 cars, a highly efficient, reliable and well integrated transport system ensures that 75 per cent of commuters, some 1.3 million people, choose to travel by the 'surface metro' bus system, giving Curitiba the cleanest urban air of any Brazilian city. It can be done.

Jaime Lerner, an architect, engineer and urban planner, became mayor of the city in 1971. Rather than treating urban problems in isolation, Lerner realized the need for a systemic approach, seeking synergistic solutions for social, environmental and economic issues. When he arrived, the city was moving towards gridlock. Scrapping plans for an overpass, he pedestrianized the entire central boulevard, where fruit trees and flowers have replaced the cars. Articulated buses collect and drop passengers in seconds. The system is entirely self-financing, with a flat rate fare covering the whole city. Fares are distributed to the private bus companies in proportion to the number of miles travelled, encouraging wide coverage rather than competition for passengers. The investment required for the system was about 1 per cent of the projected cost for an underground, allowing huge amounts of money to be directed into further social improvements.

In terms of integrating any of these role models at Samakanda, or more widely within Sri Lanka, our choices are limited. There might be applications for the Walking Bus concept, although the general lack of roadside verges in many areas might merely increase the dangers.

Brewing biodiesel seemed the area in which we could make the biggest impact on local transport. Many crops in Sri Lanka could be used for this, as could the recycled cooking oil from roadside stalls. My initial research was promising, as countless testimonials extolled the ease with which cars were converted and were now running off a home-brew concocted in people's garages. I reviewed the list of chemicals and equipment required, imagining what the team at Samakanda might make of it all. Since many were brewers of an illegal moonshine alcohol known as *kasippu*, which I was constantly trying to clamp down on, I felt reluctant to launch into starting my own distillery. However, it remains part of our longer-term strategy and our planting programme has extended to incorporate suitable bio-fuels.

The potential dangers involved with making bio-diesel also concerned me. I had absolutely no experience as a chemist, beyond schoolboy pranks with Bunsen burners, and the instructions on boiling up vats of ethanol made me slightly nervous.

My father's battle cry has always been 'never trust an expert', a seemingly blinkered view that must have rubbed off. The more that time passed in Sri Lanka, the more I saw some wisdom in my father's mantra. Some of the most impressive and inspirational people I have met came to their field with no formal training or qualifications. As a result, they are able to approach the subject in an entirely original way, thinking 'out of the box'. Sometimes, if we are too close to our subject, we are unable to look at it with fresh eyes.

This can explain our collective myopia. We are so close to the tragedy of our times, so indoctrinated by the omnipresent media, that we find it hard to disengage and look at the world in a new and different way. I know for a fact that, as soon as Yvette and I stopped having television in the house in Wales, our whole outlook changed.

Habitat

Modern man talks of a battle with Nature,
forgetting that, if he won the battle,
he would find himself on the losing side.

E. F. Schumacher

Max Lindegger was a name I had known for years, mainly from articles in *Resurgence* and permaculture magazines, but always in connection with Crystal Waters. Winner of a UN World Habitat Award and widely regarded as one of the most successful eco-village experiments in the world, Crystal Waters is an intentional community built on the principles of permaculture.

As Colin used to say: 'Permaculture is what indigenous people have been doing for millennia – solving problems in a sustainable way.' A combination of *perma*-nent and agri-*culture*, the term was first coined by Australians Bill Mollison and David Holmgrem in the 1970s. Mollison had been a conservationist and, with his top student Holmgrem, successfully transformed depleted land into productive, fertile systems. Their visionary work was also inspired by more recent developments, fusing the benefits of indigenous techniques, like intercropping in forest gardens and agro-forestry systems, with modern research and technologies like renewable energies.

I began to feel that permaculture was, in many ways, the future, presenting perhaps the most comprehensive and holistic approach to sustainable lifestyles to have emerged from the ecological movement. Nothing was excluded, from food, water and waste systems, to transport, education, energy and health. Much of what it taught was common sense. Like the concept of 'zones' radiating from around the house, starting with the herbs and vegetables most commonly used and needing the most attention, then expanding to grazing and woodland at the periphery. It was also realistic, recognizing that all life is built upon networks and relationships, exposing the limitations and consequent failures of many experiments in alternative living, where utopian attempts are doomed from the start by divorcing themselves from the outside world. A community like Crystal Waters therefore, is very conscious of the reciprocal exchanges it makes with mainstream society, dependent as they are on materials they cannot produce themselves, but then imparting knowledge and skills to those that visit and attend courses.

It was Mollison who first made the distinction clear to me about the crucial difference between self-sufficiency and self-reliance. True self-sufficiency is more or less impossible in the modern world. I'm sure that most of those living in tipis in Wales still use commodities like toilet paper, cooking oil, tea, coffee, salt: products which they cannot make or grow themselves. Self-reliance, on the other hand, is a more accurate description of the systems put in place by a permaculture community, taking control over personal energy demands, water needs, housing, sewage treatment. The community may be nearly self-sufficient in food, but will also need some products that it cannot produce. This definition strikes at the core of sustainable living and highlights some of the erroneous assumptions often made – that it entails some sort of regression to living in a cave, deprived of all modern comforts. As such, I believe that the Web of Hope database and the Project Flamingo campaign offer the tools for self-reliance, rather than self-sufficiency.

It may sound like semantics, but the distinctions are important, since we can easily be led to false conclusions. For example, there is nothing wrong with consuming per se. Rather, the problem is *what* we consume and the *rate* at which we consume it. If we are using any material faster than it can be replenished by nature, then it is inherently out of step with sustainable systems. Likewise, if we are making products, by-products and toxins that cannot be safely sequestered or absorbed by natural processes, then we are failing to live within the parameters of sustainability. This is the case with global warming, plastics, heavy metals and a host of environmental problems. We become the only species on the planet to generate waste that cannot be recycled. We've changed the rules, stepped outside the system, by creating linear rather then cyclical systems.

Another example is 'globalization', which has become a dirty word. However, in itself, I see nothing inherently wrong with much that globalization makes possible. The size and influence of the global civil society movement for example, has been facilitated by globalization processes such as communication technologies. Climate change treaties, biodiversity conventions and international agreements on protecting fisheries, are all made possible by globalization. The problem with globalization is the manner in which it has been hijacked by a powerful elite, pushing a particular agenda. So, when opponents talk about globalization as the scourge of the modern world, they usually and more accurately mean the neo-liberal economics propelled by large multinational corporations and powerful Western governments. As the writer George Monbiot says, the task for civil society is not so much to overthrow globalization, but to capture the helm and use it for 'the world's first democratic revolution'.

The analogy of comparing trees to houses was first used by Michael Braungart and Bill McDonough, in their Cradle to Cradle design process, which seeks to 'design industrial systems that emulate the abundance of nature'. So, rather than looking at raw materials and waste, their company, MBDC, sees 'biological' and 'technical nutrients' which, rather than being *downcycled*, turning plastic bottles into park benches, can be *upcycled*, retaining their high quality in closed-loop industrial cycles, like the revolutionary 'paper' on which their book is printed, designed to be used, broken down and recycled indefinitely as 'paper' or other products.

MBDC sees the next industrial revolution as being the application of these principles to design buildings that, like trees, produce more energy than they consume, accrue and store solar energy and purify their own waste water; factories where effluent water is cleaner than influent; products that decompose as food for plants and animals, helping to rebuild topsoil in the process. As the eco-economist Paul Hawken says, rather than designing products to be recycled, we need to use materials that can be thrown away, going directly to the compost heap and, thereby, turning into soil. That's a closed loop, which removes waste from the equation entirely. Pollution becomes a moot point and zero-waste becomes a tangible goal.

The ING bank in Amsterdam is a working example of MBDC's philosophy. Built in 1987, the building has both indoor and outdoor gardens fed by rainwater captured from the roof. Every office is fed by natural air and light. Water cascades down 'flow-form' sculptures in the bronze handrails of the staircases, 'harmonized' in the process by the aerobic conditions and charging the air with negative ions, conducive to 'good vibes'. The complex uses 92 per cent less energy than the bank next door, which was constructed at the same time. This represents a saving of $2.9 million a year and makes it one of the most energy-efficient buildings in Europe. It is estimated that the energy saving systems paid for themselves in the first three months. Another systemic benefit is that employees actually enjoy being in a bank. In fact, they hardly seem to want to go home. Absenteeism has dropped by 15 per cent, productivity is up and social events are held at the bank during weekends. As always, this intelligent design not only works, but works really well on many levels.

In our enthusiasm for modern technology, we often overlook the merits of traditional methods. Air-conditioning is a good example. AC is a phenomenally inefficient way of keeping cool. An AC unit producing 12,000 BTUs of cooling will consume 2,400 watts of electrical energy; this means that an equivalent of 70 per cent of the total potential cooling output is needed just to run it. Air conditioning accounts for 16 per cent of total electricity use in the US and, on hot summer afternoons, it takes more than 200 enormous power stations to keep American buildings cool, costing $3.3 billion for the city of Houston alone, a figure which eclipses the combined GDP of 42 African countries.

In addition, AC has led to house design that abandons all the traditional architectural devices for keeping buildings cool. AC is also far from healthy, producing pools of very dense cold air in lower parts of the room, affecting blood circulation and respiration, particularly in children and the elderly.

Yet, for at least 8,000 years, aboriginal tribes in Australia have created buildings that reject unwanted heat, keeping indoor temperatures as much as 19° C cooler than outside. In hot countries, traditional devices for keeping buildings cool, like louvered shutters, high ceilings and features that encourage a cross- or through-draught, have been abandoned in favour of energy intensive concrete boxes.

Many ancient technologies are proving to be at least as efficient as their modern equivalents. A sustainable and energy efficient air-conditioning unit has been developed in India, incorporating woven matting made from *khus-khus* grass, which gives off a pleasant fragrance when kept moist by a controlled drip from a water reservoir. The cool air is then circulated through the room by a small solar powered fan.

In Nigeria, a fridge has been developed that does not need electricity and costs 30 cents to make. It consists of an earthenware pot nestled inside a larger pot and packed with a layer of damp sand. When stored in a dry, well-ventilated place, the water held in the clay and sand evaporates, taking the heat with it. In trials, the fridge kept tomatoes fresh for weeks. In the rural areas of Upper Egypt, the *maziara* is a traditional water-cooling and purification system that also utilizes the evaporative cooling properties of large, porous ceramic pots. Heat is continually drawn out of the jars by the dry desert climate – 580 calories of energy for every cubic centimetre of evaporated water. The *maziara* requires no energy except filling it with water in the morning.

There's no doubt that many of these ways to reduce the Ecological Footprint are easier in the tropics than in the harsh conditions of northern Europe. Few of us would relish the idea of a British winter without central heating. In Wales, we had under-floor heating.

Yvette would never have lasted five minutes of winter without it. Although some 40 per cent more efficient than radiators, we still had weighty fuel bills.

One of the many revelations exposed by the Ecological Footprint analysis is just how unsustainable the current trends are. Our economic model promises something it cannot deliver, since we do not have another three planets to provide the resources. London's Footprint covers some 20 million hectares, about 125 times its surface area. The city needs two supertankers of oil each week and consumes 2.4 million tonnes of food per year, which requires the equivalent of the country's entire productive land area to sustain itself.

Yet a housing development in the UK has recently proved that sustainable lifestyles are indeed possible, even within the parameters of urban northern Europe and with what we might call the non-negotiable demands of modern life, like cars, fridges and washing machines. In the south London borough of Sutton, BedZED is the country's first carbon neutral housing project, making no net contribution to global warming from fossil fuel use.

Wood chips from an urban forestry programme provide the necessary fuel for a combined heat and power station (CHP). A car-pooling scheme (ZEDcars), has reduced car dependence and saved each member an average of £1,500 a year. BP Solar's photovoltaic panels are integrated with double-glazing in the top-floor conservatories, generating electricity while providing shade and preventing over-heating in the summer. This electricity powers 40 vehicles, providing 8,500 kilometres of carbon neutral driving for each car. Rainwater is harvested from the gardens and the roof surfaces, stored in tanks in the foundations of the terraces, then used for flushing toilets and irrigating gardens. A Living Machine reed bed system treats sewage on site, recycling water for flushing toilets again. Combined with water-efficient appliances like dual-flush toilets, BedZED has reduced mains water usage by 40 per cent. Other initiatives include a sustainable local paper cycle, hemp cultivation for clothes, and barbeque charcoal from coppiced woods in Croydon.

Initial estimates suggest that by living at BedZED, without any major lifestyle changes, residents have reduced their Footprint by one-third from the UK average. Those that join the 'green lifestyle services', like car-sharing and organic box schemes, can reduce their Footprint to the fair-share target of 1.9 average global hectares. So, BedZED proves that it can be done, even in the suburbs of south London.

Energy

*There's a time when silence becomes
betrayal. That time is now.*

Dr Martin Luther King

Conscious of the carbon Footprint created by my journey to London and back, I decided to work out how many trees I would need to plant to offset the emissions. Various estimates from online carbon offset schemes placed this at between 6 and 12. This added further incentive for me to finally visit Rainforest Rescue International's nursery and buy a selection of climax and sub-climax rainforest trees, to accelerate diversification of the land.

Although I liked the fact that it placated my conscience to some degree, I could not help feeling that the basis for some carbon sink schemes was slightly spurious. Was this not obfuscating the real issue? It would take decades for trees I planted now to sequester the carbon emissions generated from my recent flight. 'Systems lag' ensures that fossil fuels burnt today will affect the climate for decades to come, by which time we will have crossed the tipping point, having triggered runaway climate change.

And what trees are being planted? Another monoculture spruce or eucalyptus plantation is hardly helping the planet if it replaces what was once diversified forest. Bjorn Lomborg, the discredited 'sceptical environmentalist', refers to more trees being planted than felled each year, revealing his ignorance of basic ecology in the process. Climax forests are the most diverse ecosystems on the planet, maintaining a wide spectrum of the planet's essential life-support mechanisms. Monocultures not only fail to do this, but actively promote ecological disasters, from shrinking biodiversity to disrupting watercourses, making such comparisons meaningless.

It also struck me that carbon trading was turning pollution into just another commodity for financial speculation. Is this really a solution to climate change? George Monbiot makes it clear. 'Perhaps the most destructive effect of the carbon offset trade is that it allows us to believe we can carry on polluting. The Government can keep building roads and airports and we can keep flying to Thailand for our holidays, as long as we purchase absolution by giving a few quid to a tree planting company.'

However, I find myself sounding fundamentalist by not acknowledging that some carbon offset schemes are at least a step in the right direction. Rather than planting trees however, the concept of installing renewable energy systems seems to be far more immediate. If a community or a company really wants to help the planet, it seems much more effective to pay for the installation of wind or solar technologies in rapidly developing countries with a relatively low carbon Footprint, like India. This at least prevents them coming on-stream with fossil fuels. Sri Lanka's per capita carbon Footprint is very low, about 0.4 compared with a world 'fair share' of 1.9. In the UK, the average is just below 10, in the US, nearly 20.

Through the concept of micro-trading, twinning schools and communities between the so-called First and Third Worlds, it becomes possible for us all to have a direct impact on tackling climate change, by investing in tangible renewable energy sources, rather than planting trees. This model, known as Converging World and developed by WoH supporter John Pontin, began to emerge as a key strand within WoH projects.

The other bonus presented by micro-trading is the way it coheres with the 'Contraction and Convergence' model, widely accepted within environmental circles as being the most realistic global framework for dealing with climate change. First developed by Aubrey Meyer and the Global Commons Institute (GCI), the model proposes that all countries must cut or limit their carbon emissions to 'contract and converge' on the per capita fair share figure as the only equitable way forward.

However, as we well know, this concept is anathema to many of the most powerful people on the planet, most notably the US administration and the major energy corporations. It is hard to believe that the idea of a decentralized energy industry, of people generating their own clean energy for free and selling the surplus to the national grid, is greeted with much enthusiasm in the White House, where the science of climate change has been rewritten on a regular basis. The fact that anyone can see a justification for gambling with the fate of the planet speaks volumes. Talk about the abuse of power.

The very word 'power' has become synonymous with governments, corporations, the media and other forces that appear to shape our world. We lose sight of the definition – the ability to act or do – which places the word squarely in the hands of the individual.

We have been conditioned to believe that the individual has been completely disempowered and there is little he or she can do to prevent the inevitable: the onward march of 'progress', the outbreak of wars, world poverty, the destruction of the rainforests, global warming and the extinction of species. That is precisely the notion we need to confront, as we work towards a new definition of 'power' in the modern world – one which dispels the illusion that the individual is powerless.

One area in which I believe we can actively prove this is by 'taking power of our power', thereby playing our part in tackling climate change. Anyone in the UK can make the switch to a green electricity scheme. It takes all of five minutes online, or by filling in a form. It's a no-brainer. As is the installation of solar hot water, which may only work intermittently in northern Europe but still pays for itself very quickly. More challenging, but more rewarding, are possibilities for community wind power cooperatives, or covering your house with solar roof tiles, both of which may even provide a return when you sell excess power back to the grid.

Personally, I find the whole notion of going 'off-grid' and generating my electricity needs tremendously appealing. I would rather not be dependent on a corporation for anything, especially one like ExxonMobil.

At Samakanda, mains electricity was already connected to the bungalow and, at the moment, we just cannot afford the switch to solar. Likewise at Inland Hills. With the Cottage in the bowl however, it did make sense, since connecting to the grid would have cost the same as the photovoltaic panels we have installed. Solar hot water however, made sense for all three buildings.

One of the main drawbacks of solar is that energy is being generated during the day, when the demand is very low. Hence the need for batteries, which are expensive and filled with heavy metals, making them far from ecologically sound. As a way round this, I started looking into another option. We could circumvent the need for batteries by using solar power during the day to pump water uphill, store it in a holding tank, then run a micro-hydro system at night to generate power when we need it most.

The staggering potential for a decentralized solar economy strikes home when one considers that as much solar energy falls on the planet in one hour as the total population uses in one year. Since photovoltaic cells rely on light rather than heat, studies show that even cloudy climates like southern England's could generate some 80 per cent of household electricity from solar power. In Norway, 50,000 homes are powered by these cells and more houses in Kenya now receive their electricity from solar panels than the national grid.

Similar potential exists with wind, wave and bio-fuels. More than 100,000 families in Denmark are members of wind energy cooperatives. At times, the country has received 15 per cent of its electricity from wind power and the turbine industry employs over 15,000 people. It has been estimated that the UK could generate its entire electricity requirements by tapping just 1 per cent of the wave energy around the coast. And if 30 per cent of UK agricultural land were devoted to energy crops, two-thirds of the country's power demand could be met.

Why then was James Lovelock, the originator of Gaia Theory, being so outspoken about nuclear power as the most viable option? I asked Web of Hope supporter Zac Goldsmith for his opinion. 'As ever, the arguments have stuck to the polarities,' he said. I agreed, now seeing this 'black and white' division being used as a diversion from other possibilities.

'It's a manufactured debate,' Zac continued. 'The turbines-in-every-field argument is largely the work of a nuclear industry in the final spasm of a struggle to survive. Nuclear, after all, has been roundly discredited on every level. It's so dangerous that even before the onset of a new type of terrorism, the insurance industry wouldn't cover it unless governments capped the liabilities. And contrary to assurances by the industry that nuclear power is clean, it's hard to imagine a dirtier energy source. In Britain alone, we face a £50 billion clean-up bill. What's more, nuclear is the most expensive form of energy in the history of energy. In a genuinely free market, nuclear simply wouldn't exist.'

'What do you see as the alternative then?' I asked. 'A portfolio of different renewables, according to the situation?'

'Exactly. No one wants Britain to be coated in wind turbines. But equally, no one is suggesting it should be. One recent US study showed that spending $5.2 billion on energy conservation in the federal Government's 500,000 buildings would lead to savings of more than $1 billion each year, indefinitely – an enormous return by any standard.

'Already we're seeing whole villages in Britain's West Country on the verge of being powered by environmentally benign small hydro projects. Biomass is emerging, solar power is becoming cheaper and more efficient. Wind is just one solution among many. But because the Government remains fixated on massive centralized one-size-fits-all projects, and because of its refusal to let local people have a say, people who might very well have been champions of wind energy are being turned against it.

'If there were no alternatives to nuclear, we'd no doubt have to accept it. But there are alternatives, and despite pitifully small investment, they are already proven. If we do decide to pursue the nuclear option, it will be because of the Government's fixation with one-size-fits-all solutions. And sheer laziness.'

Many of us suffer interminable guilt about our car use. I know I do. There seems to be no alternative as we wait for hydrogen fuel cells to revolutionize the industry. However, biodiesel is proving to be an increasingly attractive option for ecologically conscious motorists. As well as being cheap, it ensures that you cease to support the oil industry.

The concept of using vegetable oil as a fuel dates back to 1895 when Dr Rudolf Diesel developed the first diesel engine, demonstrating it at the World Exhibition in Paris in 1900 using peanut oil. Biodiesel has many advantages over conventional fuels. It can be used in any diesel engine, produces about 80 per cent less carbon dioxide and almost 100 per cent less sulphur dioxide than conventional diesel and can actually extend the life of diesel engines since it is more lubricating. Fuel consumption, auto ignition, power output and engine torque are all relatively unaffected.

Biodiesel is as biodegradable as sugar and 10 times less toxic than table salt. It can be made from domestically produced, renewable oilseed crops such as soybeans and, when burnt in a diesel engine is said to replace exhaust fumes 'with the pleasant aroma of popcorn or french fries'! It is a proven fuel with over 30 million successful US road miles and more than 20 years of use in Europe.

Enthusiasts maintain that running a vehicle on vegetable oil should be preferred over biodiesel because it is more carbon neutral. At the time of writing, it is possible to walk into a supermarket in the UK and buy a litre of vegetable oil for 46 pence. Once you have paid the 25.82 pence duty to the Government to make it a road fuel, your total cost is 71.82 pence per litre, which is cheaper than petrol or diesel. This price falls even further if you use waste vegetable oil from restaurants. With free waste oil it soon becomes possible to recover the cost of engine conversion. Running a diesel car on vegetable oil is easily achievable for those wanting carbon neutral motoring today, as thousands of people in Germany and the rest of continental Europe are already proving.

With prophetic insight, Jules Verne alluded to the potential for hydrogen as an energy source in his 1874 novel *The Mysterious Island*. 'And what will they burn instead of coal?' asks one of the characters. 'Water,' replies another. 'But water decomposed into its primitive elements. Yes, my friends, I believe that water will some day be employed as fuel, that hydrogen and oxygen which constitute it will furnish an inexhaustible source of heat and light. Some day water will be the coal of the future.'

Much has been touted about the transition to an economy running on hydrogen, the most abundant element in the universe. However, it must be remembered that hydrogen is an 'energy carrier' rather than a primary source. In the same way that the electric car is not necessarily a solution to the emissions problem, hydrogen production still requires electricity at source. Of course, if this electricity is generated by renewable technologies with zero emissions, like wind, solar, wave or the Icelandic option of geothermal, then we really will enter a new energy era.

Perhaps the most exciting prospect of the hydrogen economy, and the most challenging for the existing energy corporations, is what the writer Jeremy Rifkin calls the Worldwide Energy Web, a decentralized and democratized energy industry built upon renewable energy technologies and hydrogen fuel cells. He explores the possibilities that will unfold when energy flows in two directions within networks, rather than from the top down. When our hydrogen fuel-cell cars can generate energy while parked, then sell it back to the national grid, an entirely new energy system will have emerged. Whether or not governments and industry would be prepared to cooperate in such a process remains to be seen.

Water

*Blood has fingers and it opens
tunnels under the earth.*

Pablo Neruda

One of Vimal's first projects at Samakanda was to excavate a small
holding tank below the boulders where the spring issues from the
side of the ridge. It would serve mainly as an aesthetic feature, planted
with flowering lotuses. A tangle of roots from surrounding trees
spread across the surface and a pit was dug beneath them. Assuming
this worked, we would then divert any excess water into buried plastic tanks, which could then supply the cottage.

The more I became familiar with the land, the more I realized
the importance of managing the water efficiently. As in any project
of this kind, it all comes down to water, the most precious resource
of all. Although the abundance of wells, the spring and the natural
catchment area of the bowl had all been factors that had drawn me
to the land in the first place, I also knew that we needed to be intelligent about how we used it.

I was convinced that large amounts of water could be harvested
during the two monsoons from the expanses of exposed rock on

the summit of the ridge. A combination of gullies below the boulders and swales (run-off ditches dug almost parallel to the contours) could be used to divert water into buried holding tanks, from where water could be directed to any part of the property, either for irrigation, household use or running micro-hydro turbines for generating electricity. This could co-exist with a series of exposed ponds, connected by pipes or gullies running down the ridge and used for aquaculture projects, like breeding fish or growing water chestnuts.

Water is essential for all life. It covers some 70 per cent of the planet's surface and makes up 70 per cent of our bodies. However, despite its apparent abundance, very little is safe to drink – less than half a per cent worldwide. Due to increasing pollution, this limited amount of safe water is decreasing all the time. The world is entering a fresh water crisis, with some urban centres like Mexico City predicted to run dry within 10 years.

We contaminate water with linear sewage systems that carry our waste straight out to sea rather than returning nutrients to the soil, already stripped by intensive agriculture. Modern sewage systems were first introduced to the city of London when the stench from the river became too severe for parliament to convene. In the 1840s, the German scientist Justus Liebig tried to persuade the London authorities to build a sewage recycling system for the city. Unfortunately, the system that was adopted, mixing waste with water and diverting it into the Thames, was replicated all over the world, ensuring the gradual loss of soil fertility which a cyclical system would have preserved. When London adopted a linear system, Liebig and others set to work on developing artificial fertilizers to replenish the soil, creating the foundations of the modern agro-chemical industry.

As rainforest expert Ranil said, this process necessitates ever more artificial fertilizers and chemicals to maintain fertility but, because we only apply a limited range – potassium, phosphorus and nitrogen – we overlook the 80 or so other trace elements that the soil should contain.

We also pollute water with toxic by-products from heavy industry, along with heavy metals like mercury, some 15 per cent of which is released from the amalgam tooth fillings of cremated bodies. The mercury ends up in the water and the food chain, building up in concentrations through a process known as bio-accumulation. The UK Government recently issued a health warning to pregnant women about eating tuna, due to high levels of mercury. This should extend to all fish at the top of the food chain, like shark, swordfish and marlin, in which concentrations of heavy metals or PCBs, the most carcinogenic substances known, can be 25 million times greater than when they are first released into the environment. One gram of PCBs – a chemical used in products ranging from pesticides to cosmetics – is enough to make one billion litres of water unfit for freshwater life. Due to bio-accumulation, eating a single trout from Lake Michigan will expose you to more of the chemical than a lifetime of drinking the lake's water.

By incinerating plastics, we release highly carcinogenic dioxins into the air, food and water. This is common practice at the roadside in Sri Lanka. For some reason, Sunday mornings seem to be a preferred time to burn off the week's garbage and we wake every weekend to the smell of melting plastic wafting through the children's bedroom from neighbouring houses. Our effort to curtail this met with hostility, despite the fact that the perpetrator was a cancer specialist at the nearby hospital.

The facts about the scarcity of water make for a sobering read. Nearly half the world's major rivers are going dry, or are badly polluted. In 2001, Mexico's Rio Grande failed to reach the sea for the first time and the Nile, Ganges, Colorado and Yellow Rivers are all dammed, diverted or over-tapped to such a degree that little or no water reaches the sea. Some rivers in Taiwan are polluted with chemicals to the point of being combustible and 80 per cent of the rivers in China no longer support fish life. One in three people in the developing world do not have access to safe and reliable water, and waterborne diseases account for 80 per cent of all illnesses in developing countries. The WHO estimates that 25 million people die every year from polluted drinking water. One flush of a standard US toilet uses more water than many families in the world consume in a day. It takes 105,000 gallons of water to make one car, 6,000 gallons to make a computer and 100 gallons to make a cotton T-shirt.

Then there's agriculture. The huge Ogallala aquifer that supplies water for American farms from West Texas to South Dakota, the US grain base, is being depleted 14 times faster than nature recharges it. The underground water table has dropped by more than 30 metres in parts of Texas, Oklahoma and Kansas over the last 30 years, and wells have gone dry on thousands of farms in the southern Great Plains. Rather than capturing and harvesting precious rainfall in urban areas, it is channelled through concrete sluices and drains, polluted in the process, then flushed out to sea.

Transnational corporations are now busy buying up the world's water companies. The process began with the Thatcher-Reagan fixation with privatization, starting in the UK, where water prices immediately rose by 250 per cent. In a sense, this is an inevitable consequence of an economic system obsessed with the illusion of infinite growth, but depending on finite resources. At the root of this delusionary state is the concept of free market capitalism, as laid out by the Washington Consensus.

After the collapse of communism, the deregulation of trade, investment and services became the one-size-fits-all ideology of the New World Order. It requires goods, capital and services to flow freely across borders without government intervention. As a result, more and more of what many of us may regard as fundamental human rights, from herbal medicines to safe water, are being monopolized by non-human entities. The corporate institutions we invented now effectively control most of the planet's resources.

By looking at water conservation and purification, some of the ways in which communities can bring this basic human need back within their grasp come to light. Ways of harvesting rain have been revived throughout the developing world. In India, rainwater harvesting systems on 83,000 hectares, a little more than half the size of Delhi, could provide clean drinking and cooking water for the billion-strong population of the country. In theory, there isn't a single Indian village that could not meet its drinking and cooking water requirements with this low-cost intermediate technology.

Since 1998, communities in the Moneragala district of Sri Lanka's dry zone, have been using tanks to store rain channelled by gutters and pipes as it runs off the houses. Despite an indigenous tradition of rainwater harvesting and irrigation systems going back to the third century BC, modern policy-makers have overlooked the value of such systems. The UK's Intermediate Technology Development Group's South Asia team, now known as Practical Action, worked with the community to develop a bottom-up approach to the project, aiming to build local skills among builders and users, creating systems that allow communities to manage their own harvesting schemes. The community was involved throughout. Meetings were held where villagers analysed their water problems and selected the technology. Local masons were trained to build the 5,000 litre storage tanks. Each system, including tank, pipes, gutters and filters, costs $195 – a month's income for an average village family.

A more recent innovation is the concept of harvesting fog. The remote fishing village of Chungungo in Chile has been transformed by the installation of a fog collection system, after relying solely on water supplied by truck. With a dependable, affordable water supply, the population not only have domestic water, but are able to cultivate commercial crops and plant trees.

The technology of fog collection is amazingly simple: massive vertical nets are erected in high-lying areas close to water-short communities. As fog blows through them, water droplets are deposited on the net. These run down into gutters attached at the bottom of the nets, from which water is channelled into reservoirs and then to individual homes. In Chungungo, this system got water flowing from the taps for the first time ever in 1992.

Purification techniques can provide another way of maintaining control over water. The ecological designer John Todd is a global leader in the field of water purification, developing technologies to replicate and accelerate the processes found in rivers, ponds and wetlands. By passing contaminated effluent through a series of tanks, populated with a variety of bacteria, algae, plants and fish, Todd's 'living machines' not only provide clean drinking water, but also generate fertilizers and maintain a miniature ecosystem. No chemicals are required, and some of the systems even double up as miniature fish farms. With a higher degree of biodiversity than the filtration achieved by a reed bed, the living machine treats a much wider range of toxic effluents. Some of the plants, such as bullrushes, also sequester heavy metals and secrete antibiotics that kill pathogens. The 'machines' can treat sewage from anything between one and 10,000 households – one in Vermont handles 80,000 gallons per day. The systems are just as suited to heavy industry, transforming toxic pollution into a beneficial resource.

A recent initiative in Nepal has paved the way for sustainable and affordable water treatment by taking small, silver-saturated ceramic water purifiers into low income, vulnerable communities. Pottery Media Purifiers are made from red firing clay, an affordable material for poor nations. The water purification systems are effective, cheap to produce, user-friendly and can be replicated almost anywhere.

The water crisis is very real indeed, but there is hope. Every one of us, regardless of where we live, should be conscious of what we use. On average, we need about 10,000 litres each a year to live, although many in the developed world are using 500,000.

As usual, the main problem lies not with us as individuals, but with industry and agriculture. Households and municipalities account for only 10 per cent of total water use, with 25 per cent going to industry and the rest for irrigation. Some industries have been able to dramatically reduce their usage in recent years, and saved millions in the process. American steel producers have cut water use from 280 tonnes for every tonne of steel down to 14. Some industries in California have made savings of as much as 90 per cent through conservation measures like recycling cooling water, monitoring for leaks, changing water nozzles to reduce flow rates, and switching from continuous to intermittent flows in some manufacturing processes.

Similar advances are possible in agriculture. Drip irrigation, pioneered by the Israelis, is 95 per cent efficient compared with the 80 per cent lost through evaporation and run-off in traditional systems. It is currently only used on 1 per cent of the world's irrigated land and, if practised more widely, could dramatically alter the equation. By implementing the water management system suggested by Ranil, it would theoretically become possible to drip irrigate any crop in any part of Samakanda, thereby ensuring the most efficient use of this precious resource possible, delivering water directly to where it is needed.

Economics

*Growth for the sake of growth
is the philosophy of the cancer cell.*

Edward Abbey

With a population of 28,000, the community of Ithaca in NewYork State is one of the world's leading examples of the alternative local economy in action. In addition to printing their own currency, Ithaca Hours – of which millions of dollars' worth have already been traded – the community now has a stock exchange, gathering money for regional eco-development. Then there's a credit union, dozens of farmer's market vendors, Community Supported Agriculture schemes, an organic home delivery service, a large food co-op and a regional food-processing centre. There are several housing co-ops, an eco-village, a natural home-builders network, a health fund which covers emergencies and hundreds of holistic healers, most of whom barter.

In Sri Lanka, the Sarvodaya movement provided me with role models closer to home. Sarvodaya began as an educational experiment in the mid-1950s, when a group of high-school teachers in Colombo decided to turn their convictions into action. They organized camps in which students from relatively affluent urban homes gave up their vacations to share their time, thoughts and efforts to work in the country's poorest villages. They went wherever they were invited and by 1970 there were a hundred villages involved. Now more than 15,000 of the country's 30,000 villages participate.

In the summer of 2003, nine months before moving to Sri Lanka, I was invited to the Colombian Amazon, to see the fruits of a similar but smaller initiative and offer advice on other possibilities that the community could incorporate. The invitation came from renowned anthropologist Martin von Hildebrandt.

Like Ranil, Martin is a man whose energy and looks belie his age, appearing a good 15 years younger than 65, his sturdy, robust frame and rugged looks etched by years spent living and working in the Amazon. Once a minister in the Colombian Government, Martin had won the Right Livelihood Award, or 'alternative Nobel prize', after campaigning for the rights of indigenous peoples to self-governance on their own land.

He wanted me to visit Letitia, a town in the middle of the Amazonian jungle, on the border with Peru and Brazil. A network of women had started a 'Savers Scheme' that had produced remarkable results. The success of the initiative was now translating into a sustainable housing project.

As soon as we stepped off the plane, the overpowering humidity zapped my strength. I was soon struggling to keep up with Martin, as he set off on a whirlwind tour of the town. We stopped at roadside stalls to chat with his friends and be plied with a constant stream of bizarre Amazonian potions. A few hours later we had visited several houses and spoken with members of the Savers network. They all had impressive stories to tell, having either built new houses or renovated what they had. These improvements had all been paid for by sales of various products they made.

The 'localization' of Ithaca, the Letitia Savers network and Sarvodaya's cooperatives are a direct contrast to the homogenizing effects of a globalizing economy. Money, goods and services are circulated within the local community, improving local people's lives. Conventional economics takes no account of these benefits. Instead it makes sweeping assumptions based on simplistic, linear indicators, most notably equating an increase in Gross Domestic Product, growth, with an increase in prosperity and well-being. Growth has become the modern mantra for politicians, economists and business leaders. Yet it exists only in the realms of fantasy, since infinite growth is impossible on a planet with finite resources.

The insurance industry predicts that the costs incurred by global warming will exceed global GDP by 2065. Some say if we continue to lose topsoil at current rates there will be none left in 50 years. What will it take to dispel the illusion that our current economic model can be sustained? What will it take to bring world leaders to their senses? How can we make the transition from a twisted economic model to one that works within ecological limits?

The distinction between 'growth' and 'development' was first made by the economist Herman Daly: 'To grow means to increase in size by the accretion or assimilation of material. To develop means to expand or realize the potentialities of; to bring gradually to a fuller, greater or better state. A growing economy is getting bigger, a developing economy is getting better.'

Economic growth is measured in rates of consumption, the speed with which we are taking natural resources, turning them into products – often creating toxic by-products in the process – which are then used and consumed before being flushed into water courses, or sent to landfills. Many of the processes involved in mining and refining these resources may be very clever. However, they can hardly be described as intelligent. We are rabidly extracting materials, many of them highly toxic, which have been safely sequestered in the earth's crust, or by trees and plants over millions of years, and dispersing them into the atmosphere. They are not supposed to be there. We use more and more energy to extract ever less material, while generating more and more toxins which we do not know how to sequester.

Instead, these poisons accumulate in the air we breathe, the food we eat, the water we drink. Most of us are exposed to at least 300 toxic chemicals every day. 'The underlying assumption,' Paul Hawken says, 'is that we will continue to need increasing amounts and different types of poisonous chemicals in order to live in a "healthy" and civilized world, a belief whose ironies are rarely addressed by industry.'

Measuring growth by rates of consumption, taxing the things that are meant to be positive – like jobs, creativity and income – and not the negatives – like toxic pollution, fossil fuel use and resource depletion – means that our economic system is back to front. What use is an economic indicator like GDP if it increases every time we turn on the air conditioner or drive a car, every time there is an accident, an insurance claim, a divorce, a hospital bill, an environmental disaster?

A range of new economic indicators reflect quality of life rather than rates of consumption. The Ecological Footprint analysis reveals the true impact of the global economy, measuring the systemic impact of a product, lifestyle or activity in terms of the 'average global hectares' required to support it indefinitely. It exposes the fact that most northern economies are 'parasitic', draining southern economies of their life-blood. For example, 9.6 hectares are required to support the average American lifestyle, five times the per capita share of the planet's ecological carrying capacity.

To bring eco-nomics back into synergy with eco-logy, markets will have to stop externalizing social and environmental costs and start to reflect the actual cost to soil, air, water, society and human health. Surely it's time to come to our senses, to change linear polluting industries into cyclical industrial ecologies, or phase out those that cannot adjust.

Biodiversity

Man did not weave the web of life;
he is merely a strand in it.
Whatever he does to the web, he does to himself.

Chief Seattle

Although it is often seen as superfluous, or of secondary importance compared with issues like climate change or poverty, biodiversity could be seen as nature's version of the immune system.

Ecosystems achieve balance and stability through the complexity that develops between species over millennia. By removing a link of the chain, or introducing 'exotic' foreign species, we can unwittingly unravel the whole system. Biologists estimate that extinction rates are now between a hundred and a thousand times more rapid than before humanity evolved. We have driven up to a million species into extinction during the last decade. Some projections suggest that there will not be a single living coral reef left in 20 years. One in three primates are endangered, one in four mammals and one in eight birds.

An example of what can happen when a link in the chain is removed occurred in 1955, when the World Health Organization

(WHO) sprayed dieldrin – a DDT type pesticide – over Borneo, to try to eradicate the mosquitoes that had left 90 per cent of the population suffering from malaria. The programme was so successful that the disease was almost eliminated. However, unexpected things then started to happen. The dieldrin killed other insects, including the flies and cockroaches living in people's houses. Small lizards died after eating the dead insects, followed by cats that ate the dead lizards. Without the cats, rats flourished and began threatening the population with sylvatic plague. Then the roofs of the houses began to fall in, because the dieldrin had killed wasps and other insects that preyed on a type of caterpillar. This caterpillar was not affected by the chemical and, with most of its predators eliminated, its population exploded. The situation was only brought under control when the WHO parachuted healthy cats onto parts of the island and the balance was partially restored.

The Irish potato famine of the 1840s is a reminder of the importance of biodiversity. *Phytophthora infestans*, an airborne disease causing potatoes to wither and rot, spread through Europe in 1845 after crossing the Atlantic in a diseased tuber. Since all the potatoes grown in Europe were descended from the few plants originally brought from the New World, no resistant varieties had been developed. The ensuing famine left nearly a million people dead and forced more than a million others to emigrate. By 1851 the population of Ireland had dropped by 23 per cent.

The extent to which political and economic power is being concentrated into global institutions and multinational corporations, is now having a major effect on the world's biodiversity. Peasant farmers in India, having saved seeds for millennia, are now banned from doing so. Instead they are locked into contracts with corporations like Monsanto that provide them with sterilized seeds that depend on chemicals from these very companies for their germination. According to the noted Indian scientist and campaigner Dr Vandana Shiva, India used to grow up to 200,000 varieties of rice, each perfectly adapted to the soil and climate of a particular region. That has now been reduced to less than 15.

Modern industrial farming methods and the standardization demanded by supermarkets, has shrunk the genetic diversity of our staple food crops. Some 90 per cent of the human population now survives on just 30 crop varieties. The UK has lost 97 per cent of its fruit and vegetable varieties since 1900. The US has lost the same proportion in the last 80 years. There are 550 varieties of pear native to Britain, but 94 per cent of eating pears grown in the UK are made up of just three types.

This restricted diet is now controlled by a handful of corporations, with just four companies – Syngenta, Dupont, Monsanto and Aventis – accounting for not only 60 per cent of the global pesticide market but also 25 per cent of the global seed trade. Two companies, Cargill and Archer Daniels Midland, control virtually the entire global grain market.

One of the greatest threats to biodiversity and the genetic diversity of our food crops is the genetic modification (GM) biotechnology peddled by these corporations. Before embracing the notion that GM crops are helping to 'feed the world', we need to look at the facts. UN figures show the global food surplus is enough for an additional 800 million people. Even with population growth, no global shortages are forecast for decades. Much as we are told about the need for GM to avoid mass starvation, the real problem is distribution: India, with tens of millions of undernourished children, has a grain surplus of 59 million tonnes. Even the US, which exports 60 per cent of its food, feeds some 26 million people with hand-outs, while 25 per cent of the food sold ends up in the trash.

The claim that GM crops are producing bumper yields seems far from the reality. In the Indian state of Rajasthan, Monsanto claimed their maize yielded 50 tonnes per hectare – some local farmers put the real figure at closer to three. *Seeds of Doubt*, a report produced by the UK's Soil Association, catalogues the disastrous results of GM crops from around the globe, revealing that before GM crops were introduced, US maize farmers made a profit of $1.4 billion. In 2001, they lost $12 billion. The claim that the crops need fewer chemical applications has also been shown to be spurious: even US Government statistics confirm that GM crops have led to increased herbicide use.

The extent to which a few corporations now control the world's food supply does not just encompass seeds, chemicals and fertilizers. It involves the entire food system. Take the seed–giant Cargill for example. A farmer buys an 'inputs package' that may include seeds from Cargill and a herbicide from Monsanto and signs a contract to deliver the harvest to Cargill at a specified price and quality. Cargill buys the produce and processes it into animal feed, which is then exported to Thailand, where it is fed to chickens by a farmer, also under contract to Cargill. Cargill then buys the chickens, processes, cooks and packages them before selling them to fast food outlets or supermarkets in the US or Europe.

The evangelical promise of 'feeding the world' ignores the fact that most of those dying of starvation in the developing world are victims of famine caused by climatic changes and non-traditional, unsustainable agricultural systems.

There are also health implications of introducing a technology which has yet to be adequately tested and has found its way around the world, by-passing the few regulations that are in place. If it ever got out of control, genetic pollution would be virtually impossible to contain, for the simple reason that it's alive and self-replicates. Monsanto was issued with eight notifications for deliberate release of GM potatoes, but sued farmers like the Canadian Percy Schmeiser after GM pollen blew onto his crop from a neighbouring farm, contravening the corporation's contractual obligations. I met Percy at the World Summit on Sustainable Development in Johannesburg in 2002 and was deeply moved by the story of what he and his family had been through.

Despite the industry's repeated efforts to reaffirm the safety of biotechnology, there are numerous studies to suggest otherwise. The Max Planck Institute has been amongst those to report that GM potatoes produce changes in the bacterial communities of the soil, the consequences of which remain unknown; a study by the *New England Journal of Medicine* revealed that when a gene from a brazil nut was engineered into soya beans, people with nut allergies suffered serious reactions; a GM maize plant from Novartis includes a gene resistant to ampicillin, an antibiotic used to treat a wide variety of infections in humans and animals.

The Korean geneticist Dr Mae Wan-Ho is one of many eminent scientists to discredit the science behind biotechnology, which overlooks the role of so-called 'junk DNA'. A report published by Amory Lovins and the Rocky Mountain Institute highlights some of the dangers of ignoring this. 'Division into species seems to be nature's way of keeping pathogens in a box where they behave properly (they learn that it's a bad strategy to kill your host). Transgenics may let pathogens vault the species barrier and enter new realms where they have no idea how to behave. Shot-gunning alien genes into random sites in the genome is like introducing exotic species into an ecosystem. Such "invasives" are among the top threats to biodiversity today. It's unwise to assume, as genetic engineers generally do, that more than 90 per cent of the genome is "junk" because they don't know its function.'

Similar assumptions have been made about the role of genetics in treating disease, ignoring the fact that what is being identified is the 'genetic component' of a disease, not its cause. The gene merely predisposes someone to certain diseases – it is not the root of the problem. Professor Samuel Epstein from the University of Illinois has estimated that no more than 5 per cent of cancers are genetic in origin, while Dr John Higginson, an epidemiologist from the International Cancer Research Centre in France, believes that up to 90 per cent of all cancers are caused by environmental factors under human control.

Like so many of the issues we face, whether it is terrorism, drug addiction, disease or soil erosion, we continue to address symptoms rather than causes. This failure is indicative of an obsolete model. Rather than controlling the pests which are an inevitable product of chemically dependent monocultures, farmers are now using diversified organic farming techniques like intercropping to prevent the imbalance ever occurring. Likewise, rather than bombarding cancerous cells with toxic pharmaceutical drugs, unleashing damaging side-effects, or using invasive surgery, methods like integrated biological medicine are shrinking tumours and healing cancer patients by addressing the root causes of the disease.

As Colin used to point out, biotechnology is a classic example of what may be clever, but might not prove very intelligent.

Science writer Ivan Illich once calculated that when you add the time taken to work to buy a car to the time spent repairing it, maintaining it and driving it, then divide that by the distance travelled, the average car owner travels at an average speed of 5 miles an hour – the same as a brisk walk or a leisurely cycle. We sit in little metal boxes, nose to tail, while we double-glaze the planet, increase rates of asthma and pollute our lungs, brains and other body tissues, all so that we can travel at walking speed. This can hardly be seen as an intelligent use of our resources.

Clearly, certain technologies can play an important role in improving quality of life and creating a sustainable future – solar power, zero emissions transport, cyclical sewage systems. However, important distinctions need to be made between science and technology, between reductionist science and holistic science, between a science of arrogance and a science of wisdom, humility and understanding, between being plain 'clever' and being 'intelligent'.

Central to this, I believe, is the realization that a linear causality does not convey the true picture of how things operate in the world. We need to see every action and reaction within the grander vision of an interdependent universe. Ultimately, everything is connected to everything else, in one eternal and infinite 'feedback loop'.

During the Second World War, the chemical industry was dominated by the production of nitrogen compounds for explosives. When the war was over, agriculture became a convenient new dumping ground for nitrates as a major constituent of artificial fertilizers. In the alimentary tract, nitrate breaks down to nitrite, a toxin, and sometimes to nitrosamines, a powerful carcinogen, extremely small doses of which cause malignant tumours in rats.

The agro-chemical industry goes to great lengths to reassure consumers that their products are entirely harmless. Zac Goldsmith observes how ICI distributed thousands of brochures which claimed that their herbicide Paraquat works in 'perfect harmony' with nature and is 'environmentally friendly', despite the fact that some experiments suggested the chemical to be 'fatal to frogs and tadpoles at the lowest doses tested … kills honeybees at doses lower than those for weed control … is extremely toxic to hares'.

More recently there was a health scare over a chemical called acyclamide, supposedly created in the production of everything from breakfast cereal to Ryvita biscuits. It seems none of us is safe from carcinogenic food products, however healthy our diet. In his editorial, following this announcement, Zac revealed that acyclamide is a toxic by-product of glyphosphate, the active ingredient of the world's widely used chemical herbicides, which may provide an alternative explanation

Paul Hawken claims that, by the time you have read this page, nearly 100 people around the world will have succumbed to pesticide poisoning – 48 every minute, 25 million every year.

Organization

You think that because you understand one
you understand two, because one and one makes two,
but you must also understand and.

Sufi saying

At the crux of the changes required within our political and economic systems, I believe there is one overriding question that needs to be addressed: how do we organize ourselves?

If you take a square box and pour enough little balls into it, you will end up with a pyramid, the hierarchical structure of our economic and political systems, which concentrate money and power into an elite. This is not so much the result of some grand conspiratorial design, more the result of recent evolution. However, in the same way that nature is being used to inspire design, eco-technologies and farming methods, so it is giving rise to new models in political, industrial and economic systems. These systems tend to resemble networks rather than hierarchies. Like an ecosystem, their ability to adapt, self-organize and self-regulate increases with diversity and complexity.

Gaia Theory is the first scientific model to explain the earth and the biosphere as one integrated, self-regulating organism. By linking factors like plankton in the oceans, micro-organisms in the soil and the role of tropical rainforests in maintaining a stable climate, Gaia Theory reveals the global cycles which maintain homeostasis, the balanced conditions required for life to thrive.

An exploding human population has combined with certain technologies and activities to disrupt the systems that support life. By presenting a holistic model for studying the planet, Gaia Theory has laid the foundations of a new multi-disciplinary approach called Earth System Science. Rather than the mechanistic, or reductionist approach, which seeks to understand biological systems by reducing them to their constituent parts as if they were a machine, Systems Science looks at the flows and interrelations between organisms.

Complex systems are those that cannot be explained purely in terms of cause and effect. Human organizations, from tribes to corporations, are known as soft systems. When systems are stripped apart through reductionism, they cannot perform the functions they were capable of when combined. A bicycle cannot be ridden if it is not assembled correctly – the whole is greater than the sum of the parts. In living systems, these 'emergent properties' appear in their ability to be adaptive and self-organizing, creating complex, adaptive, self-organizing systems, like Gaia or the human body.

Over the last few years, I have come to realize that the politics of anarchism, in the proper sense of the word, not the nihilistic Sex Pistols version, resonate closely with ecological truth. The roots of anarchism can be traced back to the ancient Chinese philosophy of Taoism. Ostensibly, the *Tao Te Ching* is a set of instructions for a wise ruler, the government that governs the best is the one that interferes least with society's natural evolution. As Lao Tzu said: 'The more laws there are, the more thieves and robbers.' Under the New Labour Government in Britain, some 7,000 new criminal laws have been introduced. Is the country any safer as a result? In its truest sense, anarchism allows society to evolve the capacities of self-regulation and adaptation seen within complex biological systems, rather than being bound by rigid linear restraints.

How can it be acceptable for a tiny minority to decide what is good and bad for all of us? One man's poison is another man's medicine. Should such a small number of people determine what drugs are legal, ban natural supplements while forcing questionable vaccines on our children, or 'medicating' society with fluoride compounds in the water supply? Why not replace the failed linear systems of our industries with cyclical ones we know actually work?

Various methods now exist that can create the shift from linear to cyclical systems, giving birth to new models for organization and ways of eliminating the concept of industrial waste. These systems recognize the need for cooperation between industries where previously there may have been competition. The Zero Emissions Research Initiative (ZERI) for example, uses an 'open systems' approach, in which all outputs from a process are turned into inputs for another. The elegance of the ZERI approach is illustrated by the concept of 'ecological clusters'. These work by creating cooperative networks, so that the waste from one industry becomes the raw material for another. Ecological clusters have developed around Colombian coffee farms, where farmers previously used just 3.7 per cent of the plant before burning the waste or sending it to landfill. Now that coffee biomass, which was previously wasted, is used to cultivate tropical mushrooms, feed livestock, compost fertilizer and generate domestic energy.

In Brazil, highly nutritious *spirulina* algae is grown in the irrigation channels of rice fields, generating extra income for the farmers. The algae are used to enrich a food programme in rural schools to combat malnutrition. In New Mexico, chainsaws lubricated with a liquid containing mushroom spores were the catalyst for another cluster, creating a rich humus on the forest floor, thus providing sustenance for sheep which in turn provide wool for a new business making jumpers. These are just three examples inspired by the ZERI approach, which recognizes that nature has no concept of waste.

Growth is necessary for all biological systems. However, they all reach an optimal point, at which point growth stabilizes. If it does not, growth becomes pathological. In the late 1980s, a Swedish oncologist, Dr Karl Henrik-Robert, was so alarmed by the number of childhood cancers he was diagnosing that he started to look at the root causes. He concluded that the poisoning of air, food and water by industrial chemicals was largely to blame. Dr Robert worked with scientists to develop what became known as 'the four systems conditions' at the heart of The Natural Step (TNS). Now regarded as perhaps the leading framework for sustainability in business, the four systems conditions are the result of rigorous scientific research and are grounded in the laws of thermodynamics. They state that, in the sustainable society, nature is not subject to systematically increasing

- concentrations of substances extracted from the earth's crust
- concentrations of substances produced by society; or …
- degradation by physical means.

And in that society …

- human needs are met worldwide.

These conditions have been adopted by corporations across the globe. Leading examples include IKEA, Scandic Hotels and Interface carpets.

The term Biomimicry is drawn from *bios*, meaning life, and *mimesis*, to imitate. Pioneer Janine Benyus describes biomimicry as a science 'that studies nature's best ideas and then imitates these designs and processes to solve human problems'.

Benyus sees animals, plants and microbes as the consummate engineers: 'After 3.8 billion years of research and development, failures are fossils, and what surrounds us is the secret to survival.' By studying these natural processes and systems, biomimicry shows us how to 'harness energy like a leaf, grow food like a prairie, build ceramics like an abalone, self-medicate like a chimp, compute like a cell, and run a business like a hickory forest'.

An example of how biomimicry could transform the approach to design is the comparison between the modern high-tech material Kevlar and the silk of a spider's web. The production of Kevlar is extremely energy intensive and creates highly toxic by-products. In comparison, the waterproof silk spun by a spider, manufactured at room temperature and at normal pressure and without using or producing toxic chemicals, is five times stronger than steel.

Exponents of biomimicry see a huge potential for a wide range of design applications, from architecture to agriculture: 'We can look at solar-powered transpiration in trees as a means to silently move tonnes of water up hundreds of feet, at how mangroves desalinate water, and at how termites thermo-regulate their shelters through structural design,' Benyus says.

By replicating the prairie's perennial polycultures, biomimicry could create an edible landscape of plants that would 'over winter', eliminate the need for ploughing and planting, reverse the trends of soil erosion and phase out the need for chemical applications. The mixture of crops would include species that fix nitrogen in the soil and reduce pest damage.

There's a story about a pioneering psychiatrist who would put his patients in a room with a row of mops and buckets on one side, and a row of taps on the other. Then he would turn on the taps and wait to see what happened. Those he considered mad ran for the mops and buckets. Those he considered sane turned off the taps.

The extent to which humanity is currently rushing for the mops is an indication of the degree to which we are on autopilot. Rather than looking at the root causes of a problem, and turning off the taps, we seem incapable of looking beyond the symptoms – we just keep grabbing those mops. In addition to highlighting a failure of our linear systems, the mops and buckets approach is indicative of an economic system built on competition rather than cooperation.

The Industrial Age has been dominated by the Darwinian notion of 'survival of the fittest', and now neo-Darwinian concepts such as the 'selfish gene'. However, according to many evolutionary biologists, what Darwin proposed was an evolution built as much on cooperation as competition.

Examples of cooperation taking precedence over competition occur throughout the natural world, from bacteria to sea anemones, from fungi to primates. In fact, we now know that ancient bacteria nearly drove themselves to extinction a few billion years ago through hostile competition. Then they began to negotiate with each other, forming complex cooperative communities that steered the course of life on earth. Maybe the time has come for humanity to do the same?

Food

*The definition of insanity is doing the same thing
over and over again and expecting different results.*

Oscar Wilde

My passion for growing organic produce had evolved from a passion for cooking, which in turn evolved from my passion for eating. Maybe it all just comes down to greed.

I started to cook when my parents separated. My father's culinary talents stretched to opening tins of baked beans, or throwing pre-cooked meals in the oven. I began to dabble, moving from oven-ready chips to a level of over-ambition, spending entire weekends assembling rare ingredients for the longest, most involved recipes I could find.

At university, I would spend hours walking the length and breadth of Edinburgh, looking for particular cheeses, hams and wines. With my 'foodie' friends, I roasted whole suckling pigs over open fires, smoked haunches of venison inside overturned dustbins and baked whole salmon coated in salt and buried under turf. While cycling in Africa, we perfected Bicycle Spoke Kebabs and Peaking Duck, stuffing the cavity with potent local herbs. Back in England, I invited friends for absurdly ambitious dinner parties, taking on complex recipes for unfeasible numbers of people. Slowly, I learned to simplify my tastes.

Friends offered me a job as the chef in a pub they were opening on London's Fulham Road. I had a lot to learn. I had no idea how to cook an omelette, or make a burger. Over the following years, I cooked in a number of London restaurants, learning the basics of running a restaurant kitchen while living on a diet of espressos, red Marlboros and red wine. This proved far from healthy.

During a particularly broke phase, I was offered a job as a waiter at the River Café in Hammersmith. The restaurant had been open for a couple of years and was just starting to gain fame. The waiters and waitresses all worked with the kitchen staff to prepare ingredients. We picked tiny leaves of thyme off the stalks, shaved parmesan into wispy curls, stripped large red anchovies off the bone. We were handling exceptional ingredients, many of them organic and sourced from small artisan producers. The finest prosciutto, exquisite fresh porcini, stalks of wild rocket.

Soon I was ensconced, applying Zen-like concentration to the art of chopping vegetables, slicing cloves of garlic so thin they were transparent, learning to make some of the restaurant's signature sauces. My attention to prep work did not go unnoticed and, when a vacancy appeared in the kitchen, I was offered the job. Rose and Ruth, the dynamic partnership that had started the restaurant, were patient and long-suffering as I grappled to come up to speed.

I learned a lot about this style of cooking. The rustic simplicity, the emphasis on fresh, seasonal produce, the robust Mediterranean flavours, all resonated well with me. This was real food, authentic, not messed about with.

As my love of food grew, so did my desire to grow it. Part of what propelled me to Wales was the fanciful notion of growing fruit, herbs and vegetables. The conditions were challenging to say the least. The growing season for most things was a tiny window of two or three months at the height of summer. Slugs were vast and prolific, gobbling up prize lettuces overnight. Rabbits razed whole beds when we went away for the weekend. I was not deterred.

If we had stayed in Wales, my long-term plan was to create a 'forest garden'. Yet we had barely made stage one in this process when the decision was made to move to Sri Lanka.

The forest garden is, of course, a much more viable proposition in the tropics, where more time is spent cutting things back than encouraging them to grow. On one trip to India in the mid-80s, I spent time in the hills of Kerala, living in a small mud hut surrounded by a thriving forest garden. Papayas, passion fruits, pomegranates and pepper vines were all within arm's reach of the window. Never in my life had I seen such abundance. I could have spent the rest of my life there, feasting on the exotic tropical bounty that encircled the hut.

The forest garden concept is established in various parts of the world. Some anthropologists believe that the complexity seen in parts of the Amazonian rainforest was caused by people intercropping the jungle with useful trees and plants. There are many examples of the high productivity that can be achieved. Rather than felling the existing trees, the Chagga settlers on the slopes of Mount Kilimanjaro planted bananas, fruit trees and vegetables in their shade. Now the individual plots, which average 0.68 hectares, fully sustain a family of 10.

Kerala, the most densely populated area in India, has some 3.5 million forest gardens. One plot of just 0.12 hectares was found to support 23 coconut palms, 12 clove trees, 56 bananas and 49 pineapples, with 30 pepper vines trained up the trees. Associated industries in the area include the production of rubber, matches, cashews, furniture, *pandanus* mats, baskets, bullock-carts and catamarans, along with the processing of palm oil, cocoa and coir fibres from coconuts. Many families meet their own energy requirements through biomass systems fed by human, animal and vegetable waste, while the forest gardens provide full-time occupations for families.

Kerala contradicts many of the current assumptions made about wealth, quality of life and standard of living. On an average annual income of around $350 – 70 times lower than his American counterpart – the life expectancy for a Keralan male is only two years less. Kerala's birth rate is reducing from 18 per 1,000 to fall in line with the US figure of 16. Kerala is now considered 100 per cent literate. According to the Physical Quality of Life Index, Kerala rates higher than any other Asian country except Japan.

Much of the success of forest gardens lies in diversity and intercropping. Many traditional agriculture systems controlled pests through diversification, planting a mixture of crops rather than the intensive monocultures of the modern agri-business. Companion planting, or intercropping a variety of species, has many benefits: it protects against pests; makes use of synergistic properties, like deep-rooted crops that bring water and nutrients up from below; modifies micro-climate conditions; encourages cross-pollination and preserves genetic diversity.

For me, this has all the qualities of an 'intelligent' approach. Monocultures of GM crops cannot compare in sophistication. As we have seen, diversity in an ecosystem is what builds resilience. Left to itself, the traditional paddy field will yield for thousands of years, maintaining inherent fertilization and insect control processes.

The introduction of just one chemical however, will unravel the entire system.

Few things connect people more than food. Food brings us together, unites us in a common experience that is perhaps our most direct contact with the rest of the natural world. It comes as no surprise to find that most of the people I meet who share a passion for the issues in this book also share a passion for food.

It is only natural that we should be concerned about the levels of toxic chemicals we are ingesting, or the additives linked to hyper-activity in children, or the provenance of the meat we serve at Sunday lunch. Food is part of our essence. One only has to look at the revolution in British attitudes to food over the last decade to see the direction of public opinion – the rise of the celebrity chef, 'foodie' TV programmes, the endless supplements in Sunday papers. More and more people now accept the link between healthy soil, healthy food and healthy people. Good nutrition is recognized as an important aspect of preventative medicine and the rapid rise in allergies has forced many to reconsider their diets.

Through informed shopping and eating choices, the consumer has increasing influence over corporate global decision-making. Despite the bleatings of government and corporate funded scientists defending research budgets, the GM debate is all but over. Overwhelming research has shown that not one GM crop has made commercial sense to date, none has produced the promised high yields and farmers across the world are suffering as a result. Far from being the hysterical over-reaction of an ignorant public to so-called Frankenfoods, the GM debate has shown that the power of activism has forced a major re-evaluation throughout the biotechnology industry. It is concrete evidence of our power.

Biotechnology is just one of myriad issues. Most of us are now aware of the many other horrors caused by mass production: the legs of over-fed chickens breaking beneath their own weight; pigs or farmed salmon in atrocious cramped conditions; the prolific use of hormones and antibiotics in the meat industry; the over-exploitation of fisheries by inappropriate technologies; the food miles inherent in globalized trade. The average UK Sunday lunch travels 26,000 miles, or once round the equator.

Many of these problems are daunting. But, as we have seen with the GM debate, they are far from insurmountable. There are many things we can do to bring food back under our control. Local food initiatives, like using farmers' markets and organic box schemes to connect the producer directly with the consumer, reduce food miles and leave us with a clear conscience about the provenance of our food.

Food is the area in which, as consumers, we have perhaps the greatest power to effect change, simply through our shopping patterns. If we shop only at supermarkets, even if we are buying organic produce, we are always contributing to food miles, the embodied energy that has gone into the processing, packaging and transport.

But if we buy most of our food locally, we not only reduce food miles and our Footprint, but support the local economy. We are also ensuring a higher level of nutrition, since our food will be fresh, seasonal and free of chemical preservatives. As ever, the rule is: 'Think global, act local.'

Farmers' markets have been springing up in the US and UK for some years. The ethos of farmers' markets is that growers and artisans are selling produce direct to their local public. 'In terms of accountability and transparency there's no better way to shop,' says WoH patron Hugh Fearnley-Whittingstall.

There are legitimate excuses for not boycotting supermarkets and relying purely on farmers' markets and organic box schemes. The area in which you live may not be serviced by such enterprises and, even if they are, supermarkets still provide products that you cannot find easily elsewhere.

One way to overcome this is by starting or joining a local food group. The idea is that, by pooling together with neighbours, you can make bulk purchases at wholesalers. A recent study conducted by *The Ecologist* compared the costs of a wholesaler with Tesco's online store over a range of 10 basic products and found the whole-saler's price 29 per cent cheaper. Not only will you be saving nearly a third of your average spend, you will also be saving the planet by cutting down on food miles, processing, packaging and, as a result, on carbon dioxide emissions. These sort of initiatives make sense, both economically *and* ecologically.

Health

A multiplicity of hospitals is no test of a civilization.
Rather it is a symptom of decay.

Gandhi

The practice of handing out medicine like Smarties has been universally adopted around the world. Drug sales in the US suggest up to 80 per cent of adults ingest at least one prescribed drug every 24 hours, while the average doctor in the UK writes a prescription every few minutes. Most insanely however, the side effects from toxic 'medicine' are now the fourth leading cause of death in the US. Millions are dying from the drugs that are supposed to cure them.

I do not reject the stunning advances of modern medical technology; I have experienced the benefits myself. When I returned from cycling through Africa with a testicle the size of a tennis ball, surgeons removed a tumour with awesome precision and skill. Sholto needed antibiotics to avert a potential disaster with his infected knee. In terms of the mechanics, Western medicine is a wonder, replacing limbs, removing tumours, fixing broken bones. However, when it comes to the complexities of systemic illnesses, like chronic eczema, or degenerative conditions like ME, Western medicine fails to address the root causes, bombarding and repressing symptoms with toxic drugs instead.

The biochemist Ernest Krebs Jr highlighted this persistent illusion of pharmaceutical drugs in the 1970s: 'In the history of science no chronic or metabolic disease has ever been prevented or cured except by non-toxic factors normal to the diet. The corollary is that no disease has ever been prevented or cured by factors foreign to the diet.'

In the same way that we cannot add chemicals to Gaian systems without creating a systemic impact on the surrounding ecology, so the introduction of toxic drugs to the human system will always produce systemic side-effects.

Instead of constantly addressing the *symptoms* of planetary and bodily dysfunction, so-called 'new paradigm thinking' directs energy and resources towards the *causes* of our malaise. For example, many alternative health practices place an emphasis on preventative medicine, using nutritional supplements to build a healthy immune system. In the same way that biodiversity provides resistance to pests, and healthy soil produces healthy food, so good nutrition can boost the resilience of the human body.

The history of allopathic medicine can be traced to 1856 and the accidental discovery that hydrocarbon by-products of the fossil fuel industry could be used as the basis for a variety of drugs. As the petro-chemical industry grew, so did the range of drugs, creating the corporate cartels and centralized monopolies that exist today.

The 'technological determinism' that now dominates healthcare in the industrial world – providing the problem and solution in one package – is constantly apparent on US television, where more than 20 per cent of advertising is for over-the-counter drugs to treat everything from headaches and arthritis to more modern complaints like Generalized Anxiety Disorder. The list of apparently 'minor' side-effects of these drugs highlights their own shortcomings – migraines, nose bleeds, vomiting, even epileptic seizures.

In fact, there is considerable evidence to suggest that many allopathic drugs are inherently dangerous, either exacerbating conditions they are supposed to cure or triggering new ones. A study by Oxford Professor Martin Vessey proved that almost every known illness is increased by the birth-control pill. As long ago as 1975, researchers at Oxford University conducted studies that compared no treatment with single- and multiple-agent chemotherapy. Their report, published in the *Lancet*, concluded that 'no treatment proved a better policy for patient's survival and for quality of remaining life'. To ensure that their drugs are prescribed, the pharmaceutical industry employs a variety of tactics, including offering doctors bonuses, holidays and conferences in exotic locations.

Most allopathic medicine is fundamentally at odds with biological systems. By relying on synthetic chemicals to treat disease, it introduces alien, toxic substances which, rather than addressing the root causes of the problem, systemically creates new ones. To illustrate the way in which corporations concoct markets for both industry by-products and their own drugs, we can look at three substances: the artificial sweetener aspartame, mercury-amalgam fillings and fluoride.

In 1965, a scientist working for Searle Pharmaceuticals was conducting tests for a new drug designed to treat ulcers. After licking his fingers, he discovered that the chemical tasted sweet. In July 1974, the US Food and Drug Administration granted approval to aspartame as a food additive, despite the fact that it had been shown to cause epileptic seizures in monkeys, blow microscopic holes in the brains of rats and cause brain tumours. Six months later the FDA retracted and the product was withdrawn, initiating a long battle and numerous further studies. Yet the FDA again approved the drug for use in dry foods in 1981 and in beverages two years later. 'It was approved in a completely nefarious, completely unacceptable manner,' Washington DC attorney James Turner said at the time.

By 1987, a US Senate hearing found that the FDA had already received 4,000 complaints relating to aspartame, and the incidence of virulent brain tumours continues to rise at a rate of 10 per cent a year. Nutrasweet and Equal – the trade names for aspartame – continue to be the sweeteners used in thousands of diet products from fizzy drinks to yoghurt while the use of Stevia, a naturally sweetening herb from South America, was discouraged by the FDA, which approved it as a dietary supplement rather than a food additive.

Alongside cadmium, and various radioactive isotopes, mercury is the most toxic heavy metal on the planet. Why then, one wonders, have dentists been busy stuffing it into our mouths for the last hundred years?

Contrary to what the US, UK and Australian Dental Associations would have us believe – that mercury is made stable when amalgamated with silver in your teeth – it is now known that fillings continue to emit mercury vapour which accumulates in spinal fluid and brain tissue. A recent study of 3,600 cases of multiple sclerosis found concentrations of mercury in the spinal columns of all but six patients. Mercury secretion, combined with a history of broad-spectrum antibiotics, is known to disturb the delicate balance of gut flora in our digestive systems, leading to the proliferation of *candida albicans*, the bacteria that many alternative practitioners regard as a precursor to cancer and a host of modern diseases, from ME to Chronic Fatigue Syndrome and auto-immune dysfunctions.

Despite being known to be poisonous since the 1830s, mercury-amalgam was adopted by the American Dental Association in 1859 as the preferred material for the dental profession and its use has been defended ever since. Mercury-free dentists report that their studies are ridiculed and denied by the mainstream profession. Although the use of mercury-amalgam fillings has now been banned in many European countries, the UK Government still maintains that it is perfectly safe – like depleted uranium.

In October 1985, the British Government rushed legislation through parliament which allowed water authorities to fluoridate water supplies. As scientist Peter Bunyard observed, one would have thought that an issue like doctoring the national water supply would have brought a serious response from our politicians, but only 130 out of 650 MPs chose to vote.

Fluoride is a by-product of the aluminium industry, and its intro-duction has been supported by the sugar industry, based on the speculative assumption that it fights tooth decay. Water fluorida-tion has been banned in Holland and Sweden, discontinued in Yugoslavia, the former West Germany, Hungary and Belgium, while it has never been practised in Austria, Denmark, France, Italy, Greece or Norway. Two doctors in the US have published reports that blame 35,000 cancer deaths a year on fluoride. Others main-tain that the use of tap-water containing fluoride accounts for the incidence of 'cot death' amongst bottle-fed infants. A study by the Australian Kidney Foundation reported a 63 per cent increase in the incidence of renal failure from 1977, the date when fluorida-tion was first introduced.

The list of corporate sponsors in an annual report from the

Dental Health Education and Research Foundation in Australia, one of the main fluoridation-promoting bodies in the country, gives one some idea of those who feel they benefit from the practice: the Coca Cola Export Corporation, the Wrigley Co., the Australian Council of Soft Drink Manufacturers, Arnotts Biscuits, Cadbury Schweppes, Kelloggs and Scanlens Sweets. Fluoridation in the UK is promoted by the British Fluoridation Society Ltd, which operates under the auspices of the British Dental Association and is funded by the Government through the Department of Health. Robin Whitlock, who has been researching fluoride for many years, observes how the BFS maintains close connections with chemical companies involved in the supply of fluoride and continues to push for nationally enforced fluoridation, despite the fact that the British judicial system has ruled, on at least two occasions, that fluoridation is essentially unlawful. 'Fluoridation does not make medical or scientific sense, is extremely dangerous and is downright immoral,' Whitlock said. 'The fluoridation lobby knows this all too well and so it is in their interests to maintain a permanent cover-up of the facts.'

There is no denying that cancers of the lung, throat and larynx can be attributed to smoking, especially when tobacco acts synergistically with other airborne pollutants. However, while the cancer industry increasingly points the finger at smoking as the primary cause of the disease, they overlook the fact that lung cancer rates in non-smokers have more than doubled in recent decades, an increase which cannot be attributed exclusively to passive smoking.

Chinese studies have found no difference in lung cancer rates between smokers and non-smokers in the rural population. Studies in the US have found that lung cancer rates in black men are 40 per cent higher than in whites and have been increasing more rapidly in recent decades. Some people suggest that this is due to a higher proportion of low-income black workers coming into contact with occupational carcinogens like arsenic, chrome and nickel, or industrial processes such as copper smelting, mining, spray painting and tanning. It was once estimated that workers in foundries inhale levels of polycyclic aromatic hydrocarbons equivalent to smoking up to 20 packs of cigarettes a day. As Samuel Epstein says, smoking and diet have been made the corporate scapegoat for spiralling cancer rates, diverting attention from the thousands of carcinogens within their products. The inference is that it's your fault for getting cancer, due to smoking or eating badly.

Over the last hundred years, the petro-chemical industry has synthesized some 10 million new chemical compounds, of which 150,000 have found their way into commercial production and a tiny percentage of which have been thoroughly or reliably tested. A study by the journal *Cancer Prevention News* once estimated that fewer than 10 per cent of new industrial chemicals have been adequately tested for carcinogenicity. These chemicals continue to enter the environment at a rate of roughly a thousand every year. Despite constant assurances from both industry and government, that all chemicals are submitted to stringent tests before being given approval, it is increasingly apparent that these are inadequate. Some studies suggest that the time lapse between exposure to a carcinogenic mutagen and the appearance of a cancerous growth can be anything up to 20 years, not the matter of weeks in which laboratory tests are conducted.

Also, chemicals are tested in isolation, ignoring the synergistic effects. Macrobiotic nutritionists maintain that the reason why the Japanese have low rates of lung cancer, despite a heavy incidence of smoking, is the absence of refined sugar and dairy products in their diet, factors which work in synergy with tobacco to increase its carcinogenic impact.

The power of the pharmaceutical industry and corporate-funded healthcare are frequently defended by the illusory notion that quality of life and average life-spans have been immeasurably improved by allopathic drugs. The cancer industry claims that cancer was rife in traditional societies, but went largely unrecognized, and that the higher incidence of the disease in modern times is due to other diseases being brought under control.

In their study of the Hunza tribe, in what is now northern Pakistan, Dr Allen Banik and Renne Taylor reported that the people live 'in health and happiness to the age of 120 years ... the healthiest, longest-lived people in the world'. The same has been said of the Inuit and the Kogi Indians of Columbia.

Zac Goldsmith also notes how the rare incidence of cancer among indigenous people has been observed by hundreds of anthropologists, explorers and medical researchers. In 1960, Rene Dubos concluded that 'diseases like dental caries, arteriosclerosis, and cancers are so uncommon among certain primitive people as to remain unnoticed – at least as long as nothing is changed in the ancestral ways of life'. On his arrival in Gabon in 1913, Albert Schweitzer 'was astonished to encounter no case of cancer'. Dr Eugene Payne examined 60,000 people over 25 years in Brazil and Equador and 'found no evidence of cancer'. George Leavitt, a ship's doctor, worked with 50,000 Inuit over many years and reported that 'no native cancers would be found in the Arctic'.

The efficacy of alternative treatments for cancer have been supported by many well documented cases from around the globe. The

Danish doctor Kristine Nolfi cured her own cancer with an organic and raw vegetable diet and continued to heal others at her health farm. Ann Wigmore pioneered and promoted wheatgrass juice after using it in conjunction with an organic vegetarian diet to cure her cancer. Stories like this are greeted with derision by allopathic doctors and the cancer establishment, who claim they are the result of spontaneous remissions, an outcome that usually occurs once in every 10,000 cases.

The limitations of the old paradigm in healthcare, the bullying tactics of the drug industry and vested interests of corporations peddling carcinogenic products are increasingly apparent. More and more evidence suggests that cancer will never be cured through bombarding malignant cells with toxic chemicals. Despite the fact that only 5 per cent of cancers can be attributed to genetic traits, spokesmen for the cancer industry continue to extol the benefits to be gained from biotechnology. Rather than funding research into cancer prevention, or ways to detoxify our environment, removing chemicals from our water supply and food chain, the industry maintains its pursuit of a 'miracle cure'. Instead of researching the potential of alternative plant and herb-based medicines, the future of cancer research is controlled by the likes of Monsanto, the company responsible for unleashing probably more carcinogens into the atmosphere than any other.

A variety of ground-breaking new technologies also help to shatter obsolete concepts about health, the human body and the treatment of disease, exposing causes rather than symptoms. As the results of many studies have proved, dismissing alternative health systems as nothing but New Age quackery is simplistic in the extreme. In fact, these technologies are proving to be the ultimate validation of ancient and traditional healing concepts developed by tribal shamans, vedantic teachers, Taoists, ayurvedic doctors and yogic masters. Rather than treating the symptoms of disease when it manifests in the body, they seek to prevent the incidence of disease by maintaining a balanced equilibrium of the human energy field. In short, they are dealing with causes rather than symptoms, with prevention rather than treatment.

When it was first developed over half a century ago, Kirlian photography purported to reveal the human aura in a black and white image, but was dismissed by mainstream scientists as showing the heat generated by the body. A Kirlian image is created by exposing film in the presence of a high electrical charge. The fact that it captures some kind of energy field invisible to the human eye, rather than body heat, was proved with an experiment in which a leaf, with one corner torn off, was shown to be complete in the Kirlian photograph. For the exponents of the technology, this was seen as proof of an etheric body.

Now, with the PIP scan aura camera, it is possible to view the human aura in real time on a TV monitor. Any abnormalities which might, for example, develop into tumours, are easily detected. By using any number of healing techniques, from the laying on of hands to electro-crystal therapy, these imbalances can be repaired and balance retuned.

In a similar vein, two Californians have developed the Q-Link, a specially programmed crystal pendant that develops a 'sympathetic resonance' with the wearer. Again, the indications are that this revolutionary technology could have shattering implications for the future of medicine.

Professor Kim Jobst, a homeopathic doctor and Visiting Professor of Healthcare and Integrated Medicine at Oxford Brookes

University, told me how the Q-Link was curing high blood pressure among many of his patients within a matter of days, producing astonishing results that would be hard to replicate with high strength drugs and without any apparent side effects. William Tiller, Professor Emeritus at Stanford University and a Guggenheim Fellow, believes that this technology 'will be an important part of humanity's future'.

Technologies like the PIP scan and the Q-Link are supported by new research into the Systemic Memory Hypothesis, as presented by Dr Gary Schwartz. The concept of cellular memory explains various scientific anomalies, like heart transplant patients inheriting memories from the donor, and homeopathic remedies, which increase in potency as the preparations are diluted.

Despite industry efforts to discredit complementary and alternative medicine, more and more of us are seeking alternatives. The number of people visiting naturopathic, ayurvedic or homeopathic doctors, discovering alternative therapies, are increasing exponentially every year. Despite repeated insurances from government and industry, more and more of us are suspicious of genetically modified and chemically produced foods.

Who really believes that pesticides are safe, that radioactive material is not inherently linked with cancer? Surely we must have severed contact with our ancient evolution and basic common sense to think that we can continue to fill air, soil and water with synthetic compounds and not suffer the reactive consequences?

Oceans

We're not borrowing the earth from our children.
We're stealing it from them – and it's not even
considered to be a crime.

David Brower

The state of the world's oceans is truly lamentable. Sri Lanka is no exception, noted for dynamite fishing that destroys whole reefs, and the use of cyanide to stun large fish. Once again, our myopic ignorance has effectively destroyed entire ecosystems. The oceans, being vast, unexplored and out of sight, were also out of mind. Now they are out of stock, with many of the world's major fisheries on the verge of collapse. The day that Atlantic cod joined the endangered species list was a wake-up call for many who may have previously ignored such issues. The staple of British fish and chips was on the way out. What on earth was happening?

Like many of the grand global issues we face, from climate change to biodiversity loss, the state of the world's oceans seems like another intractable problem, the human drain on resources being so out of step with what is sustainable. Since the mid-1980s we have been in 'ecological overshoot', using 30 per cent more of the planet's Net Primary Productivity (NPP) – the sum total of nature's biological output – than can be regenerated during that time. In other words, it takes 16 months for nature to replenish what we use up in one year.

By 1995, nine of the world's 17 major fishing grounds were in precipitous decline and four had been commercially 'fished out'. The EU began to decommission 40 per cent of its fishing fleet, the Malaysian Government halved the number of inshore fishers and Canada laid off 35,000 people in the industry.

The situation has hardly improved since then, with many of the world's fisheries on the verge of collapse. Blue-fin tuna and Atlantic cod have joined the endangered species list, while other white fish like the deep-water orange roughy, which only spawns after the age of 30, taking decades to build up stocks, are now being fished as a cod substitute. The North Atlantic breeding population of blue-fin tuna has dropped by a staggering 90 per cent in the past 20 years.

Over-fishing creates a vicious circle, yielding major returns to start with, but depleting resources in the long-term, since it removes the spawning stock. After three years, an intensive fishery catching 90 per cent of the stock in the first year returns the same as one that had caught only 30 per cent. By the following year, the intensive fishery catches 30 per cent less than the sustainable one, since it has removed a substantial portion of the spawning stock.

As well as regarding marine populations as inexhaustible, we have tended to think that the sheer scale of world's oceans would render them immune to pollution. A Greenpeace study once revealed that the bed of the Irish Sea is so seriously contaminated by the Sellafield nuclear plant that it should be classified as nuclear waste. Anti-nuclear campaigners claim that some 2 million gallons of radioactive liquid are discharged from Sellafield every day and the incidence of leukaemia in the area is 10 times the national average. Carcinogenic compounds like dioxins and PCBs can be traced in marine populations around the globe, from the flesh of tuna on the equator to penguins in the Antarctic. Oil spills, industrial pollutants and plastic bottles now wash up on beaches from Sri Lanka to San Diego.

Global warming is also having an impact. The excess carbon dioxide in the atmosphere causes acidification of the oceans due to the increase in carbonic acid being absorbed. This is having a serious impact on micro-organisms like plankton, as well as shellfish and other species further up the food chain, since all evolved in alkaline waters. As Lovelock's Gaia Theory proved, complex processes involving coral reefs and micro-organisms, have played a crucial role in maintaining homeostasis and a stable climate. But these are being disturbed or destroyed. In the last few decades, 35 million acres of coral reefs have been destroyed by human activities. Practices like dynamite fishing have degraded 10 per cent of the worlds reefs and, at current rates, this could rise to 70 per cent during our lifetimes.

Much has been touted about the potential of aquaculture and fish farming for reviving marine populations, but this often overlooks the systemic consequences. For example, it takes an average of 5lbs of wild fish to feed and produce 1lb of farmed salmon and the use of antibiotics in over-populated fish breeding pens has had drastic knock-on effects for other species. Even when we follow what we believe to be 'ethical shopping' guidelines, we may be supporting the continuing decimation of world fisheries. Due to different fishing techniques, the 'by-catch' created by saving one dolphin for the yellow-fin tuna labelled as 'dolphin-friendly' can include up to 16,000 discarded small tunas, 380 *mahi-mahi*, 190 *wahoo*, 20 sharks and rays, one marlin and up to 1,200 smaller fish.

The decline of world fish stocks can be attributed to the growth of industrial fishing fleets using new technologies and the enclosure of local fishing grounds as part of the drive to divide the 'global commons'. However, many traditional fishing communities around the world evolved rules to prevent over-fishing and maintain healthy marine populations in perpetuity. From the Marovo of the Solomon Islands to the Moluccan communities of Indonesia and the Cree Indian in Canada, the control of fishing resources was held by clan leaders and councils that decided who could fish where. For 450 years, the fixed gear fishery in Newfoundland caught large quantities of high-quality cod and other fish at low cost, without diminishing stocks and providing the economic basis for hundreds of often isolated coastal communities. When the Cocamilla people in the Peruvian Amazon noticed that their lake was being over-fished by commercial operations from district and provincial capitals, they ruled that only subsistence fishermen should be allowed.

During the 1950s and 1960s, fishermen in Raritan Bay in New Jersey formed their own cooperative with a system of quotas. Any boat that caught more than its quota was obliged to give the surplus to other less fortunate boats in the co-op. More recently, the Ocean Wildlife Campaign, a coalition of six US national conservation groups, worked alongside recreational fishing organizations and the Pacific Fishery Management Council to ban 'pelagic longline gear' off the coast of California, Washington and Oregon, safeguarding populations of tuna, swordfish, marlin and shark after overfishing had depleted numbers. The law details specific requirements to rebuild stocks within a set timeframe, minimizing by-catch and protecting areas of essential fish habitat.

About 75 per cent of the estimated 10 million fishermen in the developing world use small-scale, minimum impact fishing technologies and well over 100 million people are thought to be dependent on this small-scale industry for their income. Ghana's fleet of 8,000 canoes for example, catches 70 per cent of the country's marine fish. Like our erroneous fixation with the supposed efficiency of industrial agriculture, our belief in the efficiencies of industrial fishing fleets is equally misguided. A canoe fisherman using an outboard motor is thought to use 1 tonne of fuel to catch up to 40 tonnes of fish, while a modern trawler uses the same amount to catch just 3 to 4 tonnes.

Coral reefs all over Asia and the Pacific have been devastated by the practice of dynamite fishing. However, some initiatives, like coral reef gardening, have shown that these effects can be reversed.

Langa Langa Lagoon for example, on the central coast of Malaita in the Solomon Islands, is dotted with dozens of human-made islands, built from corals taken from what used to be a very rich coral reef lagoon. Despite being illegal, dynamite fishing became one of the most common fishing methods over recent years, replacing the reefs with graveyards of broken coral skeletons. In Marau Sound, the reefs are in slightly better shape, since dynamite fishing is not often employed.

However, *Acropora* corals have been harvested and burnt to obtain lime, or calcium oxide, a necessary ingredient used in the habit of chewing betel nut. This practice not only destroyed important reef habitats throughout the Solomons, but has also caused ecological shifts in coral reef communities as they lost the 'stag horn' *Acropora*. The trade in ornamental and aquarium coral resulted in additional damage to the reefs in the 1990s.

An attempt to reverse these trends was begun in 1997, with a small grant from the Pacific Development and Conservation Trust

(NZ). A partnership involving a local NGO, the Solomon Islands Development Trust and the Baha'i community in Malaita, focused on restoring reef areas degraded by generations of coral harvesting and dynamite fishing, aiming to provide economic alternatives to rural communities through the sale of cultured corals to the aquarium trade.

Two communities were initially trained in Malaita, and in May 1999 the Solomon Islands Development Trust arranged for an additional workshop during a follow-up visit. A 'no-fishing zone' was established around Malave Island in Langa Langa Lagoon, with corals replanted at several sites. The result of an educated population is the expansion of coral replanting to other communities and a large reduction in dynamite fishing in Langa Langa Lagoon.

The work in Marau Sound initially involved training more than 30 women as coral farmers, and resulted in the export of tens of thousands of farmed aquarium corals to the US between 1998 and 1999. Unfortunately, these coral farms were abandoned in 1999 during a period of ethnic strife, when homes were burnt and the people fled. The conflict has now subsided and cultured corals are being used as 'seed stock' as the coral farming and reef restoration work resumes. The resulting education and empowerment of local communities is now seen as an important step towards the coral reef rehabilitation and conservation needed regionally. Once again, a grassroots initiative has proved that 'bottom-up', local innovation can be the most effective approach to reversing the trends imposed by globalizing forces.

Peace

*The most potent weapon in the mind of
the oppressor is the mind of the oppressed.*
Steve Biko

We are told there is only one superpower now. But actually there
are at least three. Sure, there's the US, flexing muscle over the world's
resources. But what about China? And what about you and me, and
up to 30 million others who marched on seven continents over one
weekend to protest against the war in Iraq? This formidable force,
the world's conscience – the peace, ecology and social justice movements – global civil society itself, constitutes the real emerging
superpower of the 21st century, a social movement with the power
to determine the future of our species.

In the immediate term however, it seems that the US has the upper
hand. While China maintains that it will never seek hegemony, the
US makes no qualms about seeking what it calls Full Spectrum
Dominance (FSD), the global domination of every sphere of political and economic influence, from electronic cyberspace to the mil-
itarization of space.

When we combine these openly stated goals with the list of

technologies being developed and deployed by the US military-industrial complex, FSD appears to be even closer than most of us might have imagined. For example, take this extract from a piece of legislation entitled the Space Preservation Act of 2001, put before the House of Representatives and which raises questions about 'exotic weapons systems' previously confined to science-fiction films:

'The term "exotic weapons systems" includes weapons designed to damage space or natural ecosystems (such as the ionosphere and upper atmosphere) or climate, weather, and tectonic systems with the purpose of inducing damage or destruction upon a target population or region on earth or in space. Such terms include exotic weapons systems as –

(i)   electronic, psychotronic or information weapons
(ii) chemtrails
(iii) high altitude ultra-low frequency weapons systems
(iv) plasma, electro-magnetic, sonic, or ultrasonic weapons
(v)   laser weapons systems
(vi) strategic, theatre, tactical or extraterrestrial weapons; and
(vii) chemical, biological, environmental, climate or tectonic
      weapons.'

Also included is reference to weapons 'directed at individual persons or targeted populations for the purpose of information war, mood management, or mind control of such persons or populations'.

The concept of weapons designed to control the moods of populations, or even overt mind control of individuals, have circulated for many years, mainly by those parts of the underground press usually dismissed as paranoid fantasy. Pentagon programmes like

MK-ULTRA, begun in 1953, are thought to have been the continuation of work begun by psychologists in Nazi concentration camps, 'to devise operational techniques to disturb the memory, to discredit people through aberrant behaviour, to alter sex patterns, to elicit information and to create emotional dependence'.

There is little doubt that mind control programmes like MK-ULTRA have existed, and it would be naive to assume that they do not still exist. However, technology has moved these efforts into a new dimension. The miniaturization promised by nanotechnology has created bio-chip implants small enough to be injected. There are even companies in the US who will, at some expense, scan your body to see if you have been bugged by any of these microscopic devices and remove them.

Independent scientists, like the South Korean geneticist Dr Mae Wan-Ho, have already rung the alarm bells about 'stealth virus' technology, along with genetically engineered viruses designed to target certain racial groups. 'Stealth viruses' could be used to infect whole populations and triggered at a later date.

Another 'exotic weapon', and the subject of considerable conjecture over recent years, is the High Altitude Auroral Research Programme (HAARP) at Gakona in Alaska, which has quadrupled in size since the Bush administration came to power. Consisting of a series of rectannae masts, HAARP beams Extra-Low Frequency (ELF) and Ultra-Low Frequency (ULF) sound waves into the ionosphere. There seems to be considerable disagreement about what HAARP is actually for.

The HAARP Programme is jointly managed by the US Air Force and the US Navy, who claim it is designed to 'understand, simulate and control ionospheric processes that might alter the performance of communication and surveillance systems'. One of the leading independent analysts of HAARP is Dr Rosalie Bertell, a United Nations Environment Programme (UNEP) Global 500 Laureate, winner of the Alternative Nobel Prize, President of the International Institute of Concern for Public Health (IICPH) and Editor in Chief of *International Perspectives in Public Health*.

Bertell believes that, by beaming 3.6 gigawatts of radiated power from high-frequency radio energy into the ionosphere, the possible uses of HAARP extend to triggering ionospheric processes that could be exploited by the US Department of Defence. 'HAARP is related to 50 years of intensive and increasingly destructive programmes to understand and control the upper atmosphere,' Bertell says. She also believes it 'would be rash not to associate HAARP with the space laboratory construction which is separately being planned by the United States' and that 'the military implications of combining these projects is alarming' since their integration would allow the US 'to deliver very large amounts of energy, comparable to a nuclear bomb, anywhere on earth via laser and particle beams'. She concludes that the project is likely to be sold to the public as 'a space shield against incoming weapons'. Many commentators echo Bertell's conclusions, suggesting that there is considerably more to the Strategic Defence Initiative, dubbed Star Wars, than the White House might lead us to believe.

A Washington think tank, called Project for the New American Century (PNAC), provides an overview of the current administration's influence on global events. Founded in 1997 by the now Vice President Dick Cheney and ex-Defence Secretary Donald Rumsfeld, as well as others who have come to prominence under the current administration, such as Richard Perle and Paul Wolfowitz, PNAC's directors include men like Bruce Jackson, a Pentagon official during the Reagan era and then in a senior position at the weapons manufacturer Lockheed Martin.

PNAC's ideology can be found in a White Paper produced in September 2000, entitled *Rebuilding America's Defenses: Strategy, Forces and Resources for a New Century*, in which it outlines what is required of America to create the global empire, or Pax Americana, they envision for the 21st century. Many of these plans however, were considered too difficult to implement without 'a significant threat to American homeland security'. Key strategies include repositioning permanently based forces in southern Europe, southeast Asia and the Middle East; a global missile defence system; the strategic dominance of space and control of cyberspace; an increase in defence spending to a minimum of 3.8 per cent of GDP, up from the then current 3 per cent. In the wake of 9/11, that 'significant threat to American homeland security', Bush increased the defence budget to almost exactly this figure.

The PNAC document proposes that advanced forms of biological warfare could target specific genotypes, or racial groups, and thereby 'transform biological warfare from the realm of terror to a politically useful tool'.

Technologies from computer games to the Internet have all percolated through to society from military research programmes. However, these are examples which are usually regarded as benign. But what about nanotechnologies, such as surveillance cameras smaller than grains of sand, which can be dispensed to the four winds? What about genetically modified microbes designed to eat metals, plastics and fuel? What about self-replicating genetically modified organisms that could denude a forest in minutes?

Who really benefits from this sort of technology other than the corporations that maintain control over it? The same research teams making biological weapons are synthesizing the drugs to provide immunity for those considered to be worth saving. Does anyone really believe that this sort of technology is making the world a safer place? Most of the nuclear, chemical and biological weapons technologies that now threaten US national security were first developed by their own military programmes. The arms industry is the core of the US economy. As many have observed, every time the US economy takes a turn for the worse, they find an excuse to go to war, thereby justifying increasingly massive budgets for military expenditure. When the Bush administration came to power, it announced a projected spend of $3 trillion in the next five years.

The petro-chemical and pharmaceutical corporations are now virtually indistinguishable from the military-industrial complex itself. Edward Hammond, co-director of the Sunshine Project, an organization dedicated to biological weapons control, says it should come as no surprise to learn that Donald Rumsfeld is a veteran biotechnology advocate and former CEO of Searle Pharmaceuticals, now part of the Monsanto-Pharmacia complex, the corporation responsible for such delights as Agent Orange and now hard at work on developing biological warfare vaccines.

A few years back, the Sanger Institute, an organization funded by the Wellcome Trust, announced that in partnership with Porton Down, it had sequenced the genome of the bacteria responsible for bubonic plague and that this will 'enable new treatments and defences from its use as a biological weapon'. As Hammond concludes: 'There is no biotech solution to the threat of biological weapons. Quite the reverse. Accelerating the proliferation of biotechnology and subsidizing the expansion of its military role will simply line industry's pockets with public money and lead to greater instability and fear, a self-fulfilling prophecy that suits industry just fine, but harms citizens, the environment and hopes for a more peaceful world.'

The pursuit of technologies like the Star Wars programme, self-replicating 'nanobots' and genetically modified viruses, makes little contribution to international security. In reality, these technologies merely hasten the day when they will be deployed, either by terrorists, the so-called 'rogue nations', or the US themselves. What 9/11 made so apparent was just how vulnerable the US is, despite such a vast array of sophisticated military hardware and a defence budget that eclipses most of the world's combined GDP. How can world peace ever be possible while countries like the US and UK continue to sell arms to both sides of conflicts? How can world peace ever be possible when the military-industrial complex produces ever more devious technologies which can never be reversed once released into the biosphere? Rather than promoting peace and stability, the illusion of power is instilling paranoia into the global mind. To be free of it, we must step outside it, transcend it altogether. A world of peace will be a world without the manipulation of fear.

It is clear that our entire value-system needs to change. Perhaps human nature is too fundamentally twisted for us to change, and we are destined for extinction as a species. Or perhaps there needs to be a global collapse before a new model can arise from the shell of the old. Given the current evidence, this collapse looks inevitable. That's why the most effective work we can do is to put the new model into practice. By disengaging from the prevailing monoculture, by ceasing to be in conflict with it, we are instantly in a new space. Energy once wasted through confrontation can be redirected into restoration. At that moment, we cease to be part of the problem and become the living solution. This approach can be likened to aikido, the martial arts system that harnesses the energy of an aggressor.

In 1945, Aldous Huxley published *The Perennial Philosophy*, tracing the single strand of ancient truth at the heart of all the world's religious and mystical traditions. In essence, this strand claims that we are not separate individual entities but are in fact just expressions of one universal consciousness, which is ultimately all that there is. The great illusion is that of being a separate little self, not the manifestation of one universal and absolute Self.

This is reflected in the teachings at the core of all major religions. In the Old Testament, we find 'I Am That I Am' and Yahweh, the Hebrew term for God, literally translates as 'I Am'. In the Hindu Upanishads, '*Tat tvam asi*', 'Thou art That'. In Taoism, 'the Tao that can be named is not the true Tao'. But this essential message, that consciousness is primary and not secondary – that you are within consciousness, it is not within you – has been obscured by institutionalized religion.

Now we find that it is not only resurfacing in a spiritual context, but within a scientific one. For example, Nobel prize-winning scientist Ilya Prigogine says: 'Today the world we see outside and the world we see within are converging. This convergence is perhaps one of the most important cultural events of our age.' His words seem to echo those of Jesus in the Gospel of St Thomas, replying that the kingdom of God arises 'when the two shall be one, when that which is without is within, and the male and the female shall be one'. Peter Russell, a prominent physicist, has reached similar conclusions, along with many others from a variety of disciplines, ranging from biologists to transpersonal psychologists.

In other words, a new way of seeing ourselves in relation to others, to the natural world and even to the entire universe, is starting to germinate within the academic world. From ecology to quantum physics, the message is the same: *we are not separate.*

With his theory of Inclusionality, Alan Rayner has introduced a new conception of space that brings with it a new understanding of self and how we relate to each other: 'The logical trap that leads humanity to war with itself can be avoided by becoming aware of the visual illusion of "independence", and feeling the receptive space that permeates within, through and around everything. This loving feeling of "inclusionality" or "spatial togetherness" transforms our understanding of the nature of self, as having both local and non-local aspects, and so enables us to move from "the logic of one or other to the logic of one with other".'

This shift from 'exclusional' to 'inclusional' logic lies at the core of our collective problem. If there is a philosophical shift in the way we view ourselves and each other, in relation to the rest of nature, then perhaps there will be a shift in the current trajectory of Spaceship Earth. Without it, there seems to be little hope for restructuring our political and economic systems in the ways that are necessary for human survival. As I write this, there are 84 different wars being fought around the globe and Sri Lanka seems poised to make it 85. It seems a sad and desperate reflection on humanity that still, at the start of the 21st century, we can find no alternatives to settling our differences than killing each other.

Education

*What we need now is not Christians or Buddhists,
but a few million people like Jesus or Buddha.
What is needed is a 'critical mass' of individuals
who are in the process of transforming themselves.
To hear this call is not arrogance so much as
the first step on the path of emulation.*

Rudolf Bahro

It all starts with education, with being informed. Only when we are informed, can we be mindful and truly empowered. More than any generation before them, Sholto and Xan will face the full-scale fallout of the industrial age. If they are to have a chance of ameliorating the mistakes made before them, they will need to embrace a new way of looking at the world. One that is inclusive, cooperative, non-linear, 'bio-mimetic' and ecologically informed. Some of the tools at their disposal have already been mentioned. The question is, will our current educational systems be able to absorb this?

Anita Roddick, founder of the Body Shop and long-time Web of Hope supporter, was once a teacher. At a meeting we had in London, I asked her how that period had shaped her ideas about education.

'Thirty years ago, it didn't take me long to work out that education philosophy can be divided into two schools of thinking,' she said. 'The first states that the child knows little, and is essentially a raw material to be processed: years of structured education will make children useful to our society, and also to themselves. This thinking asks kids to listen unquestioningly to authority; asserts that education is to prepare children for their roles in the economy; to make them good workers.'

'And the second?' I asked.

'The second school sees children as a unique set of potentials, and it helps them develop the habit of freedom. It encourages them to celebrate who and what they are. This is the type of education we find in the Steiner or Waldorf schools, or the fabled Summerhill, or the schools of the Human Scale Education movement. In "transformation education", we see imagination as more important than knowledge and that education is about a route that encompasses the mind, body and spirit – not a collection of computer-like facts, data, memories and rules. Education should be concerned with the *whole* being.'

'So what do we do?' I asked.

'I see a groundswell happening: people taking charge of their education, looking for an alternative. I see a growing sense of wanting something different; an emergence of a fundamental shift in our practice of education. What we must have as teachers, as parents, even as business people, is a moral sympathy with everything we do. All of us here should work to develop free human beings who can develop purpose, imagination, a sense of truth and a feeling of empathy and responsibility.'

The groundswell that Anita spoke of is indeed happening. I was stunned to discover that some 200,000 families in the UK choose home-schooling in preference to the state system. That disaffection is creeping in everywhere. People want change.

The question is the same: change to what? There were certainly some progressive models appearing in the UK, from Satish's Small School network to the innovative Room 13 arts project in Scotland, run entirely by the children themselves, both of which conformed well to the criteria. At the same time, I felt the need to look further. How can we all trigger deeper and more systemic change within society as a whole? How can we make that change 'go viral', through the nodes and networks identified by Jacquie McGlade, who I met at the summit in Johannesburg?

Jacquie had studied the way HIV was spread from areas of infection by 'carriers', such as truck drivers, who travel out from the community and infect others. These carriers return periodically to the areas of infection, the 'nodes', where they are re-infected, maintaining their potency.

Just for a moment, put aside the virus's negative associations and compare its spread with the process of awakening that is developing around the globe. The areas of infection are the nodes: the World Social Forums, the social justice organizations, the ecological learning centres, the research institutes, the sustainable farming systems, the pioneers of eco-technologies and ecological design processes, the peace activists, the alternative communities.

These nodes are developing the solutions, the blueprints, which are then replicated around the world through their contact with others. As we enter the 21st century, the future of our planet depends on the rate at which we can accelerate this 'infection' process. Rather than the old habits of conflict or competition, we will enter a paradigm of cooperation, usurping those that are now at the helm, adjusting the sails and setting our sights on another world.

One answer may lie in Sri Lanka, with the Sarvodaya movement. Sarvodaya means 'the awakening of all', a process that is realized when farmers and landless labourers join university trained managers and civil servants to initiate community projects. They identify their real needs, develop their capacities for cooperation and become empowered through increased self-reliance. Sarvodaya projects include windmills, bio-gas systems and developing new products from local materials. A personal awakening is integral to that of the community, which in turn reflects on the country and the world at large. In this way, the virus-like transmission of change becomes a healthy contagion.

The movement's founder, Dr Ariyaratne, is clear about where this process starts. 'It's not enough to parrot Sarvodaya philosophy. We've got to live it. Our revolution has got be spiritual; no amount of tricking will get us there. We don't divide people, we show them how they can change.'

Sarvodaya's ideals give rise to the sort of 'Buddhist Economics' first suggested by visionary economist E. F. Schumacher, making the crucial distinctions between growth and development, or standard of living and quality of life: 'This definition of development goes beyond those that confine themselves to measuring gross national products, growth rates, per capita income … It represents the process necessary for total happiness.'

As the Canadian environmentalist David Suzuki points out, environmental destruction, such as the collapse of an ecosystem, often follows an exponential curve. As an example, he asks us to imagine the spread of lilies over a lake during a 60-day period, at the end of which the surface is completely covered. If the lilies spread at an exponential rate, doubling their surface area every day, then on day 59 the lake is only half covered. All appears to be fine. The next day however, there is no sign of the water. The lilies have deprived the lake of oxygen and the ecosystem dies. In terms of climate change, biodiversity loss and the global water crisis, there is much to suggest that we may well be living through day 59.

This analogy can be applied to the critical mass required for an evolutionary shift in our business practices, in our economic and political systems, in our scientific views and use of technologies, even our basic relationship to the planet. Right now, it may not appear that there is much sign of that shift but, like those first few lilies on the pond, the seeds of a new way of doing things are germinating across the globe. We have the blueprints, the role models, and they can be replicated at an exponential rate. Day 60 will dawn when these new models have replaced the old. Like the 'flip-over' that climatologists refer to – the possibility of a sudden shift in the global climate from one steady state to another – an equally sudden shift is necessary now if we are to have any chance of avoiding catastrophe.

Ultimately, the space in which that shift occurs is within each and every one of us. It all starts here, with that one simple step, when we get off one boat and on to another. In that instant, we cease to be part of the planet's destruction and become part of its restoration, joining a growing global movement for positive change.

The decision rests with each of us.

Glossary

Analog forestry – A scientific term for the forest garden concept, pioneered by Sri Lankan biologist and rainforest expert Dr Ranil Senanayake (see **Forest garden** below).

Aquaculture – Water-based agricultural systems that can integrate fish farming with edible plant species, like water chestnuts, or food supplements, such as the nutrient-rich *spirulina* algae.

Biodiversity – The diversity of all biological life within a specific region, from entire ecosystems to individual mammals, plants, insects and bacteria. A 'biodiversity hotspot', like Sri Lanka or the Amazon, is noted for its rich biodiversity.

Biomimicry – A new science that studies nature's models and then imitates or takes inspiration from these designs and processes to solve human problems, for example the solar cell, where designers are hoping to emulate the efficiency of the leaf. It marks the beginning of an era based not on what we can extract from the natural world, but on what we can learn from it.

Biotechnology – Any technological application that uses biological systems to make or modify products or processes for a specific use. Most commonly used with reference to the science of manipulating particular genes across the species barrier in genetic modification (GM), or genetic engineering (GE).

Carbon neutral – A term to describe any activity that makes no net contribution to carbon emissions by offsetting the 'carbon footprint' through tree-planting schemes or investment in clean, renewable energy technologies like wind, wave and solar.

Ecological Footprint – An 'ecological accounting tool' that calculates the bio-productive space required to maintain an activity indefinitely. It can be applied to anything from a specific lifestyle to a manufacturing process, taking into account the production, transport, assembly, use and disposal of a product. The calculation expresses the result as a measure of land used – 'global hectares' – per capita.

Forest garden – A method of food production and land management based on natural systems. Trees, bushes, shrubs, herbs and vegetables that yield products useful to humankind are intercropped. By exploiting the premise of 'companion planting', these can grow on multiple levels in the same area, like the plants in a forest. The technique is sometimes known as three-dimensional farming.

Gaia Theory – An ecological theory which proposes that the living earth functions like a single organism. It was first scientifically formulated in the 1960s by the independent research scientist James Lovelock and named after the Greek goddess Gaia, a suggestion from his friend, the novelist William Golding.

Homeostasis – The property of open systems, especially living organisms, to self-regulate their internal environment so as to maintain stable, constant conditions, such as temperature in the human body, or a global climate that supports life.

Monoculture – The practice of relying on a very small number of genetic variants of a food crop in commercial agriculture. Modern agriculture relies on this standardization so that the technology for tilling, planting, pest control, and harvesting can be used over large geographical areas to obtain an economy of scale. The term is also used to describe the homogenization of world culture through the forces of globalization.

Nanotechnology – A field of applied science focused on the design of materials and devices at a molecular scale – the diameter of a human hair is about 80,000 nanometres. Two main approaches are used: one is 'bottom-up', where materials and devices are built up atom by atom, the other 'top-down', where they are synthesized or constructed by removing existing material from larger entities.

New Paradigm – The science philosopher Thomas Kuhn used the term 'paradigm' to define the set of practices that describe a scientific discipline during a particular period. New Paradigm describes the emerging 'ecological worldview' presented by a wide variety of scientific disciplines but which share similar concepts.

Permaculture – A design system that aims to create sustainable habitats by following nature's patterns. It seeks the creation of productive and sustainable ways of living by integrating ecology, landscape, organic farming, architecture and agro-forestry. The focus is not on these elements themselves, but rather on the relationships created among them by the way they are placed together, the whole becoming greater than the sum of its parts.

Systems Theory – A trans-disciplinary theory that studies the structure and properties of systems in terms of relationships from which new properties of wholes emerge. First established as a science in the 1950s, Systems Theory has applications in numerous fields from geography to economics and organizational theory.

Index

THE WEB OF HOPE

The Web of Hope is an expanding on-line educational resource, designed to empower people and communities around the globe with sustainable lifestyle solutions and tools for self-reliance.

To be more effective, we need you to become another active strand in the web. Every person and every action counts. Together, we truly can make a difference, turning a time of crisis into one of opportunity.

If you resonate with the core issues raised in this book, PLEASE consider becoming a Hopester by joining as a member.

WWW.THEWEBOFHOPE.ORG

'Hopesters. Hipsters with a conscience. So very now.'
—UK Sunday Times

PROJECT: FLAMINGO
A WEB OF HOPE CAMPAIGN

The Project Flamingo 'journey' provides practical 'toolkits' for engaging with change, at home, at the workplace and within your community.

WWW.PROJECTFLAMINGO.ORG

Samakanda is The Web of Hope's first 'Bio-versity', an ecological learning centre developed on the site of an abandoned tea estate in south-west Sri Lanka.

Rather like a conventional 'Uni-versity', the Samakanda 'Bio-versity' provides the space for a shifting population of teachers and students, demonstrating living examples of sustainable lifestyle solutions, inspired by the natural 'intelligence' of biological systems.

For more information about Samakanda, details of events, courses and accommodation, please visit

WWW.SAMAKANDA.ORG

The Web of Hope is a registered UK charity (reg. no. 1101462) specialising in environmental education.